P9-BZT-328

Mr. John Simi
Charles C.T. Community College
La Plata,
Md.
20646

Silver Spring, MD 20902

Mike Roberts Color Productions
Emeryville, CA 94608

"RIVETING!" —USA Today

"EXTRAORDINARY!" —The Boston Globe

"DRAMATIC!" —St. Louis Post-Dispatch

"FASCINATING!"
—The New York Times Book Review

EXIT THE RAINMAKER
Jonathan Coleman

EXIT
THE
RAINMAKER

JONATHAN
COLEMAN

A DELL BOOK

For my parents,
for Amy,

and in memory of
Irvin Ehrenpreis (1920–1985)
Shiva Naipaul (1945–1985)
Thomas Victor (1937–1989)

PROLOGUE

First, you should probably know, there was a little pink-cheeked music man, name of Homer, cute as the dickens. Back in the days when money was real, in such whistlestops as Muleshoe, Texas, and Ada, Oklahoma, he barnstormed with the Sells-Floto Circus and the Jesse James Show, playing a trumpet, wearing spats, riding the rails, and keeping company with show gals who invariably had him busy until sunup. That was before he settled down, more or less, to a different sort of life. Now, nearly ninety-one, he was determined to set the record straight.

"There is nothing in that boy's background, from the time he was a squalling baby, to indicate that he would break out in the way that he did."

That boy, raised simply in small towns in Texas, was Homer and Bea Carsey's first child, their only son.

The mass of men lead lives of quiet desperation.
                    —Henry David Thoreau

Sometimes you hear, fifth-hand,
As epitaph:
He chucked up everything
And just cleared off,
And always the voice will sound
Certain you approve
This audacious, purifying,
Elemental move.
                    —Philip Larkin

ONE

I T WAS THE SORT of fine spring morning when you feel the urge to hop into a red convertible, flip on the radio, and drive forever. It was a Wednesday, May 19, 1982.

Twenty-five miles south of Washington, D.C., a tall man with china blue eyes was preparing to leave his twenty-three-room Georgian house shortly before eight. He told his wife that he might be home for lunch. Half asleep, she remarked that his light gray suit looked a bit crumply. Carrying a scuffed briefcase, he got into a black Caprice Classic and headed down the driveway, stopping to talk to some maintenance men who were not cutting the grass to his satisfaction. He had lived here at Green's Inheritance since Christmas of 1974. He was forty-seven years old, the local college president, a government consultant, a person so well liked that he was affectionately referred to as "Uncle Jay" by both children and friends. In Charles County, Maryland, hunt and tobacco country grudgingly giving way to bedroom community, he was so prominent that everyone knew him—or thought they did. His name was Julian Nance Carsey.

On the tree-lined back roads toward Washington, roads he had traveled hundreds of times, he drove carefully, very carefully, until he reached the bank. He calmly withdrew about twenty-eight thousand dollars, converted the amount into traveler's checks, then phoned his secretary.

"Katharyn, would you please cancel my dental appointment? Also, I may not get back in time for that meeting this afternoon. Something's come up with my sister's two boys and I may have to go to Philadelphia. Please call Nancy and tell her." After a long pause he added, "I bet you didn't even know I had a sister."

She didn't. But Katharyn Jones did know that in all the years she had known Jay Carsey, he was always more the compassionate listener than someone who revealed much about himself.

After a drink at the Army & Navy Club, Jay crossed the Potomac and arrived at a National Airport parking lot just after eleven. He put the car keys and his checkbook into the glove compartment, left the current issue of the *New Yorker* and his umbrella on the front seat, and made his way to North Terminal. Just before entering he stopped. He pulled five letters and one postcard from his jacket pocket and dropped them into the mailbox. He bought two expensive pieces of luggage, put one inside the other, checked in, and made his way to the Pan Am Clipper Club. To his immense relief, he saw nobody that he knew. A few vodkas and one additional letter later, he called the secretary of a man for whom he did consulting.

"Hi, Joanne, Jay Carsey. I can't meet with Bob today because I have to go out of town on family business. I haven't been able to reach Katharyn at the college, and was wondering if you could try her. Just tell her that I *did* go to Philadelphia, and that she should phone Nancy."

Within an hour, Julian Nance Carsey—low-key, dependable Uncle Jay—was gone.

TWO

No sooner had Katharyn Jones received Jay's phone call that morning than Nancy phoned. There was nothing unusual about that. Often Jay would arrive at his office at Charles County Community College and Nancy would be on the phone, wanting to speak to him.

"Jay's not here," Katharyn said. "But I'm sure he'll be calling you." Even though Jay had told Katharyn to phone Nancy, she felt certain he, the most attentive husband she knew, would contact her himself.

An hour later, Nancy phoned again.

"Have you talked to him?" Nancy asked.

"Yes."

"Well, he hasn't called."

For the first time all morning, Katharyn, a mother hen by nature, began to worry. For some strange reason, she suspected Jay might have made up the story about his sister—*if* he had one. When she received Joanne's phone call in the afternoon, she became more suspicious, but kept those feelings to herself. Why hadn't Jay phoned her directly before he left for Philadelphia? His saying he couldn't get through was ridiculous; the president's office had more than one line.

John Sine, the dean of the college, had asked Katharyn why Jay had missed the budget meeting, and she told him what little she knew. Just before she left the office to go home, Nancy phoned again. She still hadn't heard from Jay.

"Jay went to Philadelphia," Katharyn said, as convincingly as she could. "Something to do with his sister and her two children. I'm sure you'll hear from him."

THE LIGHT LUNCH Nancy had prepared hours earlier was still on the table, and she was perplexed. In the fourteen years Jay and she had been married, he had always been so good about letting her know where he was. When he went out of town, she usually went with him, especially in the past five years, after she resigned her position as a school principal. But it was Katharyn's mention of Jay's younger sister that made Nancy uneasy. Though Jay had practically raised Susie, he had had little, if any, contact with her for years, and there were reasons for that.

Nancy was planning to attend a political fundraiser that evening for Mike Sprague, a state delegate and friend of the Carseys', and she couldn't decide whether or not to go. At six-thirty, and again at seven, she phoned Katharyn Jones at home, hoping for some word.

"I think you ought to go," Katharyn said, trying to conceal her own fear that Jay had been kidnapped. "There's no use sitting around. I'll be home all evening. If Jay can't get you, I'm sure he'll call me."

Nancy put a message for Jay on the answering machine, left him a note, got into her white Mercedes, and drove to the American Legion Hall. Once there, she expressed her worry and puzzlement to everyone she saw, and said she wouldn't be staying long. She didn't want to miss Jay's call. In Charles County, everybody seemed to know everyone else's business, not to mention their patterns of behavior. If there was one thing women like Karen Sprague and Bobbie Baldus—both of whom talked to Nancy that night—knew about Jay Carsey it was this: Nancy didn't need to be alarmed.

AT ELEVEN-THIRTY the phone rang at Katharyn Jones's house. All evening she had been alternately reviewing the events of the day and trying to block them out.

It was Nancy, bordering on tears.

"Why don't I come over and stay the night?" Katharyn said. "You need to have some company."

"No, I'll be okay," she said. "Let's talk in the morning."

Nancy tried to sleep, but worried that she might dream Jay had called, then discover he hadn't. So she stayed up, pacing, reading, peering out into the rainy darkness.

THREE

THERE ARE DAYS in a person's life that stand out so clearly it can seem that all of one's life is condensed into twenty-four hours. Thursday, the twentieth of May, was such a day for Nancy Carsey, and in varying degrees, for others as well.

Green's Inheritance was still that morning. Nancy could hear the chirping of birds. Dressed in her purple robe (her trademark color), she chainsmoked as she watched the mist slowly lift from the tennis court. By anyone's standards, the house would be considered large; without Jay that morning, it seemed cavernous.

Built in 1850, the house had a long history. Not only was a murder said to have been committed on the third floor, but "restless spirits," the local papers claimed, still inhabited the place. It was essentially a white elephant when the Carseys bought it, but Nancy had devoted her considerable talents to making it one of the showpieces of the county ("Smithsonian South," some called it, with a mixture of awe and criticism), filling it with everything from Cambodian temple rubbings and green Chinese carpets to African masks and a suit of armor. Wherever the Carseys went (they had traveled all over the world), they acquired things. Nancy was the push behind that, and Jay, eager to please, would get caught up in her infectious enthusiasm. From childhood on, she had been a collector—dolls, boxes, canes, what have you—and that passion only increased as time went by.

She loved taking visitors on a tour of the house and she loved to entertain, so much so that Jay thought of her as the Perle Mesta of Charles County. Though forty-five, it would be fair to say she was still girlish, and true to say you wouldn't miss her tall, athletic figure when she entered a room, her long red hair swinging from side to side.

Nancy was perched on a stool in the kitchen when the phone rang at eight-thirty. It's about time, she thought.

But it was Katharyn

"Did Jay get in? Everybody all right?" Katharyn was going to a meeting in Frederick that day, and wanted to remind Jay she wouldn't be at the office.

"I haven't heard a word from him," Nancy said, trying to keep from shouting. "I was up all night. I *know* something has happened to him."

"Nancy," Katharyn said slowly, as if to a child, "I'm going to hang up and make a few calls. Then I'll phone you back."

Katharyn called the college and spoke to Jane McCloy, who also worked for Jay. "Listen carefully," she began. "You may get some inquiries about Dr. Carsey. I think it would be best if you just said you didn't know anything." Katharyn had been a secretary long enough to know the importance of telling white lies to cover for one's boss. And she also knew how secretaries love to get together and gossip. "Something has happened," she continued, almost as if she knew precisely what, "but there's nothing to be talked about until it's a little more concrete."

Katharyn hung up and dialed the main number at the Pentagon.

"Virginia Foster's office, please," she said. Virginia Foster was

Jay's aunt. Only ten years older than Jay, "Toodge," as she liked to be called, was the only relative Jay felt close to, yet he spoke with her only once or twice a year.

When Toodge got on the line, Katharyn asked if Jay had a sister.

"Yes, he does," Toodge said. "What's this all about?"

"Does she live in Philadelphia?" Katharyn pressed on.

"No, she lives in Northern Virginia. She's a nurse at one of the hospitals."

"Well, that's funny," Katharyn said. "Do you happen to have her phone number?"

"What's happened?"

"Does she have children?" Katharyn would not be deterred.

"Yes, two sons. Now *please* tell me what's going on."

Katharyn finally related the events of the day before. Toodge said she would call Susie, but was not optimistic. "I doubt if she knows anything. To the best of my knowledge they haven't spoken for years."

"KATHARYN, THIS IS JANE, the mail just came in. There is a letter for Ed Loeliger with Dr. Carsey's handwriting on the envelope. What should I do?"

Ed Loeliger was the college treasurer. Since he worked only part-time, he did not come in on Thursdays.

"Don't open it," Katharyn said. "Let me try to reach Ed at home."

"HAVE YOU HEARD from Jay?"

Nancy was surprised to hear Louis Jenkins, the chairman of the college's board of trustees, on the other end of the line.

"No," she said, "not since he left the house yesterday morning. He's gone to Philadelphia."

"Well," Jenkins said in a measured voice, "I have his letter of resignation on my desk. It's postmarked yesterday from Washington:

Louis—

Effective 15 May 1982 I resign as President. I am proud of what I have accomplished but it is time for new leadership.

J.N. Carsey

Nancy was dumbstruck. Each word out of Jenkins's mouth pierced. *This can't be happening*, she thought. *Sure the last year was tough—the federal budget cuts, the people who had to be laid off, the phone calls . . . God, it was hard for both of us, for Jay especially. He'd never experienced failure. The college was his baby. He was everyone's golden boy, most of all mine. Graduation's in three days, we were looking forward to the summer, to getting away and doing things together. But this . . .*

"I think you better check your mail," Louis said, breaking her trance.

NANCY WAS AN unfamiliar figure at the tiny post office in Pomfret. As she fiddled with the combination to Box 35, her hands were shaking.

"Where's Doc?" It was Evelyn Coombs, the postmistress, surprised to see Nancy. Jay had always picked up the mail.

"Oh, he's out of town," Nancy said, trying to be nonchalant. The last thing she wanted was Evelyn Coombs trafficking in idle gossip.

There was a letter from the National Register of Historic Places (Green's Inheritance was a landmark house), an American Express bill, an electric bill, a color brochure from Neiman Marcus—and a letter from Washington, a letter from Jay.

Minutes later, sitting in the den off the kitchen where they spent so much of their time, where they had just had dinner two nights before, Nancy began to read:

N—

    I'm leaving because I know you can't. I am a physical and psychological disaster, I have no will to improve, and I don't want to drag you down with me. When you feel emotionally able, there is a tape in the right-hand drawer of my desk that you should listen to.

J

That wasn't all. There was another piece of paper in the envelope.

To whom it may concern:
15 May 1982

    I hereby irrovably [*sic*], and for the future, relinguish [*sic*] all claims to any assets and net worth relating to the estate of J.N. and N.S. Carsey. I also disclaim any responsibility for liabilities related to that estate.
    This includes cash values of extant life insurance or annuity policies.
    All properties assigned jointly or under my name singularly are Nancy S. Carsey's privileges to dispose of as she wishes.

J.N. Carsey

Holding one note in her hands, then the other, Nancy read them, and read them again.

JOHN SINE GOT a postcard.
Sine had been dean of the college for seventeen years—as long as Jay had been president. They were friends, they played tennis together, they complemented each other. If Jay was Mr.

Outside—successful at fund-raising, dealing with people, holding the lantern while everybody else chopped wood—Sine was Mr. Inside, the person Jay could count on to implement his plans. Knowing that Jay enjoyed playing pranks, Sine felt sure that the color postcard of Ronald and Nancy Reagan—and the message on the back—was precisely that. It had been a long, grueling year, and perhaps this was Jay's own peculiar way of saying so.

ACROSS THE HALL, Ed Loeliger had arrived to open his letter. Loeliger was a fastidious retired colonel who looked the part—late sixties, finely barbered white hair. He had been working in his garden when Katharyn Jones called. She told him what had happened the day before and about her conversation with Virginia Foster (who had immediately phoned back to say that Susie had not heard from Jay and that her two sons were fine and in school). She was reluctant to call Nancy back, Katharyn told him, "because I know she's going to really go into a tantrum if we tell her that there's something drastically wrong here."

Jay's note to Loeliger contained information and a request: it said the college car was in Short Term Parking at the North Terminal; and it asked him to help Nancy out in any way that he could.

BY THE TIME Loeliger went to see John Sine, Sine had already spoken with Louis Jenkins. *Under no circumstances*, Jenkins said, was anyone to discuss this, nor were the police to be notified. With graduation that Sunday, Jenkins didn't want this to mar the occasion. Anyway, the lawyer in him reasoned, they didn't know all the facts.

Once Loeliger left, Sine reread Jay's postcard. He then got up slowly from behind his large mahogany desk and stared out the window. Though he saw students playing frisbee and walking hand in hand in the May sunshine, what filled his mind was an image of himself, directing Jay in a production of *The Rainmaker* in the early Sixties—the first time they had met. The play's hero, Bill Starbuck, is a charismatic figure who not only makes people believe he can bring rain to a parched Western town, but love to a young girl's heart. And though he does both, he turns out to be less than what he seems.

Perhaps, Sine wondered, Jay saw himself in life that way—as someone who had wrought miracles, who could see not only to the end of the street but around the corner too, yet who had felt it was time to move on, to begin again. Jay had often said, "You know, John, when it isn't fun anymore, we ought to go tend bar and be a lot happier." As well as anybody, John Sine knew that in the twenty-three years Jay Carsey had lived in Southern Maryland, he had always been someone for whom life seemed to come easily, someone who never seemed to have a problem.

But Sine, like Katharyn Jones and countless others, also knew that Jay was a man who lived inside himself, who never really opened up. Perhaps the burden of trying to be all things to all people had become intolerable, Sine thought; perhaps Jay had been walking along the edge of a cliff and nobody had fully realized it.

All things begin in dreams, and nothing ever ends but ourselves. As John Sine walked across the hall and stared into Jay's empty office, a wooden statue of Don Quixote on the desk, he read the postcard a third time:

John—

    Exit the Rainmaker. Good luck.

                      Jay

pls handle

FOUR

Louis Jenkins had arranged to meet a fellow board member at Green's Inheritance. He told John Parran that Jay had resigned, that something was amiss, and that Nancy was expecting them. Both men had been to the house many times before, and they, like most of the county, had often wondered how Jay and Nancy could afford to live the way they did (even though a good deal of the Carseys' entertaining was paid for by the college). This visit was different. Instead of the whirling dynamo of red and purple who always greeted them, they found a woman deeply distraught.

Clutching the two pieces of paper she had received as if they were rosary beads, repeating over and over that "something's happened to Jay, he's fallen into ill hands," she led them into the room where Jay's desk was. The tape was exactly where he said it would be. Having shown both men the notes, she proceeded to play it.

Income tax situation is clean, it began in a voice remarkable for its matter-of-fact tone, a voice clearly, and coldly, Jay's. As he went on to inform Nancy about their financial life, the details of which were largely unknown to her, her own voice, alternately punctuated by sobs and hysteria, was an odd counterpoint. There were some joint loans that she didn't know about, and, he said without apology,

13

I think you're hung with that. He elaborated about certain things she might do, steps she might take, where things were; said he had canceled MasterCard but as far as Visa and American Express (and other credit cards), *The first few days I will probably charge a couple thousand dollars against [them] and then I will throw them all away*. As for money from the college, *Ed Loeliger is your best bet. They should owe me thirty days at least leave and there is a paycheck floating around.*

For Jenkins and Parran it was a numbing experience. Here was a man they knew and admired, socialized with, had business with, had shared secrets with (at least *they* had with him). Why, Jenkins had seen Jay just four days before, on Sunday, at a party at the Dixons', and Jay was in great spirits, had even joked with Gordon Barnes, the Washington weatherman, about the forecast for graduation the following Sunday, would it be beautiful or should they plan to set up chairs in the gym? (Barnes promised to call him on Tuesday.)

But as the two men left Green's Inheritance, certain that others would soon arrive to sit with Nancy and watch over her, to keep a vigil, many thoughts went through their minds—not least of which was the sinking sense that despite what Nancy thought, Jay might not be returning soon, if at all, to their little corner of the world.

"Quite frankly," Jenkins said later, using his favorite expression, "if you would have told me that Jay was going to leave that Wednesday, I would have said you were stark raving mad. This kind of thing may happen in places like New York City, but not, quite frankly, in a place like Charles County."

FIVE

In another corner of the world, Houston, Texas, to be precise, Lamberth Carsey was readying himself for trial when he received Nancy's phone call.

A partner at one of America's most prestigious law firms, Fulbright & Jaworski, he was raw-boned, tall, and imposing, yet he possessed a soothing bedside manner and voice that put you at ease—qualities also found in his cousin Jay. At fifty-seven, he was a decade older than Jay and had known his share of tragedy: his sister, a pianist, died young and his wife, a former beauty queen, was confined to a wheelchair. His father and Jay's father were brothers. Their grandfather was an agnostic and an itinerant bandleader, so music and the wisdom of Robert Ingersoll eventually played a significant role in both boys' upbringing. Though they were not close, Lamberth was the relative Jay most admired, and that was the primary reason Nancy decided on him as the first of Jay's family to contact. Besides, she thought Texas a place he might go.

Lamberth listened patiently to what Nancy had to say. She spoke of her increasing concern about Jay's eyesight (his mother had glaucoma), recurring problems with his back, his difficulty sleeping, and his drinking more than usual.

"Did you try to persuade him to see a doctor?" Lamberth asked.

"Yes, but he refused. Told me to stop nagging him. I wonder if he found out he has some terminal disease and doesn't want to burden me. That would be just like Jay. He was always telling everyone that Houston had the best doctors in the country."

Ever sensitive, Lamberth was careful in what he said to Nancy, but so was she. Though Lamberth barely knew her, he had the distinct feeling "she seemed to be trying to say to herself, as well as to me, that 'I can't understand this,' that there was nothing she could think of in the marriage or in their personal situations that would cause him to do anything of this nature."

Instead of prying, though, Lamberth tried to give her moral support as well as practical advice: call the airlines, contact the credit card companies, involve the police, get a lawyer.

"Have you phoned Jay's parents?" Lamberth asked, just before they hung up.

"No, not yet," she said. "I don't want to alarm them." Then she added, almost defiantly, "I'm *sure* I'll hear from him."

"If there's anything more I can do," he said, "call me."

Lamberth sat back in his chair and put his hands behind his head. His first thought was that Jay might have been so severely depressed that he committed suicide. Clinical depression was not unknown to Lamberth; it had affected a member of his family, and it could certainly cause one to act in odd ways. Even if Jay hadn't committed suicide, had merely vanished, it still struck him as a desperate thing to do, though he could "understand the compulsion"—especially if Jay's life was "knotting with problems" and he was as nonconfrontational as Nancy claimed.

Lamberth had lived long enough to know that "humans are a peculiar species, and it is entirely consistent with human nature for a person to do that, to be unable to do it any differently."

He was actually thinking of a friend of his, someone he knew far better than he knew Jay, who couldn't bring himself to face difficult situations. "They may be life-threatening, or at least career-threatening or marriage-threatening or personally threatening in a nonphysical sense. The problem is simply that he cannot bring himself to deal with it and will sit and watch it go to the point of ruin. He can't reach and open the envelope that he knows he should open because it's telling him that he must do something and if he doesn't, the darn thing will have him."

But in Jay's case, Lamberth sensed there was more, more than what Nancy was telling him. There *had* to have been, he thought, or else his cousin probably wouldn't have left in the way that he had.

SIX

JOHN SINE DECIDED to go to the airport to pick up the car. He took the college's athletic director, Trevor Carpenter, with him, and they, John especially, feared the worst. They knew how increasingly distant and ineffective Jay had become over the past year, and they knew he was drinking a great deal (they could see it in his face and, occasionally, smell it on his breath). They also knew that he should not have gone to Florida the previous November, not when the college's problems and the pressure from both the board and the county commissioners were at their most intense. This, though—this was more than they could fathom.

Jay had been used to having things his way, to being a wunderkind. When he put his mind to something—be it obtaining a grant or having a building built—he usually delivered. In truth, Charles County hadn't needed a community college, but Jay had made it a source of deep pride for everyone, a showcase of progress. Back in 1965, John had wanted the job of president, had lobbied hard for it. He had been teaching English at the college, and Jay, a part-time math instructor, worked at the Naval Ordnance Station in nearby Indian Head as a chemical engineer and a member of the management board. The college had been established seven years earlier; it was a makeshift operation, with classes held at night in a high school. But by 1965, community colleges were starting up at an astonishing rate around the country, and the board of trustees wanted someone with a certain charisma, someone with vision.

John had asked Jay to put in a good word for him, and Jay went to see George Dyson, the one person John was convinced was against him. He was right. Dyson wanted Jay to take the job.

"But I'm not an educator," Jay reminded him. "I'm an administrator."

"That's exactly what we want."

Surprised, Jay said he would think it over. What Dyson didn't know was that Jay had been getting restless; the job he had was dangerous, and he simply couldn't see working for the government for the rest of his life. The first few years at NOS had been exciting for Jay. He was working on the Polaris program, making the fuel for the submarine-fired missiles, and, under the watchful eye of Joe Browning, became known as one of Joe's FHB's—Fair-Haired Boys. Then when Kennedy was elected president, Jay got caught up in the fervor of Camelot. He was single (if there was a happier bachelor in the country, he told someone, he had yet to meet him), drove a red Corvette, shot pool and played the slots at Smitty's Steak House, ate regularly at Charlie's Diner, drank beer at Joe Ann Joe's, and lived alone in a trailer behind Dick Fuchs's service station on Route 210, Indian Head Highway.

As puzzling as that last detail was to his male coworkers, the majority of whom lived together in apartments and yearned to be married, Jay simply did things differently. Always had. He was part of the crowd, yet he wasn't.

When he went to see George Dyson about John Sine, Jay had already navigated his way from outsider to a position of respect in the county—not an easy feat, given the area's inbred nature. Sixteen families had come over from England on the *Ark* and the *Dove* in 1634 and settled in Southern Maryland. None of them was named Carsey. But Jay knew how to ingratiate himself. He taught swimming, served as the local head of the Red Cross, gave up Sundays to be a lay preacher (another source of puzzlement, given his lack of faith), and became a scoutmaster. He had a way about him of making you feel that his time was yours. He was charmingly naïve and deceptively unpolished. But far from conspiring against him, his mismatched outfits and uncombed hair endeared him to all he met.

By the time he told John Sine about his discussion with Dyson, he had already come up with a scheme, an ability he would sharpen as the years went by.

"Look," he said, "why don't I go back to Dyson and say, 'I'll take the job on one condition. That you create the position of dean, so that I can appoint John.' "

No sooner had Sine agreed to this than it was done. And for seventeen years, from that day to this, they had worked together as a team. As Sine circled the parking lot at the airport, looking for the Caprice Classic, he thought again about Jay's postcard, how, in a way, it symbolized the beginning—and, perhaps, the end—of their relationship. As for the "pls handle," that was what Jay, a great delegator, would write on countless memos to him.

John spotted the car, then parked his own. Not knowing that Jay had left the keys in the glove compartment, John had brought an extra set. Having convinced himself that Jay might be lying dead in the trunk, John slowly opened it and peeked in. Had the moment not been so serious it would have been amusing. A spare tire. A jack. No body.

"It's like I told you, John," Carpenter said. "A person doesn't go to an airport to commit suicide."

SEVEN

B OB STRAUS DID NOT receive a letter from Jay that Thursday, but he did receive Nancy's troubling call. He was not exactly Nancy's favorite person in the world, and the feeling was decidedly mutual. In his seventies, Straus was cantankerous and Calvinistic. The pin-sharp head of Galaxy (an organization for which Jay did consulting—primarily on matters of energy and education—and from which he earned more than fifty thousand dollars a year), Straus had met Jay for the first time around 1960. Once Jay became president of the college, the two men found a way to help each other. Straus was one of the founders of the Accokeek Foundation, a group devoted to preserving an area of land on the Maryland side of the Potomac River. In return for the college's channeling of resources into the effort, Straus was able to give Jay entrée to

Congress and the Department of Education. Those contacts made it easier for Jay to get money for the college. (A lot easier, as it turned out. At one point, the college had one of the highest percentages of federal aid of any two- or four-year institution in the country.)

Straus was a wheeler-dealer, but so was Jay. A distinct part of his pleasure in cutting deals was the zigzag from conception to completion. The more panache, blue smoke, and mirrors, the better. The last thing Jay wanted to be was a by-the-book bureaucrat. His style was unorthodox and people came to accept it and be frustrated by it at the same time. Joe Browning and Bob Straus were the figures Jay most admired, the men he modeled himself on—but only in terms of business.

What Straus could never understand was Jay's seeming inability to say no to Nancy, to have any effect on her occasional public outbursts and displays of outrageous behavior, and his apparent desire to grant her every wish. Just two days earlier at an Accokeek meeting over which Jay presided, he disappeared briefly. Straus later learned that he had gone to pick up Nancy's dry cleaning, and had asked Straus's secretary not to tell him about it. In fact, whenever Nancy had somewhere to go or something she needed done, Jay would always take her or do it, even though she had her own car and was no longer working full-time.

But as Straus listened to Nancy on the phone, he thought back to another Accokeek meeting months before. Jay had brought Nancy, but since she was not on the board Straus would not allow her to attend. Besides, she had been getting paid to do some work for the foundation and, in Straus's opinion, was not doing it.

"I disinvited her and she went out and sat in the office and looked at papers. And something must have annoyed the hell out of her. So she came screaming into the meeting, saying to Jay, 'You've got to get out of this meeting this minute and resign right now because I've been insulted by them.' There were about ten or twelve pretty substantial citizens there. Jay got up and walked out and they had a great argument outside the door. I said, 'For Christ's sake, Jay, get back in here.' Once he did I excused myself. Nancy had left and had gotten into their car and was going to drive off and leave him there. I said, 'Nancy, first of all, you're going to kill yourself driving around in a rage like this. I think you're making a mountain out of whatever the molehill was.' " Though Straus persuaded her not to drive off, she remained in the car.

It was during this same period of time that Straus had not only observed a dramatic increase in Jay's drinking, but he had talked to him about it. Straus's first wife had been an alcoholic, and he had been a long-suffering member of Al-Anon. "If you keep this up, buster, you'll kill yourself," Straus had told Jay. But none of these things aligned with the news Nancy was now telling him. Normally unflappable, Straus was rattled. To his mind, no matter how bad things are, or seem, you confront them—you don't just walk away.

EIGHT

JAY'S CLOSEST FRIEND in the area was probably Dominic Monetta. Seven years younger than Jay, Monetta looked upon him in the same way Jay viewed Bob Straus and Joe Browning—as someone to admire and emulate. Slick, brash, and aggressive, he burned with the same ambition to make his mark that Jay did, though Monetta's was considerably more naked. His career eerily mirrored Jay's. Both were chemical engineers, both had worked for the Naval Ordnance Station, both had been on the management board there, both had doctorates in public administration. And both possessed an uncanny sense of who was traveling north, and how to hitch a ride, and who was not.

A native of the Bronx whose father had been in the produce business, Monetta was not without warmth, not without charm, studied as it might be, and not without a deep-seated Sicilian loyalty to his friends. He was a man to be counted on. Head of his own consulting firm, he was in New Mexico on business when Bob Straus tracked him down.

"Dom, we've got a problem," Straus said with characteristic bluntness.

"What is it?" Monetta asked, thinking that only an aborted business deal would result in Straus's calling.

"Jay left."

"Oh yeah, where did he go?" said Monetta sarcastically.

"You missed my point. Jay disappeared."

Jay disappeared. Monetta, to himself, repeated the two words over and over, but they made no sense. It's not that Monetta hadn't heard of people doing this. It's just that Jay Carsey—the Jay Carsey *he* knew—didn't. As far as Monetta was concerned, Straus could have been speaking in tongues.

"Did he leave a note?"

"Yeah, he left one for Nancy," Straus said, filling Monetta in on the canceled meetings and on Philadelphia.

"Is Nancy okay?"

"Well, she sounds badly traumatized."

"Listen, thanks for calling. I'll probably be back in D.C. sooner than I'd planned."

He took the next available plane. On the long trip east, he worried that something had "really gone awry" in Jay's and Nancy's marriage. In Jay's letter (Monetta had had a friend in his apartment building look through his mail) he expected word that Jay had moved to D.C. or Baltimore and was getting ready to see a divorce lawyer.

As soon as he got back, he anxiously grabbed the mail, but waited until he walked into the privacy of his apartment before reading Jay's message:

Dom—

　　Easy come, easy go. Please take care of Nancy for a while.

Jay

The expression was familiar to Monetta. Whenever something particularly difficult happened to either of them, Jay always tried to minimize it by flippantly saying this. When Monetta went

24

through a painful divorce, Jay called him every few days and often said it in an effort to lift his spirits. But, more significant, Jay's seeming insensitivity toward Monetta was actually covering his own aversion to dealing with matters of the heart.

As for Jay's request, it didn't strike Monetta as strange or unreasonable. Like Jay, he dealt in the world of chits and the mutual scratching of backs. At that point, it wasn't a question for him of understanding the reasons for what Jay had done. He not only didn't, he couldn't say for sure what they were. But that didn't matter. Monetta's philosophy was simple: with friends, you accept their actions without necessarily understanding them. And when it came to Jay, it was even simpler. Monetta felt he owed Jay a great deal; if that meant taking care of Nancy "for a while," he would do it. But not even Monetta, loyal to a fault, could know the full extent of what that would mean.

NINE

EVELYN HUNGERFORD HAD BEEN by Nancy's side when she began making her phone calls. John Parran had called Evelyn, and she had rushed over. Evelyn was Nancy's closest friend. Nancy and Jay were "Aunt Nancy" and "Uncle Jay" to Evelyn's children. The Carseys and the Hungerfords spent nearly every Thanksgiving together. They had time-sharing units in Florida, they played bridge and tennis with each other. They had been friends for many years. Evelyn and her husband Vince, a pilot who now worked at NOS, had grown up in Indian Head. They knew Nancy's first husband, had witnessed her turning from him to Jay, and had a fairly good understanding of why. Evelyn's father was Nancy's doctor; Vince's brother had been married to John Sine's wife. Each person's life in the county seemed, somehow, to touch on someone else's.

Evelyn and Nancy were alike in a number of ways. Strong-willed and outspoken, they were women chameleonic enough to be "one of the guys" one moment and altogether feminine the next, women who seemed to dominate their quieter husbands. Evie, as most people called her, knew Nancy as well as, if not better than, anyone—but that knowledge had its limitations. She felt that Nancy would tell her only what Nancy wanted her to know, would take things out of context, would level with her only up to a point.

When Nancy first moved to the area in 1958, she was Nancy Stevens Brumfield, from a middle-class Methodist family in Princeton, Indiana. Her father died just after she graduated from high school and she had been the apple of his eye. He used to take her hunting, fishing, and practically everywhere he went. Only forty-seven when he died, his heart attacks had kept him bedridden for a number of years, but didn't prevent him from controlling the daily life of the family, even the annual decorating of the Christmas tree. He had been in the insurance business, then opened a diner. Nancy, her mother, and her younger brother, Mike, all worked there, and the family had a comfortable existence in a house on South Hart Street, as well as a portion of a farm that was in the Stevens family. But with Simon Stevens's death, their financial situation deteriorated and Nancy decided to go to nearby Purdue, instead of a college in Missouri. There was also another reason: not long before her father died, she had met a handsome farm boy from neighboring Fort Branch, and he tried to fill the void that her father had left. His name was Gordon Brumfield.

Gordon had met Nancy at a basketball game. She kept dropping her coat and he kept picking it up, all the while staring at her long red hair. Things, as they say, progressed from there, and by the time she arrived at Purdue they were pinned.

Nancy was the valedictorian of her class in high school, but at Purdue an active social life took precedence over her studies. Since Gordon sensed Nancy's constant wish to be entertained, to be in the social whirl, and felt that he would not be able to satisfy this need in her, he encouraged her to date other men. But whenever Nancy came back to her sorority house after an evening out, Gordon, more often than not, would be there, hopeful for a dismal report. As much as she loved the variety of attention, she eventually decided that Gordon, solid and ever reliable, was for her, and they had a large, traditional wedding on a cold Indiana night in December of 1956.

But as joyous as the occasion was, as much as he loved "Red" and was mesmerized by her, there were two things that Gordon couldn't entirely shake from his mind. One night at Purdue he had been taking Nancy back to her dorm so that she would be in before curfew. They had been having a discussion about something, a discussion she felt had not been resolved, and she refused to get out of the car. Nancy had violated her parietal hours before, Gordon reminded her, but she was not listening. In fact, the more Gordon tried to reason with her, the more incensed Nancy became. So, his patience exhausted, he got out of the car, came around to her side, and, after smashing the little window that turned inward, he unlocked the door and dragged her out.

The other thing involved Nancy's mother, Clo. When her husband died, Clo began working at the local factory in Princeton on the assembly line. But Nancy, wanting more for her, encouraged her to get a loan from the bank and open a clothing store for young girls, Clo's Young Miss Shop. Nancy played a large role in its design (a lavender and purple motif, of course) and in selecting the clothes (often meeting her mother in Chicago and going through the Merchandise Mart together). So it was unsettling to Gordon when Clo pulled him aside one day and said, "I hope you're not planning to have a family, Gordon, because my daughter is really too selfish."

When the Brumfields arrived at Indian Head, Gordon was a young naval officer and Nancy had plans to teach elementary school. At first they lived in a trailer, then moved into an apartment which Nancy decorated like a South Seas island. They spent a lot of time at the Officers' Club, Nancy flirting with everyone long into the night and usually telling Gordon that they would leave when she was ready, and it was there, one day in the early Sixties, that Jay Carsey first saw her. It was during a break from rehearsals of *The Rainmaker*, and Jay "practically leapt out of his chair," John Sine remembered.

In no time at all, it seemed, Gordon, Nancy, and Jay became an almost inseparable trio, and in no time at all, the word *cuckold* began to form on people's lips. Nancy and Jay appeared to have more in common than Nancy and Gordon, and Gordon seemed perfectly happy for Jay to take Nancy to museums and the theater in Washington. It didn't really occur to anyone, even Vince and Evelyn Hungerford, that Gordon was subtly encouraging the liaison as a way of getting out of the marriage.

Gordon's feeling that he couldn't measure up to Nancy's expectations—that he could never be as successful or as socially prominent as Nancy would want—had been a problem almost from the start, and it was part of what did them in. Jay, meanwhile, was going somewhere, everyone could see that, but he needed someone who would take him in hand, smooth out the rough edges, and give him an uptown image.

Nancy had also developed a reputation as someone who was going somewhere. From the moment she began teaching fifth grade at Indian Head Elementary, she was considered a teacher without peer, envied and resented by her colleagues ("Plain vanilla always dislikes a strawberry parfait," was how one admirer, Dorothy Artes, put it), idolized by the children. One time Nancy persuaded an extremely shy local artist to come to her class and paint a portrait of her. She had the artist sit with her back to the children so that they could see the painting evolve. On another occasion, Nancy noticed how well dressed one little girl was, a girl less confident than some of the other students. So Nancy went over to where she was sitting, knelt down, and said, holding the girl's hand, "Oh, Amy, tell me how in the world you were so clever to put on a dress this morning that so perfectly matches your beautiful eyes?" Amy said nothing, but she didn't have to. Her face lit up, and she trembled with pleasure.

These were only some of the things that Dorothy Artes, a substitute teacher at the school, recalled about Nancy. Yet, for some reason, she felt defeated. "You have no way of knowing the impact she had on those children. She was like the air they breathed, the sunshine they required. She played those kids just like an orchestra. When she wanted them to sing, they sang. She gave them that extra thing that makes beauty out of the world." Artes even went so far as to praise Nancy formally in a letter to the National Education Association.

But there was more that Dorothy Artes wanted to say. She wanted to say that Nancy had a Jekyll-and-Hyde personality. That the warmth and caring, the constant nurturing, she displayed day after day in the classroom did not spill over into her relationship with either Gordon or Jay, both of whom Artes had come to know. She had no trouble understanding their both wanting to please Nancy so much, but she couldn't understand why Nancy was unable to shed her "Lady of the Manor pretense." Perhaps it stemmed from a deep insecurity that neither man could ever shore up, a look on Nancy's face, captured in that classroom portrait, that reminded Dorothy of "a forlorn little girl, lonely as a hound dog on a mountaintop, wanting, desperately, to be important."

Whatever, it prevented Nancy, in Dorothy's opinion, from ever "sitting down and analyzing what Jay wanted out of life." For the longest time, they were "riding the main line and letting the good times roll. Because he was so entranced by Nancy, I think he enjoyed it so much at first that she had deluded herself into thinking that he really did want to live at that pace. And I don't think she even recognized when he began to get bored with it all or disappointed."

But in thinking about that, something else occurred to Dorothy. "I think she basically needed a masterful man because she'd been able to lead Gordon and Jay around by their noses. I think she basically wanted Jay to say, 'Now look, Nancy, we're going to slow down here. We've got a lovely home and I'm getting older, you're getting older, let's slow down the pace and put some depth in this marriage. We're just roommates and partygoers together.' But I don't think he did it. And I'll tell you, he's got a hell of a lot of nerve to leave her like that, with all the humiliation of being the woman scorned."

TEN

Throughout that Thursday friends came and went. Nancy refused to get dressed or leave the house. She wanted to be there for Jay's call, convinced it would come and ostensibly daring anyone to suggest it wouldn't. People brought food. More than one of them felt they were at a wake—without a body. No one quite knew what to say or do, but they wanted to comfort Nancy as best they could. Whenever she was asked where Jay might go, her stuporous response was always the same: "Someplace warm. Jay hates cold weather." She mentioned Texas (as she had to Jay's cousin Lamberth), as well as Mexico, San Diego, Australia, and New Zealand—places they had been to together and loved, she reminded everyone. (Jay in fact had been so taken with Sydney that he had become a subscriber to the *Sydney Morning Herald*.) She started to make a list, putting *Puerto Vallarta* after Mexico and *Hotel del Coronado* after San Diego. Though playing a role was not unusual for Nancy, she was becoming an amateur detective without fully realizing it.

When Jim and Barbara Simpson arrived, she couldn't help thinking back to the previous Saturday night and the wedding of the Simpsons' daughter. Jay, for some reason, was not able to attend the ceremony, and he was late for the reception. "I was so lonely without him until he got there," Nancy recalled. "I remember standing around that dance floor watching the couples enjoy themselves and I thought, I wish Jay would hurry, I really miss him, 'cause the music was the kind of stuff we enjoyed dancing to. I was standing there talking to Evie and I was saying, 'God, where *is* he? He really should be here by now.' " But if she was impatient waiting for him, she was also sobered by something else—seeing people she had known for years who were either divorced or widowed, who were without companionship. It made her feel lucky about what she had and long for Jay even more. "Jay used to tease me when I'd say, 'Jay, we have so much, we enjoy things to such a degree. Can it always be this way?' and he'd say, 'Why do you always think it can't continue?' He'd make me feel childish to have even thought like that."

When Jay finally arrived that night, they had a delightful evening. That, at least, was how Nancy perceived it. "I left the wedding just thinking what a wonderful time we had had together. I thought, In a week we'll have that graduation out of the way and we can do things we like together all summer. He must have been thinking, In a few days I'll have a whole different . . . I don't know what he was thinking. It just doesn't seem possible that he could be that deceptive. I always thought—I was *sure*—that what we had was special. How could he do that? How could he live with himself? It would tear your gut apart, I would think, to live with someone and deceive them like that."

HOW WELL DOES—or can—one person ever know another? Nancy wasn't the only one asking that question. If seeing the Simpsons only took Nancy back five days in time, it took Jim Simpson, a state senator, back to the previous November, when he and a mutual friend went to visit the Carseys in Captiva, Florida. They had driven from St. Petersburg and did not plan to stay the night; Jay seemed distressed and was acting as if company were the last thing he wanted. (This surprised the senator. He was so used to Jay's being accommodating—one time Jay had driven all the way to Washington on a weekday and picked up box lunches for Nancy's bridge game—that he had kidded him once, "You're spoiling it for the rest of us.") But Nancy insisted, and Simpson and Tom Posey wound up staying an uncomfortable three days. Whenever the four of them played tennis, Simpson recalled, it became more than a match. "It was life or death for them. Their competitiveness was so apparent it took the fun out of it." When others, like Vince and Evelyn Hungerford, would play with the Carseys, Nancy would often scream at Jay if he missed a shot. Eventually they took to playing on opposing sides.

The Simpsons owned a wholesale beverage business, and one of their drivers had told them, not long after that, he had seen Jay at a bar in the middle of the morning. At the time, the senator dismissed it from his mind, sure the driver had either made a mistake or that Jay had just stopped in for coffee. As far as Simpson was concerned (as well as many of the Carseys' friends), Jay didn't drink any more than anyone else in Charles County, which is to say that people in that part of the world enjoy bending their elbows quite a little bit. In fact, Jay always seemed to be the one driving other people home.

But what Simpson didn't know, nor did the other people who saw the Carseys in Florida that November, was that Jay not only was drinking heavily, he was trying to conceal it from Nancy. She would be looking for something in a drawer and come upon a martini at nine in the morning. "My heart would just start pounding and I would lash out, 'Jay, what is this? What *is* this? Let's talk about it.' And then he would clam up, I would try to quiet down, and he would have a nice, rational reason." Nancy suggested that he seek help in Washington, so that his image could be protected, "but he just totally blocked me out. I couldn't get to him. He wouldn't communicate. I just wanted to help him, 'cause I thought that he and I could solve anything together."

Jay and Nancy against the world. That was how it had always been, and it had seemed to work, but by the fall of 1981 their united front was crumbling.

THERE ARE SOME who have no nickname, and others who have one. But aside from criminals, very few people, it seems, have two. John Sprague was known to everyone as "Buddy" and to some as "Slick." His boy-next-door, fresh-faced good looks would have made him an excellent candidate to understudy Wally on "Leave It to Beaver." He owned a good deal of real estate and a liquor store that was across the road from where Jay used to have his trailer, which, by the way, was still there, a monument to his past, radically simpler life.

When Jay and Nancy first considered buying Green's Inheritance, 188 acres came with it. Since they couldn't afford what that would have cost, Jay put together a limited partnership and asked Buddy to become an investor. Jay also put Buddy on his board of advisers to the college, and Buddy did his best to be an extra set of eyes and ears in the community, a troubleshooter of sorts.

Buddy was as aware as anybody of the problems Jay was having at the college; in addition to the federal cutback of funds, enrollment, after years of soaring growth, had dropped off considerably.

In the past six months Jay would often stop by the liquor store to shoot the breeze with Buddy in the late afternoon. And even though Buddy began to notice that Jay didn't look well and was becoming increasingly withdrawn, he attributed it (along with Jay's drinking) less to the pressures at the college than "living with that goddamn redhead." It wasn't that Buddy didn't like Nancy. What he couldn't abide, though, were the times Nancy would get angry at Jay and begin berating him, and the way in which "the more Jay tried to avoid her wrath, the more she belittled him." These incidents, which Buddy found both ugly and embarrassing, would either happen on the tennis court or after Nancy had had a few drinks, and would often concern the one thing they didn't have—a child.

Buddy was only one of the many people who put Jay on a pedestal (except when it came to his dealing with Nancy), who thought of him as the Dale Carnegie of the county, as a magician when it came to doing the impossible. But few of these people, including Buddy to some extent, had been calling Jay to give him a vote of confidence. If he had brought rain time after time in the past, the thinking went, then of course he would find a way to solve the money problems without a loss of jobs. Perhaps if his friends and supporters had known Jay was receiving hostile mail and phone calls at home, they might have been on the phone themselves, reminding him that, no matter what, day or night, they were there for him.

But they weren't used to being there for him. Jay didn't let them be. If he had, he would have been admitting weakness and vulnerability and they might stop coming to him with *their* problems. He had set up this one-way dynamic, this role of priest and father-figure, and now he was gone, a victim of his own unwillingness, perhaps, to appear fallible, to appear human, to allow anybody in. So as Buddy Sprague stood in the house that Thursday, he was sad, he was upset, he was concerned, but he didn't feel particularly guilty. Once Jay started coming by the store, Buddy said he was sorry that Jay was having a rough time, and asked if there was anything he could do. But Jay essentially brushed him off, thanking him for his concern, saying everything would be fine, and then changing the subject.

But things weren't fine. When the Carseys went to a party a few weeks before Jay left, they arrived fashionably late, as always. As Nancy made her customary grand entrance, Jay trailing a few feet behind, she tripped and fell. Much to everyone's surprise, Jay didn't help her up, or even ask if she was all right. He walked on, oblivious, as if she were a total stranger.

"Buddy, could you come upstairs with me?" It was Nancy, her commanding voice bringing him back to the present.

"Sure," Buddy said, wondering what she wanted, or couldn't say in the presence of the other people there.

As they made their way to the stairs, Buddy took in all the things he had seen a hundred times before—the armor, the masks, the carvings, everything in its place—but found he was now looking at them in a different way. It wasn't that he had never wondered how Jay could go from living in a trailer to a house that many considered more a museum (or, in one person's opinion, mausoleum) than a home. It was just that he found himself wondering to what extent all of these trappings had affected Jay, to what extent he may have felt driven out by these possessions alone, to what extent he may have felt he could no longer afford the way of life he had partly created, that he could no longer afford Nancy. Once they got to the bedroom, Buddy couldn't contain a little smile, a welcome moment of comic relief. Straight ahead of him was the fountain everyone joked about, the one they knew Nancy loved, the one that was supposed to induce a sleep full of sweet dreams but which resulted in countless trips to the bathroom instead.

"Buddy," Nancy said, "on the tape Jay left he said that the college owes him a check. Now, I *know* he's coming back. But just in case something has happened to him, or he has done something to himself, I want you to see if you can persuade Louis to not only release that money, but to keep Jay's salary coming in."

"I'll see what I can do, Nancy," he said, taken aback by the timing of her request, by her ability to be terribly upset one moment and coldly talking dollars and cents the next.

THE TIMING OF that request had something to do with Spencer Matthews. In his sixties, Spencer was a retired admiral and former naval aviator who had fought in three wars. In every conceivable way, from his clipped, yes-sir-no-sir manner to his deep, booming voice and his equally deep sense of right and wrong, he was a military man, medaled and ribboned. Words and phrases like *courage* and *moral obligation* were the bedrock from which he looked, humanly but somewhat imperiously, at the world. He and his wife, Jackie, were relatively recent friends of the Carseys, and he and Jay had a number of things in common: the Navy, an interest in the various uses of computers in education (Spencer was a trustee of the Naval Academy Foundation), and a love of travel.

Two nights earlier, the night before Jay left, Spencer had called Jay and they had talked of getting together for lunch the following week at the Army & Navy Club. The conversation, Spencer recalled, was as normal as any they had ever had, and that made the fact that his friend had left without a word all the more shocking, hurtful, and ultimately disappointing.

"As a flier," Spencer said later in struggling to understand why Jay hadn't confided in him, "my life was dependent on—literally in the hands of—my friends. I think some of us in the military, who fought in all these wars and have seen friends die, develop personal relationships that are so much more meaningful and valuable than perhaps some people who are not exposed to that environment. It could be that Jay had a different attitude toward our friendship. Maybe it didn't mean as much to him."

Perhaps it didn't. If so, it seemed Spencer would have to accept that, upsetting as it might be. But he had been around enough years and enough people to know that, more often than not, "you're only exposed to various compartments of their lives, not to the full spectrum."

That still, however, left the question of Nancy, and what Spencer considered Jay's unfair treatment of her, "his moral obligation to not leave her in such a traumatic way. First there was the shock, then the feeling of ultimate rejection—and it will always be there. I can never be convinced that Nancy had any indication of a lack of communication or of a deteriorating relationship." What he was convinced of, though, was that Jay's leaving demonstrated an odd combination of courage and gutlessness. "There are a lot of Jay Carseys sitting out there, staying in a relationship, who don't have the courage to do what he did, which he did that way because he lacked the courage to do the right thing, what basic human values would indicate that you ought to do."

And the admiral was convinced of something else: that Jay was too stable an individual to take his own life; and that Nancy was a strong enough person, enough of a survivor, to eventually accept what Spencer had told her that Thursday— that she had to pull herself together and forget Jay, that there was no reason in the world that she should suffer because of his weakness.

For Spencer, Jay's leaving was like a sneak attack, and everyone had been wounded, not just Nancy. Harsh as his advice to her was at the time, he was merely fighting back, trying to respond to an enemy he couldn't see, to comfort himself as much as he was trying to help Nancy.

ABOUT THE QUESTION of communication, Spencer Matthews was only partly right. Friends see what they want to see, believe what they want to believe. And even if they sense something is awry, the majority will let it pass. It's easier, it's safer, and besides, confrontation doesn't always work, is often taken for prying. Nobody knew that better than Nancy.

From the moment she met Jay she found that certain areas of his life were simply not open for discussion. She would ask about his growing up in Texas and the scant details he reluctantly offered would be as fuzzy as a poor photograph. He seemed proud of saying he had "weaned his parents early" so that they wouldn't expect too much of his time. When Jay and Nancy decided to marry in April of 1968, he not only didn't invite his parents, he didn't tell them about it. That would only have drawn attention to the fact they had been living together, something he knew his mother would not have approved of. And if Jay's sister had not come to live with him in his trailer during the summer of 1963, it is likely that Nancy never would have learned the full extent—the truth—of his importance to Susie.

When Jay talked to people he seldom looked directly at them, and that concerned Nancy. How could he ever expect to gain their trust? she would ask him, but somehow he always did. As a nostalgic reminder of the many Sundays he had traveled around the county as a lay preacher, Nancy had bought him a portable pulpit, only to find out much later, when they were discussing death (and what might happen to you afterward), that Jay had serious doubts about the existence of God.

If these things concerned Nancy, it was Jay's inability to express his emotions that truly upset her. "Jay had a hard time telling me he loved me," Nancy admitted, bowing her head. "It was a difficult word for him to ever get out. He could write it easier than he could say it." (Before they were married, Nancy spent two summers in Europe and Jay wrote her letters and poems. After they were married, he would send her monthly anniversary cards, letting the message on the card speak for him.) For the most part, Nancy was eventually able to transform her upset about this into rational acceptance, into wishing they could have talked more but claiming "we always seemed to get along without a lot of feelings kind of talk. Besides, you get so busy with your daily routines that these kinds of things don't surface that often anyway."

But occasionally they would, and they would involve more than talk. One night, not long after they had moved into Green's Inheritance, Nancy got a phone call—a call telling her that her younger brother, her only sibling, had suddenly died of a heart attack. "I remember that evening," Nancy said, running her hands through her hair, "just sitting and shaking on the side of the bed, feeling my guts had been torn out. I thought, I wish he could sense that I want him to just hold me, that I need it. And I tried to put my arms around him, and he gave me a little hug, but I *needed* to be held. He didn't understand that. These kinds of things might have happened a lot, but I had gotten used to them. That was Jay. It just wasn't in him to give hugs. I'm a much more emotional person than he is. Even though I hit both peaks and valleys, there is a lot of emotion in me, and I probably gave him a lot more of me than he ever knew, because I don't think he had that much to give of himself."

A few years before Mike's death, Jay and Nancy had gone to Maine for two weeks of "sensitivity training." (Nancy was a principal in Prince George's County at this point; since her school system was beginning to experience the turmoil of desegregation, they paid for her to go and Jay went along.) In the group therapy sessions, Nancy learned that it was perfectly all right to express herself with four-letter words, and she learned the importance of being open to people, that "every human being has something positive to offer." What Jay learned, she felt, was less clear. She thought he was made uncomfortable by everyone baring his soul, and saw it as nothing more than a two-week vacation. "To tell you the truth," she said later, "I don't know what he thought, because he would never talk about what he thought."

IT HAD BEEN a long, exhausting day, and by the time it ended Virginia Foster had finally learned from Katharyn Jones what had happened. She had had time to think about her conversations with Jay over the past year, and she recalled three things that gave her pause, things she was not conscious of at the time. One had to do with President Reagan and how Jay felt he was "ruining everything" in terms of money for education. The second had to do with Nancy, and Virginia's realization that Jay "had stopped talking about 'Nancy and I' or 'we.'" The last had to do with a call Jay had made to the house during a workday just a few weeks before, a call which her husband had answered. Jay *always* phoned Virginia at work, and it made her wonder if the call had been his odd way of saying he was leaving without having to speak with her. She didn't know for sure, but what she did know—what she strongly felt— she told Jay's sister in no uncertain terms on the phone that Thursday night.

"Susie," she said, "that boy is crazy. He's lost his mind."

"No, Toodge," Susie said, "he's found it."

ELEVEN

SUSIE WAS LYING IN BED when she talked to her aunt on the phone, and when she hung up she continued to lie there, smoking one cigarette after another, wondering where her only brother had gone with his newfound sanity. Susie had lived in Northern Virginia for nearly twenty years, but in the sense that people can never really disentangle from their past and the experiences that shaped them, much as they might desperately want to, she had never left the small, East Texas town of Bryan.

Back there, back when she was "a little bitty," born an unwelcome eleven years after Jay, his—not her mother's, not her father's—was the first face she remembered, smiling down at her as he wound up a stuffed animal that proceeded to play "Mary Had a Little Lamb." He was "Doodie" then (her version of Julian), but she continued to call him that until he made her promise that she would stop. As far as she was concerned, that was the least she could do. She owed him a lot.

When he was thirteen, he started saving his pennies for a life insurance policy—with her as beneficiary—and when she started school, he worked with her on her primers and read to her before she closed her blue eyes at night. He played jacks with her on the porch of the family's modest stucco house, showed her how to tie a bow, and put her in his bike basket on trips to the library. In summer, when he was a lifeguard at the local pool and she was old enough to swim, he would give her a Baby Ruth every time she dared to go off the high dive.

To Jay, Susie was his responsibility, one he dutifully shouldered. To Susie, Jay was the sun and the moon. If he was at all resentful, she was not aware of it.

What she became aware of, though, was that she had not been a wanted child, and that her mother, forty-four when Susie was born, had considered having an abortion, a pretty radical step at the time. Jay was the one, Jay was *always* the one, whom their mother's world revolved around, the one who carried the burden of meeting her high expectations—ones their father couldn't manage to, hard as he tried.

Bea Nance had come from a well-to-do, God-fearing Baptist family in the sunbaked West Texas town of Ballinger, roughly halfway between Abilene and San Angelo. She was thin, petite, and rather plain, but what she may have lacked in surface good looks was more than made up for by her bubbling personality. Whatever passed for West Texas aristocracy at the time, the Nances were a proud and definite part of, and Bea's was an upbringing in which she and her sisters were expected to become proper ladies

41

and land a man with good prospects. She took piano and violin lessons, faithfully attended church and Sunday School, learned how to play a mean hand of bridge, but went off to college in Abilene and returned home without a husband. She began working at the local picture show, selling tickets for a nickel, and it was there, in 1922, that she caught the eye of a handsome little devil named Homer Carsey.

Twenty-seven at the time, Homer was seven years older than Bea, had blond hair and blue eyes, and had been living a life that could best be described as fast and loose, colorful and adventurous. His father had run away from home at thirteen, learned how to make everything from boots to cabinets, and to live by his wits. Crazy about music, he became a traveling musician and bandleader, moving his family around so much that Homer felt too young to know whether he was supposed to enjoy it or not. "He moved anywhere he could organize a municipal band," Homer said of the time when towns had their own bands and schools did not. "Lampasas. Rising Star. Fort Stockton. Sweetwater. It would be hard to tell you how many towns we did live in. We rarely stayed in one place over a year. A band would peter out. Adults would give up the ghost of trying to learn to play instruments, and if someone quit and he didn't have a replacement, he put me in that section."

So it was hardly surprising that when *Billboard* magazine began advertising for musicians ("they were so dadgum scarce") that Homer, age fourteen, took his inherited love of music—and wanderlust—and joined a tent show called Renfro's Jolly Pathfinders for the princely sum of fifteen dollars a week. But Homer's father didn't let him leave until he was sure his son understood that music was not all that tent-show life was about, that "certain evils might befall me."

Needless to say, Homer soon became acquainted with the ways of the world, but not, according to him, because he took the initiative. "I never did chase the girls," he said. "I don't know why. They just never seemed to occupy my mind that much. I was always more interested in reading. I've often wondered why I wasn't more bullish about sex. I remember being in Manhattan, Kansas, once. It was during World War I. After the show a woman was standing by the exit and struck up a conversation with me. Before I knew it, she told me to go home with her. She lived in a two-story house, and I remember walking through the downstairs and there were a bunch of sleeping children and we went upstairs. That gal kept me busy until sunup and I decided to try and get out of there, and besides, I didn't feel so good about it. She was one of those women who can't get enough. That's the reason, I guess, the lower floor had so many children. Anyway, things like that happened. I never did chase anybody."

But they happened enough that Homer eventually burned all the evidence—all the photographs and letters (including a goodly number from a college president's wife, some twenty years older than he)—from his circus days, and he had his reasons. "I just didn't want posterity to see some of that stuff," he explained one day, getting red in the face. "If I passed first, I didn't want anybody crying."

By the time he met Bea Nance he was in between seasons with the Sells-Floto Circus and tiring of his vagabondish life. He had been at it, off and on, for about thirteen years, and he yearned to do what his father had done—organize a band. His parents were living in Ballinger at the time, and he discovered that its town band (a sorry group of thirteen, all male, all adults) was in dire need of a good director. When Homer went to talk to the people in charge, he had learned enough from his father's experiences to say that he would take the job on one condition: that he could start classes (and charge money) in order to train children to play, the only way, he felt, to ensure the life and success of the band. Once the town fathers agreed, Homer's years on the road, for the most part, came to an end. But not his troubles.

Anyway, he had seen Bea at the picture show a few times before, but had never spoken with her, and the only reason he decided to approach her, so he said, was that a friend of his named Roy Power, a ladies' man, had come to visit and was eager to have a date. So Homer went right up to the ticket window and told Bea his name and his problem: "I've got a friend visiting here and I have no way to entertain him." Bea said that she had a girlfriend who would like to go out, and over the next few days the four of them rode around in Roy's car and went dancing. Aside from going to church and the picture show, there wasn't much else to do in Ballinger. Except have a drink or two. Even though it was the heyday of Prohibition, nearly everyone, it seemed, had concocted a pretty potent home brew, usually getting the key ingredient—whiskey—by slipping a doctor three dollars for a "prescription."

Roy Power eventually left town, but Bea and Homer stayed together and made plans to marry, over her father's objections, in November of 1924. It wasn't that Mr. Nance was worried about Homer's supporting Bea. By this point in time, Homer had not one, but five town bands, and was raking in the cash, primarily through selling the band members their instruments, which he would get from New York. No, what troubled Bea's father was the wayward life he felt Homer had led, and he made it clear to his daughter that he was sure she could do better, that society girls simply didn't attach themselves to circus performers. But there was something else that bothered him, even more than his fear that Homer would turn out to be a scoundrel, and that something had to do with Homer's lack of faith. The idea of W. A. Nance's daughter getting married to an agnostic (and socialist to boot) who was always going on about Robert Ingersoll and Thomas Paine as if either of them could have been God himself made his skin crawl. But Bea was determined, the marriage went forward, and Homer put his bride, "all ninety-eight spicy pounds of her," into a brand-new Ford with a rumble seat and pointed it east, to Dallas and Fort Worth, for their honeymoon.

Within the year, though, she was back in her father's house.

. . .

"I HAVE NO more idea what that was all about than that little ol' jackrabbit," Homer said, pointing out the window. "I can't remember what in the devil happened. Just got crossways or something, and she went home. Funny thing is, we never argued about anything—at least not that I know of."

What he did know was that he hadn't been all that keen to marry in the first place. But he was twenty-nine years old and that was old to be a bachelor in those days, and he sure didn't want anyone questioning his sexual persuasion. What attracted him to Bea was her charm and her ability to make friends easily and permanently, an ability Homer didn't have—or could ever understand. "She knew everybody and everybody was crazy about her. Everybody that was ever associated with her for five minutes would like her. She had that about her. I don't know what it was. I still don't."

What Bea found attractive about Homer was the glamour of what he did, but she soon learned, to her dismay, that he was not the gregarious social animal that his public life had led her to believe. He would take her dancing in San Angelo, but, for the most part, he was not comfortable around people. She would often complain about his lack of social graces when her bridge partners would come to call, or how late he often made the two of them when they had somewhere to go. As far as he was concerned, Bea was "too goddarned social," but he quickly found that she would bear very little criticism of her tea-and-parties lifestyle. Since he loved her—"to the extent I could love anybody, or even knew what love was"— he went along, by and large, with the things *she* wanted to do. Went along because it was in his nature (as it would be in his son's) to "fall in the line of least resistance."

Nevertheless, Bea went home and began to go out with a young man whose father was the prosperous owner of the local lumber company. And Homer, whose "pride was offended," retaliated by starting up with the pretty daughter of a rancher. But no sooner had word spread that "Bea didn't like that Higginbotham boy," than Homer decided to swallow his pride and invite her to go away overnight. "We had a sexual party at a hotel in Coleman, Texas," he recalled, "and came back home. Stayed home. She was disillusioned with her separation and it didn't make much difference to me.

"To tell you the truth," he went on, "women expect too much out of you—especially in the first year of marriage. We never kissed each other much. I'm just not a very affectionate fellow. But hell, mothers tell their daughters that that fervor can't last forever."

As to what Bea's expectations might have been, Homer didn't have a clue. "I don't even know what mine were," he confessed, shaking his head. "I think about things like that."

BUT EXPECTATIONS—OR the lack of them—continued to play a role in their lives. Nearly ten years after Homer and Bea got married, they received the unexpected news that Bea was pregnant. Like Homer, she had not particularly wanted a child. On the contrary. She did not want anything to hamper her social life. Nonetheless, when Julian Nance Carsey was born on May 13, 1935, they were delighted, even though their circumstances—and the country's—had changed.

But it wasn't only the Depression that made it difficult for Homer to make ends meet. As his municipal bands began to fold and give way to school bands, the fact that Homer didn't belong to a church prevented him from running the school band in Ballinger, or in any of the towns nearby. "It's plain and simple," Homer said. "If you weren't religious, you were dangerous."

So in 1937 the Carseys moved clear to the other side of the state, to a dot on the map called Rusk, in shouting distance of the Louisiana border and not far from where Homer's brother was living. Homer managed to get a job directing the school band there—provided he would do one thing: play his trumpet at the Methodist church every Sunday. Since he had a family to support, he reluctantly agreed.

If the expression "Children should be seen and not heard" could be traced to any one particular child, it would be traced to Jay Carsey. He was the epitome of goodness, his mother's idol, her pride and joy. She would read to him and then, once he could, he would spend as much time reading as his father, who bought him the Harvard Classics when he was thirteen. He was such a superb student that one of his teachers told Homer they had "a genius in the household." He collected butterflies, made friends as easily as his mother did, played softball and the cornet, and became an Eagle Scout. "He was the best kid," Homer recalled. "Bridge players never even knew the little booger was around. In fact, I don't remember him crying much as a little ol' baby. I'm sure he did, but I don't remember it. Why, he was so good he would rock himself to sleep at night." And so independent that Homer felt Jay "raised himself."

But in saying that, Homer was more ashamed than proud. "As a papa, I was a failure. I never did take enough interest in Julian's activities. He was always closer to Bea. She couldn't have asked for more in a son. I'm just not sensitive enough to other people. I just let him manage for himself. Raised him like my daddy did me. I didn't take him hunting or fishing, didn't play softball with him, didn't help him build anything. He was an Eagle Scout, but couldn't build a bird cage."

Yet along with this streak of independence was a self-containment that bordered on the secretive. "Julian always kept his information to himself," Homer said. "And like me, he was always so good at hiding his feelings. He would never defend himself or blame anybody else. He just didn't relish confrontation with anybody."

THE SAME COULDN'T be said of Susie, and when she accidentally came along, in 1946, Homer had to make a decision about the family's financial future. During the previous few summers, to make extra money, Homer had worked in Houston and in Louisiana for various pipeline companies. Since his was an office job, he became a good typist, and when he returned to Rusk in the fall, someone at the local newspaper told him he could make a lot more money as a linotype operator than he could as a schoolteacher. So he began to practice any chance he could, and the following summer he got a job on a newspaper in Dodge City, Kansas. From there he was hired by the newspaper in Bryan, Texas, and began work on the *Daily Eagle* in the fall of 1947, moving his family from Rusk a few months later.

For all his self-deprecating talk about not being sensitive to others, Homer had a good and selfless reason for choosing Bryan. When Jay would be ready to go to college, in the fall of 1952, he would be able to attend nearby Texas A&M and live at home.

STATUS CAN OFTEN be more important to a person than money, and to Bea Carsey, Homer's new job meant a considerable drop in the former. She had, for the most part, been happy in Ballinger and Rusk, but her unhappiness with having had a second child was now compounded by the move to Bryan, a hundred miles northwest of Houston. To compensate, she once again took refuge in bridge (playing nearly every day), in keeping an almost neurotically spotless house, and in her hopes for Jay. Whatever pedestal she had put him on in Rusk was being raised higher and higher.

Jay didn't disappoint her—and didn't want to. He was editor of the high school newspaper, president of the band, a member of student council as well as the National Honor Society. He finished at the top of his class. In his high school yearbook, below a picture of a studious, blond-haired boy with glasses who looked older than his years, was the claim that "His day is filled with work but he finds time for pleasure."

It was hard to see how. Aside from caring for Susie and his job as a lifeguard, he picked cotton and worked in a cafeteria as a busboy. Since Bea didn't have a job, whatever Homer earned, they lived on; if Jay wanted anything extra, he had to work. There was no money for luxuries.

As for social life, Jay found it through the Methodist church. In this, and in so much else he would later do, he was more pragmatic than anything else. Bluntly put, he realized that by singing in the choir he would meet girls. Since he was far less outspoken than his father about religion (the *only* subject on which Homer didn't hide his feelings), nobody would have to know he was an agnostic.

But like his father, he apparently didn't chase girls. They gravitated toward him—two in particular. Their names were Nelda Bruns and Jean McDonald. Like Jay, they had come to Bryan from somewhere else, and found that it was not the easiest place to fit in. To Jean, a smart, sassy, petite blonde who dreamed of becoming Marilyn Monroe, Bryan was a place in which there was little to do but dream, a layered society in which "nasty little people with white socks"—Rotary and Chamber of Commerce figures, mainly—ruled the day. What attracted her to Jay was that he stood apart and didn't conform, didn't do "the President Eisenhower–type thing." And the fact that he didn't seem the least bit interested in Jean naturally made her want him all the more. As far as she was concerned, Jay had erected a wall that he was tantalizingly hiding behind, and she was going to do whatever she could to bring it down.

So along with Nelda, a brunette who was considerably less flashy than Jean but who shared a "joint crush" on Jay with her, they would often drop by Jay's house unannounced and flirt with him on the front porch. Homer, of course, thought they were pushy, and they knew he disapproved of their advances toward his only son. But that didn't stop them. They did silly adolescent things, like leaving a bra on the front doorknob and squeezing glue onto his trigonometry paper, and they occasionally "kidnapped" Susie in an effort to pump her for information, any morsel would do. After a while, though, even they began to wonder why Jay put up with them.

Nevertheless, they would go to the Methodist church on Sundays because he did, and gradually, their zeal in pursuing him began to work—for Nelda more than Jean. Even though he had told them both, "Please leave me alone. I don't like to talk about myself," he would drift over to Nelda's house and they would sit on the porch, talking well into the night about books, about poetry, about getting away from Bryan (though not necessarily together).

"In high school," Nelda explained, "there are only two people, in my opinion, who are happy: the captain of the football team and the girl he is dating. The wonderful thing about Julian was that you could sit and talk with him about things like, 'What is love?' and 'What is death?' because in those days if I had said that to any of the boys I dated, they would have looked at me as if I was crazy."

In Jay's last year of high school, he and Nelda, along with Jean and two boys named Gary Goodwin and George Shearer, became known as the Motley Crew, and Jay was its undisputed leader. Even though there was precious little to do in Bryan, whatever he wanted to do they did. And whenever he tried to learn something, like dancing, he refused to let Nelda or Jean show him how to do it. He had to figure it out himself, in private, as if doing otherwise would be seen as a fatal sign of weakness or dependency.

The opposite, however, was never true. Jay wanted to show the way, and that was why Gary, especially, felt so indebted to him. Whenever Gary had to study for a test, Jay would help him so much that he came to think of Jay as his guardian.

Between his mother's expectations (and his own), his continuing care of Susie, and his rescuing Gary, time and time again, he was carrying a lot of bricks on his seventeen-year-old shoulders as he prepared to enter Texas A&M.

TWELVE

THREE YEARS LATER Jay nearly died.

It happened one unforgivingly hot summer day, the kind that not even Texans ever get used to. A deceptive wind was blowing. Not strong enough to bring much relief, but powerful enough to cause a bizarre sort of trouble. So bizarre, in fact, that the incident made the front page of the *Houston Post*.

Jay was working for the U.S. Division of Entomology, and had gotten up at four that Tuesday morning in order to toil in the cotton fields and be done before the heat made him feel like he was inside an oven. He had picked cotton before, but now he was spraying it, using an experimental poison designed to kill off the Mississippi boll weevils that had been ravaging cotton in Texas for the past few years.

But the wind kept blowing as much poison back at Jay as he was spraying on the cotton. He didn't think much about it at the time—after all, he had on a protective suit and mask—but later, when he got back to the lab at A&M, he threw up in the bathroom and slurred his words when he made a phone call. Because he was so looking forward to playing softball later, the highlight of his day and summer, he tried to ignore how unwell he felt.

He got no further than the front seat of his '41 Ford. He couldn't move his hands. Or his head. Or anything. To make matters worse, he began retching and couldn't stop, even though he had had nothing more than some fritters for breakfast. For the next five hours, he slipped in and out of consciousness, convinced his young life had come to an end before he could even get out of Texas, and somehow even managing to find some black humor in his predicament. He had a belief in fate that ran wide and deep, and, as a result, death (as Nancy found out to her dismay) did not particularly scare him.

Nevertheless, when he was conscious, he was trying mightily to turn the car lights on and, eventually, miraculously, he was able to do so. The Ford was spotted by an employee of the State Entomology Department, who just happened to be driving along Farm Highway 60 and who wondered if the car's proximity to the department building had anything to do with some burglaries that had recently occurred there. Within minutes, Mr. Knox Walker pried Jay out of the car and delivered him to the hospital.

For the next four hours, doctors, nurses, and his father worked feverishly, bathing him and administering glucose, oxygen, and other drugs. Urgent phone calls went out to specialists, and military chemical warfare experts were brought in. Tired as Jay was, he was not permitted to sleep. The poison was apparently a lot more potent than anyone had realized. In fact, if the doctors had gotten to him one hour later than they did, he would have been dead.

ON THE SURFACE, that incident was easily the most dramatic thing to happen to Jay during his years at Texas A&M. But there were other things that would affect the way he looked at the world, and they had to do with dreams. He set out to become a chemical engineer not, as it turned out, because of any burning desire to do so, but through a process of elimination he would later question. He had toyed with the idea of a career in music, but Homer was vehemently against it. His argument was that the chance to make any money at it was long since past; that since people could now listen to records they no longer had to depend on live music for entertainment. The world had changed, Homer reminded him. Even so, saying that to Jay was not easy for Homer, especially since a part of him, a crucial one, had long ago been lost to and changed by it.

The other thing Jay thought about was journalism. He had won a couple of awards in high school and had begun to fantasize about having his byline be one of consequence in the outside world. But once again, Homer was discouraging. He had worked at the local paper long enough, he told his son, to see there would never be any "real money" in it, and to watch reporters come in with high hopes and go away disillusioned.

So the pragmatist in Jay gave up those dreams, rationalizing he would do whatever was necessary to get a good degree—and propel himself out of East Texas. After all, Jay was a Depression baby, something he was—and would always remain—extremely conscious of, and the fact that Homer had sacrificed something of himself for him made Jay feel indebted to him. He may not have been that close to his father, but he certainly wasn't going to let him down.

And he didn't. He graduated from Texas A&M, in January of 1958, with not one but two degrees—one in chemical engineering, the other in business administration. But aside from his brush with death, he had one other close call that could have changed the course of his life.

AT THE TIME Jay went to A&M, the school was not only all male, but all military. Jay was a terrible soldier, and was always getting demerits for having his tie askew, his shoes not shined brightly enough, and his rifle in the wrong position. When these things happened, he would have to atone for his sins by marching in the "bull ring." Nevertheless, Jay wanted to get his commission—not because he desired a life in the service, but because he didn't want to get drafted. In order to get that commission, he had to spend six weeks at Fort Hood in the summer of 1956 (the summer after his accident), six long, demanding weeks under the relentless Texas sun. The same things that plagued him at A&M plagued him at training camp (with the added problem of having to make his bed, which he hated to do at home). But fortunately, there was a leadership element to the whole process, and that is where he distinguished himself, as he would in the years to come. Still, he needed an overall performance score of at least 120 points in order to ensure his commission as a second lieutenant.

He got 121. Fate, once again, had been on his side.

THIRTEEN

J AY FINALLY GOT OUT of Texas, but he didn't get all that far, taking his college degrees and a '53 Chevy to Anniston, Alabama, where he had to fulfill his obligation to the Army. Glad to be escaping a home situation, between his mother and sister, that had become increasingly difficult (and, at times, violent), he took an administrative position at Fort McClellan, and a more aggressive one with women than he ever had in Bryan. Anniston was a dry, docile town, but with the Women's Army Corps school and a surplus of local girls far from diffident about the attentions of a second lieutenant, Jay found plenty to do, eventually with one girl in particular.

Her name was Jessica Ross, and she was surrounded by children in a park when Jay came upon her one summer day in late June. A student at the University of Alabama, she had dark hair, sea-blue eyes, and the kind of clean-cut, All-American looks that would make most men want to rush her home to Mother, and to have her as the mother of their children. If that wasn't enough, she was a proud member of the Methodist church, and belonged to a prominent family. But there was a problem. She was engaged.

That didn't stop Jay. He had come to Alabama with boundless Texas optimism and a sense of being special—a healthy, reasonably good-looking WASP on his way to better things in Eisenhower's America, the sort of young man with fine prospects that his mother had been expected to find nearly forty years before. He and Jessica got to talking and when she said that she sang in the choir at church, Jay said that was some coincidence, that he used to sing tenor in his church back home, and it sure would be nice if he could continue praising the Lord right there in Anniston.

"Why don't you just come to choir rehearsal?" Jessica suggested.

"Oh well, if you think it would be okay, I'll do it," Jay said. "But I'll only be in Anniston a little while longer."

"That doesn't matter," she said in her sweet Southern voice. "We've got a lot of people who don't come in the summertime. We need replacements."

Jay went back to the barracks that afternoon with one thought on his mind, and it had nothing even remotely to do with his vocal cords. He told himself that he could make Jessica fall in love with him and break off her engagement. It was a reckless thing to do; he knew that, didn't exactly understand what prompted that impulse in him, but decided to go ahead with his scheme anyway.

They began to keep company and become more and more attached. When the autumn came and Jessica, no longer engaged, returned to Tuscaloosa, she came home on weekends and Jay would dutifully drive her back to school on Sunday nights, not telling her, of course, that he was occasionally seeing other girls during the week. While she was hoping for him to ask for her hand in marriage and her grandfather was trying to persuade him to work for his company, Jay was plotting his next move.

Just as his required stint at the base was ending (he had been promoted to first lieutenant and was doing so well that his commander encouraged him to stay), he discovered that another officer was driving to Boston. From reading the Harvard Classics Jay had dreamed of attending Harvard someday, and that dream now began to strike him as a possible reality.

As it turned out, his stay in Boston was a short one. While the Harvard Business School told him he could probably get admitted—not because he was so dauntingly brilliant, but because they were looking high and low for people who weren't from the Northeast—they also told him he couldn't get a scholarship. End of dream. Jay had five hundred dollars with him and no overcoat. He wasn't going to Harvard.

So he hitchhiked to Detroit, where he had a good friend working for Ford. Not even a promising interview, though, could alter the negative impression of the city that he had quickly formed, one that wasn't entirely Detroit's fault. It was too goddamn cold, and it was only November. Jay was not used to weather like that, and he didn't want to get used to it either. He'd rather broil in Texas than freeze his ass off in Detroit.

Once again, he put his thumb out and headed in a southeasterly direction, to the nation's capital. He remembered so well the trip that he and Gary Goodwin had made there a few years earlier, a pair of awkward Texans come east for their first look at a new and different world. Virginia Foster had put them up, they'd had a grand time, and Jay had even said that he might want to return someday, to seek the proverbial, and limitless, fame and fortune that a college education had led him, and others like him, to believe would ultimately be theirs.

In a sense, it would be, but Jay hadn't a clue about what any of it would mean—or personally cost him in human terms—when he arrived in Washington one week before Thanksgiving in 1958.

FOURTEEN

"I SAY WE START *calling him Walter*."

"*I don't think that's terribly funny, Marilyn,*" Joe Browning said, *unhinged by her response to the news of what had happened. "Jay could be lying out there dead somewhere, and you're making jokes.*"

"*All I'm saying is that I'm not surprised. He's not dead, I assure you of that. He's like Walter Mitty with one exception. He's actually gone to chase his pipe dreams.*"

PERHAPS MARILYN SOUTHWELL was right. Maybe Jay was like the James Thurber character who would sit in his armchair night after night, dreaming of a life far more adventurous than the one he had, only to be brought back to harsh reality by the unwelcome cadence of his wife's voice calling him to dinner. And if she was right, that he was different from Walter in that Jay actually did what Mitty could only dream of, then she and Spencer Matthews, unknown to each other, were both essentially saying the same thing—that there are a lot of Jay Carseys out there, ready but unable, for reasons good and bad and gray, to do what Jay had apparently done.

Marilyn had known Jay a long time, from those early days at Indian Head, when she was working in public information and he was working on Polaris. But she viewed him in a far different way than his boss and mentor Joe Browning did—or had at the time. After all, in making Jay the first chairman of the assistant management board (created to involve nonmanagement people in the decision-making process) Joe was essentially crowning him as the fairest of all his Fair-Haired Boys. In Joe's eyes, Jay could do little wrong.

By the time Jay met Marilyn Southwell, a handsome Irish Catholic girl who had come down from the hills of Michigan to work for John F. Kennedy's presidential campaign, he had broken things off with Jessica Ross. Jessica had come to Maryland to visit a few times, but when she eventually forced Jay's hand about his intentions to marry her, things came to an end. Hard as he tried, he couldn't understand why all his friends were so afflicted by "the Marty complex" (referring to the Paddy Chayefsky movie *Marty*), by the notion that they couldn't function unless they were attached to a girl, that they couldn't be alone without being lonely. Even in high school, if a girl broke their heart, nearly all of Jay's friends would swear to him that they couldn't live another day. They would go out into the woods, beat their breasts under a tree somewhere, write passionate poems, and pine away. Why they did it, he could never figure out. Why he didn't remained a mystery to him also, but not a total one.

The inability to express rich, deep emotion was a Carsey trait. His father, in words and actions, had always stressed the importance of head over heart, just as Homer's father had to him. The first you could count on. The second could only get you into trouble, make your palms sweat, and force you to lose your grip. Sure, Jay could sit on the front porch of Nelda Bruns's house and talk and talk about what love is. And he could express outrage when he learned that Jean McDonald was going out with a boy six years older than she was, which seemed to Jay, who was twenty then, a lifetime. But Jay wasn't about to open himself up in a way that counted. That wasn't his table. That is, until he met Marilyn. At least that's how she remembered it.

Even though Marilyn was from a world as provincial as the one Jay had come from, working for the Kennedy campaign had given her entrée to Camelot, and she became an intimate part of the glamorous social whirl that that administration created in Washington. Hoping for an eventual appointment in the administration itself, one that she said "Bobby promised me," she viewed her job at the Naval Ordnance Station, putting out the base newspaper, *Missile Laneous*, as a temporary one at best. Jay and she would spend hours at Charlie's Diner the day after some big party Marilyn had been to, and he (like so many others affected by the contagious spirit and romance of Camelot, especially after the crashing dullness of the Eisenhower years) would never tire of her regaling him with stories about who was there and what was served.

Since Marilyn lived in Washington and commuted every day, she became more than just a woman who intrigued Jay. She symbolized a bulletin from the front, from the kind of world that had drawn Jay to the East in the first place. Given the kind of company she was keeping, it was easy for him to forget that they were the same age and that she was as dazzled and wide-eyed as he was. It was especially easy to forget when they drove to New York once, and Jay stayed at the YMCA and Marilyn wound up with her picture in the *New York Times*.

Occasionally Jay would tag along to these social events in Washington (Marilyn thought it was like taking the bat boy to a World Series party), but for the most part he remained aloof, deriving his pleasure vicariously. Marilyn would often tease him that there was an empty apartment in her building on Capitol Hill and that he should move up there, wondering why in the world he would want to go on living in Indian Head. "But he never did," she said, "and I got to thinking that he probably liked being a big fish in a small pond, where he could control things. He was very shy, but he was also very secretive. For instance, I knew him for more than a year before I knew he was from Texas. Almost as if it was something he was ashamed of. He never said a word about his parents, not a word about either of them, and I thought that was strange, but I never asked about his background. Being from the Midwest, I have a very strong respect for a person's privacy."

Nevertheless, it made Marilyn feel more and more uncomfortable to be around Jay. "I don't enjoy talking at long length with some-body that doesn't share," she insisted, despite her irrecoverably Irish gift of gab. "In other words, I talk and then you talk, right? If you're just going to sit there and I'm going to do all the talking, then pretty soon I'm going to quit talking, because it becomes a confession, not a conversation."

Marilyn, as it turned out, was right about Jay's feeling self-conscious about Texas, particularly A&M. It was his Achilles' heel. When someone at the base predicted that Jay would never go very far because he hadn't gone to an Ivy League school, he got word of it and bristled, silently taking that as a personal challenge to prove the man wrong (in the same way Lyndon Johnson always felt put down by the Kennedys, by the attitude of *We know him but we don't associate with him*). And prove him wrong Jay did, rising from a GS-5 to a GS-13 in a New York minute, all the more impressive given the glacial nature of the government.

But there was something missing, and Marilyn claimed to know what it was. She felt Jay, contrary to the impression he tried to give, was not only enormously insecure but very lonely. "I would often come home at three or four in the morning," she recalled, "and the phone would be ringing. It would always be Jay, telling me how lonesome and restless he was, how he needed more, even though he couldn't say and didn't know what that *more* was. I remember one night, this was after he had met Nancy, he called me from a pay phone near Andrews Air Force Base. He had been drinking, they apparently had had an argument, and he had run his car off the road and straight into a billboard. He begged me to come out and help him. I was involved at the time with a man I was hoping to marry, a prominent surgeon, and I knew he wouldn't be too happy about this if he found out. But I went anyway.

"He was driving a red Corvette then, and that is one of the reasons I think of him as Walter Mitty. He was always talking about getting into his red Corvette and driving off into the sunset."

EVEN THOUGH MARILYN had mentioned Walter Mitty to Joe Browning in order to dispel the notion in Joe's mind that Jay might have killed himself, she nonetheless saw what Jay did as the emotional equivalent of suicide. He may have left Nancy a note, but he didn't, in Marilyn's opinion, leave her anything to point to. "Jay is more than a poor communicator," she said, "he is a noncommunicator. And if he couldn't communicate his unhappiness to her, then he should at least have acted it out. In other words, you illustrate. You remark that things are always dusty and the dishes are always dirty, so that if some day you say you're leaving, she can at least say it was the dirty dishes or the stockings that were always dripping in the bathroom. She has something to refer to. But you don't just go for years and years and years saying nothing and then cut and run, because you leave an awful lot of people behind who say, 'What did I do? What did I do?'"

In saying that, Marilyn was not just breezily holding forth (suicide was not unknown to her; both her father-in-law and a friend of her son's had killed themselves), nor was she being sentimental about Nancy. Marilyn had gotten to know Nancy a bit when she was married to Gordon Brumfield, and didn't particularly like her. Part of it might have been jealousy—"bombshell" was the word Marilyn would use over and over in describing her and how "she thought she could get away with anything" and how "over-whelmed" Jay was by her, "the most desirable woman at Indian

Head at the time"—and part of it might have been recognizing some of her own strong and domineering self in Nancy . . . qualities Jay found attractive in both women. No, in Marilyn's view of things, "it takes a strong man to stand and fight. Only cowards, like Jay, run away."

This whole notion of running away, of flight, struck Marilyn as a fundamentally American thing to do, not a European one. "Even though Gauguin ran off to Tahiti, he eventually came back and had a big exhibit. A Frenchman cannot leave France forever. Europeans have roots, I feel, that go much deeper than Americans'." But in saying that, Marilyn didn't know whether Jay had left the country, though she distinctly recalled that he was always talking about Australia and New Zealand. (She had even suggested to Joe that all of Jay's friends put a hundred dollars into a pool and hazard a guess as to Jay's whereabouts, a suggestion Joe didn't find very amusing.) But even that was beside the point, she said. What "running away" (the term she preferred to *disappearing*) had to do with was something very basic. It had to do with commitment, a concept she felt Jay never fully understood or accepted. To her, Jay was like static—clinging to you one minute, gone the next—always suiting himself. "Just because you have somebody in the harness," she pointed out, "doesn't mean you have him. Jay had a great deal of discipline, he could get things done. But you needn't think that just because somebody is disciplined and turns up every day that you have a total commitment on their part. I wouldn't be surprised if in all those years he had been president that he would often look at the clock and say to himself, 'It's five minutes to five. If I leave now, I could get the last plane for Tahiti.' If he had called me up and told me he was planning to do what he did, I would have said, 'Go ahead and run, you bastard, you've done it before.' "

Done it before? What was she talking about?

Well, it had to do with something Jay had confided in her on one of those rare occasions when he offered anything about himself, something she had not mentioned to Joe Browning when he phoned to ask if she had heard from Jay, but which had always troubled her.

It had to do with a child Jay had apparently fathered before he left Texas, a child born out of wedlock. Even though there was some question if it was indeed his child, he told Marilyn, he had nonetheless paid support for the child—for a time. Then he broke off all contact with the mother and never saw the child again. As far as he was concerned, Marilyn recalled, Jay felt he had discharged his responsibility. Jay never referred to the child by name and never said if it was a boy or a girl. What he did say was as clear in Marilyn's mind as if he had been sitting in the room, repeating it: "If I had let myself be forced into marrying her, I was convinced that I would never get out of Texas and I would never be a person."

Though Marilyn couldn't recall how the subject had even come up, she hadn't let it pass without asking Jay if he ever wondered about the child. When Jay said that he didn't, she told him, "You know, the guilt from something like that will follow you all your life. At some point you ought to try to go back and figure out why you did what you did. I can't believe that you just ran."

If her disbelief all those years before had made his disappearing now seem plausible to her, she was convinced of something else—that Jay would never shake free of all the things he had done, that they would be a part of him wherever he went, even if he found—or thought he did—the "more" that he was always seeking.

Beneath her deep layer of cynicism, Irish blarney, and genuine disappointment, it seemed clear that Marilyn Southwell still cared about Jay Carsey, wherever he was.

"You just don't uproot a tree as old as Jay Carsey without doing a hell of a lot of damage when you pull those roots. He must have had some sort of emotional stability with Nancy or he wouldn't have stuck around that long. I hope he did, because he will never regain what he had."

FIFTEEN

IT WAS A HOT summer's day in 1968, a day that Susie will long remember. More than anything else, she was thinking of that day when she told Virginia Foster on the phone that Jay hadn't lost his mind but found it. She told her that because the day in question fourteen years before *had* been one of loss, of Susie's feeling that her relationship with Jay was about to change for a good long while, if not forever.

Susie, by this time, was married, and she, her husband, and their first child had come to visit Jay and Nancy at Marchoza, a little place they had on the Chesapeake. Jay and Nancy were themselves recently married, and even though Susie had not been to the wedding she had met Nancy on a number of occasions, beginning in the summer of 1963, a pivotal summer in Susie's life.

It was the summer before her last year of high school, and things between her and her mother had reached such a low point that Susie felt the need to get away from home. The ostensible reason for the turmoil had to do with Susie's desire to become a Catholic, to have, in the Church, a mother who wanted her unconditionally, a mother she didn't feel she had. From Bea's point of view, even though she was not by any means a churchgoing Baptist, the last thing any self-respecting Baptist could abide was a Catholic. It was almost as if Susie had deliberately decided to convert because she *knew* it would upset her mother.

Upset her it did. Bea not only wouldn't allow it, but the occasional outbursts of violence, in the form of verbal threats, that had marked their relationship while Jay was still living at home, now escalated into physical clashes between them. If Susie wore rosary beads around her neck, Bea would not only rip them off, she would flush them down the toilet. When Susie wanted to go off to Catholic youth meetings or to see friends her parents didn't approve of, she would often sneak out her bedroom window. Once Bea discovered this, she nailed the window shut. But when that didn't work and Susie tried to leave the house anyway, Bea ripped her blouse off, wrestled her to the floor, and, one time, pulled out a gun and threatened to shoot her. Susie fled anyway, and didn't return for three days.

"I could easily have forgotten my name in that house," she said. "I'll tell you, I knew how to answer to four-letter words. I could quickly respond to slut or something like it. I kept hoping and hoping I'd been adopted, and even began looking in the cedar chest for any evidence I could find." Under different circumstances, she might have resented Jay, so often was his name invoked as the embodiment of perfection. But she didn't, because she felt that everything that she knew—"from reading on up to being"—she had learned from him. But more than feeling grateful, she felt guilty, the full extent of which she realized only later.

It's not that Homer wasn't around. He was, but in a distant, unemotional way, as he had been with Jay. (And the fact is, the way Homer was was not unusual at that time: a 1928 book by the psychologist John Watson, entitled *The Psychological Care of Infant and Child*, warned parents against "spoiling" their children with unnecessary gestures of affection. "Never hug and kiss them, never let them sit on your lap. . . . Shake hands with them in the morning." While Freudian theory, for the most part, significantly changed that point of view, one wouldn't have known it from the

Carsey household.) Nonetheless, Homer's detachment didn't mean that he agreed with Bea's treatment of Susie. He didn't, but couldn't bring himself to do anything about it. Bea was the dominant one, and Homer, even though he also read to Susie and played ball with her, was resigned to feeling himself a failure, both as a father and a husband.

The ironic thing was that Susie didn't think of her father as a failure (from him she felt she had learned the importance of integrity and not hurting anyone deliberately), nor did she blame him for the things he blamed himself for. She blamed her mother for making him feel that way, for making him (as well as her and Jay) feel that material possessions were important in and of themselves, that the way the neighbors viewed you was supposed to be some sort of perverse mirror for how you were supposed to see yourselves. Day after day, Susie would watch her mother plant her feet under the bridge table and make polite small talk with her refined friends. And day after day, she would observe how Bea would escort them out the door then turn, more often than not, to harass Homer about not being social enough (claiming he was more wedded to his stereo than to her) and not providing in the way her friends' husbands provided for them.

"See," Susie tried to explain, "she didn't understand that the musician she met, all the social aspects of that, had little to do with the man he was. My mother lived in the era that she came from, and that is why she came to resent him, because he couldn't produce what she wanted. There was always a push on for a new car, for more clothes from Sanger Harris. J. C. Penney's just wouldn't do. And the really sad thing is she didn't understand how good she had it, that she had the right man all along. A lot of her friends' husbands worked or drank themselves to death, and he was keeping her alive. And I am telling you, he will die and *never* know his value as a human being, because of what she did to his ego and sense of self-esteem."

Jay didn't like what was going on between Susie and Bea and

between Bea and Homer any more than Susie did, but as was his nature, he chose not to confront his mother directly. He was much more subtle and circumspect about it, but even he, while he was still in Texas, couldn't entirely conceal his concern about the situation from Nelda, Jean, and Gary; or, once in Maryland, from Virginia Foster, who had the distinct impression that Jay resented his mother for not working.

But if a dread of confronting things head-on was a part of his nature, so was his willingness to answer a cry for help. And when Susie cried out for help in 1963, he stepped forward, encouraging her to come east for the summer and live with him in his trailer.

THE BROTHER SUSIE encountered when she arrived in Maryland was not all that different, in her mind, from the one who had left Texas more than five years before. Even though she was seeing him in a new environment, he was still leading and people were still following. A newspaper Jay had in the trailer informed her about his becoming chairman of the local chapter of the Red Cross: "Jay Carsey has stepped into our community and has made himself a vital member of our society by understanding and contributing to our needs," it read in part. She smiled a knowing smile. Something as good and wholesome as the Red Cross didn't surprise her. Nor did his lay preaching. Or the fact that he was a scoutmaster. Or his teaching part-time at the community college. Or his involvement with the Potomac Players (the amateur theater group that put on *The Rainmaker*). Or his rapid success at the Naval Ordnance Station. Or his decision to work toward a master's degree in engineering administration. None of it surprised her, because she, like her parents, had no doubt Jay would succeed in whatever he focused his energies on. After all, he hadn't been given a Good Citizenship Award when he graduated from high school for being a reclusive shut-in.

But while none of it surprised her, it did trouble her, a worry about *who* exactly he was doing this all for that only increased as time went on.

JAY WASTED LITTLE time in showing his kid sister around that summer. As he had in Texas, he included her in his activities and introduced her to his friends. He took her to Ocean City, Maryland, to New York, and to plays in Washington, enabling her to retrace his steps and become exposed to a world she had never seen.

And he made good on his promise, seeing to it that she became a Catholic. He even went to mass with her and, on one occasion, took communion—a gesture that troubled Susie not so much because of his disbelief (she was well aware that hadn't stopped Jay before), but because she superstitiously feared the ceiling of the church might fall in.

It didn't, and Susie went back to Texas happily converted. But having officially "transferred my Oedipus complex to Jay," it was no wonder that she was determined to rejoin him as soon as she graduated.

DURING THAT SUMMER of 1963, Jay had been dating a nurse named Lois Sorenson, whom he had met on a blind date. She was sweet, pleasant-looking, and down-to-earth—in other words, too ordinary for Jay. If Marilyn Southwell had overwhelmed him, Lois was someone for Jay to knock around with, nothing more. Unfortunately, Lois didn't know that, and she fell deeply in love with him.

"Oedipal problems" aside, Susie had gotten to know and like Lois that summer, and far from seeing her as any sort of threat, Susie actually became Lois's goddaughter. And by the time she returned to the Washington area a year later, she had also decided to become a nurse. (She enrolled in the same nursing school Lois had attended—and Jay paid for it.)

She was saddened by Jay's decision to stop seeing Lois, but was not surprised by it. "He loved her as best he could for that stage in his emotional development," she said. "Because our daddy was always stressing intellect, Jay's emotions were late to follow." That may be true, but once again, his lack of emotion was connected to an insensitivity he didn't fully grasp. Because Jay's need to be liked, to be approved of, by people was so strong (and so unconscious), he didn't realize how much his dropping by unannounced to see Lois after he had broken things off was hurtful to her.

But there was also Nancy. When Susie first met her, she was married to Gordon, and Susie took an instant dislike to her. It wasn't because Nancy was far more glamorous and sophisticated, which of course she was. And it wasn't because Nancy was more a man's woman, which was also true. It was something far more unsettling. Though she was miles and miles from home, Susie felt she had come face to face with her mother.

"I clashed with Nancy after the first fifteen minutes," Susie recalled, "in the same way my mother and I did. I thought she was phony as hell. I didn't think I would ever be able to relate to her. I didn't say anything, but I imagine she must have sensed it. The first thing I felt about her, which was probably my permanent complaint with my mother, was hypocrisy. You know, she'd smile at your face and then stab you in the back. I sensed she could be vicious and self-serving, that she was out for a game, that she wasn't real. And when I saw how she was with Gordon, I could just see he was ruined. He was as dutiful as a son."

It didn't take Susie long to realize how attracted Jay was to Nancy, to her "potential," and that things with Nancy and Gordon were not going to last. In fact, the more time Jay spent with Nancy, the more time Susie spent with Gordon. At first, they were sort of babysitting each other; he would pick her up at nursing school in his sports car and they would go for "a Budweiser sandwich." They began fooling around, but their relationship never really developed much beyond that. Nevertheless, Gordon did offer to loan Susie money, interest-free, if she ever decided to go to college, and he offered her something even more valuable—the warning that if Nancy and Jay were eventually to marry, Nancy would see to it that Jay lost his family.

Susie never forgot that, but she didn't entirely blame Nancy for what she felt that summer day at Marchoza. It was far more complicated than that.

"I remember how cool and distant he was, very ominous anonymous," she said years later, still shuddering at the memory of that day. "That was his role then, and I realized that with Nancy wedged in there, it was all changed. I didn't like it. I didn't feel like I could talk to him. I didn't feel like it was him, my real brother. It hurt, and I didn't want to be hurt anymore—especially not by Doodie. Whatever good parts I have are because of him, and I didn't want to be thrust into the role of non-sister.

"Then, there was my son," she continued. "Jay was very cold and indifferent to him. I don't know why. He may have burned out being a father to me, which had to have been a conflict with what he should have been doing in adolescence. I even remember him telling me the summer I spent with him that if he ever had kids he would send them away to boarding school and only see them once in a while. But I was his sister and this was my kid, and I decided right then and there that he would not know that hurt. He would not know that he had an uncle nearby who didn't care whether he ever saw him. I had seen how he casually 'dropped in' on Lois every so often, and I was not going to be an occasional stop on his route.

"You see, Jay was a big-time role player, even growing up. He was a model son—on the surface—but he led his own life. He only told our mother what he *wanted* her to know, nothing more. He knows people, knows what they like. He has this ability to make people believe in him, and believe in themselves. He can deliver —and he does. But I never bought this Pillar of the Community stuff. He was doing it for our mother. She had certainly taught him what a success wasn't. She pushed him and pulled him. He was her second chance. And I can't begin to tell you how much he did for her by being in that lifestyle with Nancy. He was living out *her* fantasy.

"I never thought he and Nancy were in love per se. It was a very pragmatic relationship. He had to go through all that our mother wanted, do all the things she taught us—to be a success, to make a lot of money, to go to the right places. I'm not saying that he didn't want it for himself, but I think his initial programming was the identity of *her* value system, whether or not he was consciously aware of it. Maybe he thought that's all there was.

"It sounds funny to say it, but I also realized that he *needed* to play that role and he *needed* Nancy to help him develop some finesse. Do you think he ever would have lived in that house or decorated it that way or done as much traveling as they did? No, sir. He was rough around the edges and Nancy was the perfect person to polish him. But I never ever thought that they would grow old together. And when I got home that day from Marchoza, I was convinced that Nancy was going to kill Jay, sooner, much sooner, than he would die otherwise, that he was on a course and he was going to hit bottom and he was going to die, probably of liver disease. Nancy was going to feed off him and only give him what *she* wanted to, and I did not want to stand by and watch that happen."

Susie hadn't seen Jay since that day in 1968. She did not call him, and the only word she got of him was through her parents, Toodge, and from being on the community college's mailing list. At Christmas, a formal card extended Season's Greetings to her from the president, faculty, and staff of Charles County Community College, but no personal message from the brother she loved so much.

None of that mattered to her now. What mattered was that he was going to live. As far as she was concerned, it was a case of frontier justice, Texas-style. "I'm telling you, there's an awful thin line between love and hate. Hate is easier. It's more productive. Whatever Nancy did to him was a biggie, and even though what he has done is worse than killing her, because it leaves her embarrassed on top of it, he would have done a much worse injustice had he stayed. You see, his job there was finished. It was time for him to go."

SIXTEEN

I F YOU EVER HAPPEN to go to Miami to do business with Joe Browning, he will insist on greeting you at the airport. He won't meet your plane, but will instruct you to come to whichever V.I.P. lounge is connected to the airline you have arrived on. If you are concerned about interrupting his business day, you shouldn't be. Joe doesn't allow anything to interrupt his business, and, in any case, he always carries his business with him. And if you travel on Eastern and expect to see him when you reach the rarefied ozone of the Ionosphere Club, you probably won't. But you'll hear him.

"We're up two."

There is a sea of tanned faces, colorful shirts, and white shoes, but no one comes forward to announce himself as Joe Browning.

"Hold on a minute, I'll be right there."

It's the same gravelly voice, but after a minute, no one still.

"We're down three ticks . . . we're only down two. Hey, we're up five."

Thirty more seconds pass until "Hi, I'm Joe Browning." Hand outstretched, he seems to have snuck up on you like a cat, and has good reason to be grinning like one. "Hey, we just made three thousand five hundred and forty-two bucks in fourteen minutes." Terrific, you might be thinking, but who is "we"? As it turns out, "we" is whoever Joe happens to be with, "we" in the sense of a king and his subjects. It's important for Joe that you share in his enthusiasm, but not, of course, in the money that *he*, not *we*, just made. In his left hand is an odd contraption with an antenna sticking out of it. Has this wiry millionaire entrepreneur suddenly become a detective—or developed a zombie-like addiction to television? He happens to be drawn to television all right, but the kind with figures on it—financial ones. What he is holding is his lifeline—to the commodities market; his ability (as well as his need), through the dubious wonder of modern technology, to eat lunch in Miami and watch the rise and fall of pork bellies in Chicago at the same time.

Had he been able to overhear what Susie had to say with the same ease he could oversee his financial fortunes, he would certainly have agreed with her last point: Jay's job, at least at the college, was over. It *was* time for him to move on, something that both he and Dom Monetta had been urging him to do for well over a year before he vanished. There was money to be made, real money they said, if only Jay would resign. What was the point, they wondered, in having to do so much consulting on the side, when he could do it full-time and have less aggravation? As far as they were concerned, Jay couldn't go on doing what he had always done—and what people expected him to do: make wine from water forever. The problems at the college seemed to indicate they were right.

Like Jay, Joe had been "the tall man in the bar" in Southern Maryland for quite some time. And one of the reasons he had resigned as technical director of the Naval Ordnance Station was because he understood, all too well, one of the basic laws of the jungle: the importance of getting out before "they"—whoever they are—get you. But the "cut-and-run" way in which Jay removed himself, Joe felt, was not only all wrong, but served as an uncomfortable reminder of what Joe had initially felt when he first hired Jay: that he was "a fairly complex character who came across, on the one hand, as someone you felt you knew everything about, yet who, on the other, you felt you knew nothing about." And who, Joe also remembered, had failed only once to do something Joe asked of him, a lapse that had irked Joe at the time and now, years later, seemed rather illuminating.

It had to do with an assignment, unofficial and personal in nature. Joe had recently gotten separated and happened to have his eye on one woman in particular. One day, as he and Jay were concluding some business, Joe turned to Jay and said, "There's something I'd like you to find out for me."

"Sure, Joe, what is it?" Jay asked, always eager to please.

"I'd like you to find out the availability of Nancy Brumfield and report back with the information." A notorious ladies' man, Joe had met Nancy (his daughter's much-idolized fifth-grade teacher) at the Officers' Club, and she had been flirting with him, virtually ignoring Gordon.

At first, Joe had reason to think Jay was successfully fulfilling his assignment. Joe was invited to the Brumfields for dinner. But when he arrived, Jay was already there. Since Joe knew that Jay was friendly with both Nancy and Gordon (Jay, in fact, was helping Gordon get a professional engineer's license), it didn't strike Joe as unusual that Jay was there; in fact, it may even have been Jay's way of loyally and cleverly disguising his boss's wayward intentions. But when Jay and Nancy went out to get some beer and didn't come back for nearly two hours, Joe was livid. "Here I was, sitting with a cuckolded husband. When they finally returned, I met them at the door and said, 'Don't you ever pull that kind of shit on me again.' And I left. We didn't speak for a couple of months."

But that was only a small blemish in their relationship. Both men felt they could call on each other, day or night, and Joe had maintained a close relationship with Nancy as well. And it was Nancy who tracked him down in Los Angeles, on the Friday after Jay left, and gave him the news. "Since you're one of the closest people to him," she reminded Joe, "I'm sure you'll be one of the first he'll contact. You've got to help me."

Joe hadn't yet spoken with Dom, who would arrive at Green's Inheritance later that day, but the two notes that Jay left Nancy struck Joe as extremely ominous and made him feel guilty. Even though Joe didn't live in Southern Maryland anymore (he had left NOS at the end of 1974), he still had business there, and had just seen Nancy for lunch a month earlier. Before he arrived, Dom had told Joe that Jay was in fairly low spirits—that Nancy was putting a lot of pressure on him about a baby, that the Board was all over him, that the faculty had actually stood out in front of the college and booed Jay when he walked in—and encouraged Joe to call Jay.

Known for being tight (his nickname is "Peso Joe"), he didn't phone until he got to Maryland. Nancy answered and said that Jay was down at a branch campus and was pretty busy and why didn't the two of them have lunch instead.

"Fine, but I'm concerned about Jay. Dom tells me things are not going well for him."

Ever protective of Jay's image, even with Joe and Dom, Nancy didn't deny what Joe was saying, but assured him of the same thing she had been telling herself: if they could just get graduation behind them, they would have the whole summer to relax and get back to "normal."

On the other end of the phone, Joe did his best to stifle a laugh. As long as he had known the two of them as a couple, the kind of life they led could never be described as normal. In fact, it made Joe exhausted even to think about it. Forever etched in his mind like a newspaper headline was POOR BOY FROM TEXAS MEETS BEAUTIFUL GIFTED WOMAN WHO CAN CREATE A SOCIAL SITUATION OUT OF ANYTHING. Joe used to entertain a good deal when he was at NOS (the base, not Joe, supplied the money) and he always felt it was imperative to have Nancy and Jay there: Nancy, because Joe knew she would become the "showpiece" of the occasion; Jay, because Joe could count on him to keep everyone's glass full.

But Joe also knew that his party wouldn't be the only social occasion the Carseys would attend in an evening. Whatever was happening for miles around, be it a black-tie dinner with the governor or a pancake breakfast at the firehouse, be it in Annapolis or Nanjemoy, Nancy would see to it that they got there. To Joe, this accurately reflected the way he always viewed their marriage: a "shovel brigade," with Nancy out front and shining, and Jay one step behind and filling in the ditches. When Joe later heard that Jay had told someone, months before he left, that what he longed to do was come home on a Monday evening and watch Monday Night Football in peace, Joe was hardly surprised. To him, no matter how quietly ambitious he had come to realize Jay was, Jay would always be a guy who lived in a trailer behind a service station and accidentally found himself in a place like Green's Inheritance. Even if he had looked comfortable in his new guise all those years with Nancy, he could never have forgotten who he was and where he had come from.

The reason Joe felt that way was that he saw so much of himself in Jay. A full decade older, Joe had grown up in a shack in West Virginia with coal dust on his face and the family refrigerator on the porch. While that may be the very thing that drives one to succeed and have all the worldly goods one's parents couldn't provide, it is also something that one is never free of, no matter how hard one tries to obliterate it. It may not be obvious on a résumé, but it is more telling than anything that might be.

The lunch Joe and Nancy had was inconclusive and shallow. "We talked about nothing that had any meaning in terms of the subject of Jay," Joe recalled. "She was her usual happy, outgoing, purple self."

But Joe didn't blame her. He felt she thought she was doing Jay a favor by not talking about his trouble sleeping and his drinking (things she talked to Joe about only *after* Jay left). He knew all too well that in a place like Southern Maryland, "if you start spreading that kind of stuff around you can destroy a guy's reputation." No, Joe didn't blame Nancy. He blamed himself. Despite what Dom had told him, Joe hadn't forced the issue or made more of an effort to bypass Nancy and see Jay. And now, four weeks later and three thousand miles away, he was feeling he had let his Fair-Haired Boy down, not the other way around—a feeling exacerbated by the fact that Joe had experienced this sort of thing before.

"A friend of mine was very depressed," he explained, "and called me and said, 'I need to talk to you.' I said, 'How about Thursday?' and he said, 'Fine.' But on Wednesday I called him and said, 'It would be more convenient to me if it were next Monday, is that okay?' He said, 'Yeah, that's okay.' "

But it wasn't "okay." That Sunday, Joe's friend put a shotgun in his mouth and blew his brains out.

"I had the same sort of feeling with Jay," Joe said. "Somewhere there was a cry for help I didn't hear. With the guy who killed himself, at least he made the cry for help and I thought I heard it and I thought I was going, but I made the stupid mistake of putting it off."

Along with the guilt Joe felt in both situations, there was, in Jay's case, a good deal of anger as well—anger that Jay had never given him or Dom a meaningful response when they offered him a way out from the professional and financial pressures they knew

Jay was under. They felt extremely sympathetic to the problems he was facing with the college's board ("After all," Joe said, "what the hell would that place have been without Jay Carsey?"), and they knew that Nancy was a black hole when it came to possessions. But when Joe tried to commiserate with him about those pressures on one occasion, all he got was a vague, almost dazed look from Jay. And even though Jay wanted everyone to know —or think—that he had things under control, Joe worried nonetheless, especially when Nancy unexpectedly said to him once, "You know, Joe, I sometimes wish I had married someone with real money, like you."

At the time Nancy said that, in November of 1981 when she and Jay were down in Florida, Joe took it to be just another example of Nancy's flirtatiousness. But the more he thought about it, the more he remembered other incidents—one in particular, with Jay present—that caused "a certain misery level" on Jay's part. It was at one of Joe's parties and Nancy was piqued that Jay was going off to Europe and wouldn't be able to take her. So in front of a lot of people who knew nothing more about her than that she was married to Jay, Nancy suddenly asked Joe if he had ever been to South Africa. No, he told her, he hadn't. "Well," she said, "Jay is going on this trip and says he can't take me, so I was wondering if you would take me to South Africa?"

Not exactly sure how to respond, he decided to make light of what he knew to be a serious suggestion.

"Why, sure, Nancy, I can take you to South Africa, but not unless I get Jay's permission." The old Catch-22 would surely rescue Joe from an increasingly embarrassing situation.

It didn't.

"Hey, Jay," Nancy called across the table, "Joe wants to take me South Africa. It's okay with you, isn't it?"

Jay pretended to go along with it, Joe recalled, in order not to make waves, "but I knew he was feeling the same thing I was feeling, which was, 'Why would you do something like that?' "

And now Joe found himself angrily asking the same question of his friend, even though his friend was not there to answer him. "If only he had come to me, we could have talked about it. But to leave and leave doubt in people's minds that this was a rational thing he had thought out, it sure has an impact. Look, I have a pact with someone who occasionally gets depressed and wants to kill herself. The pact's very simple. Before she does that, she'll call me and I'll come over and we'll talk for two hours. If after two hours she hasn't changed her mind, I'll walk out of the house and she can do whatever she wants to. But if she ever kills herself and doesn't give me that two hours, I'll begrudge that as much as I begrudge Jay."

But Joe was smart enough to realize that Jay may have felt it much too risky to talk about what he was planning to do, especially to someone like Joe, whose almost fatherly approval Jay had always sought and who would have been "first in line" to talk him out of it. Jay, Joe rationalized, probably knew that.

As Joe sat in Los Angeles, shaken by the news and listening to Nancy say how sure she was Jay had had a breakdown, how much she loved him and needed him and depended on him, how crucial it was that Joe help find him, he not only knew that she meant everything she said—but he was certain that she had been "oblivious to all the disaster that was about to happen," and that she didn't believe she contributed to his leaving one bit. To Joe, that was part of the problem—his uneasy notion that their relationship was always based far more on drama and excitement than on selfless love.

But "love," as Freud pointed out, is only one part of a person's life, and when Joe began to think about the other, "work," he recalled how Jay was someone who got his thrill from participating in the beginning of things, not in keeping them ticking over. And because Jay had been at the college for so long, perhaps a deep disillusionment and restlessness had set in years before. It reminded Joe of another of his friends, who told him once that there were three things in his life which had impact on him: the people he reported to, the people who reported to him, and his family. If any one, or even two, of those things went against him, he could cope. But if all three conspired to make his life miserable, he felt ruined.

In considering this—that Jay may have felt ruined and had chosen a far less conventional way of changing course than the one Joe and Dom had offered him—Joe turned inward, reviewing his own life with what he called "Browning's Theory of Evolution," his version of Erik Erikson's belief in the stages of human development.

When he was about eighteen, he set for himself the lofty goal of becoming head of a major industrial operation by the time he was thirty-five. In order to do that, he felt that he would have to sacrifice many things. So he made those sacrifices, spending little time with his wife and family, and only missed attaining his goal by one year.

But no sooner had he become the technical director of NOS than he felt he had only achieved a Pyrrhic victory. When he walked into his office on the first day, he expected that something miraculous would happen, that he would feel a sense of elation at having arrived in a position of power and privilege.

It didn't and he didn't. "There wasn't anything in there except me and the furniture," he recalled. "It took me a long time to realize that nothing had changed. And then I became a little bitter that I had made so many sacrifices and led such a narrow life in order to get there."

So he set another goal: that he would be on his own and working for himself by the time he was fifty—if he didn't die by the age of forty (which he saw as a distinct possibility). He had good reason to be morbid. He had become an alcoholic.

As it turned out, he didn't die at forty, was on his own by fifty, and became a millionaire a few times over. But none of that, not one bit, could relieve the sadness of a typical day in his life, spent in pursuit of money and nothing else. "I reached a point where I woke up at six o'clock, got ready to play the stock market, played it, and had my first drink at eleven. I would have three drinks, which is really kind of misleading because they were actually doubles. I'd have a Bloody Mary and then a vodka and tonic and then a grapefruit drink. By that time I needed to go to sleep. I'd sleep for two hours, wake up, start the vodka and tonics and drink until I had a Stinger and it was time to go to sleep at night."

But Joe felt he had an even bigger problem: he had never knocked anybody down, had never mistreated his daughter, and always made enough money so that people he had responsibilities to—be it his ex-wife, his daughter, or individuals he did business with—could never say he was shortchanging them. Some alcoholics, of course, might not see this as a problem at all, but Joe was smart enough to eventually rise above the rigid stance of denial that most alcoholics take (who don't go to Alcoholics Anonymous) and get help for himself. When Nancy mentioned to Joe that Jay was "drinking more than usual," Joe didn't know how much import to give that, because he hadn't been around Jay that much once he left Southern Maryland. And when Joe heard that someone said, "Hell, he didn't drink any more than the rest of us," that was as funny to Joe, in its own blind way, as Nancy's saying that all she had wanted was for their life to get back to normal.

Beyond all the guilt, anger, sadness, and introspection was the one thing, more than any other, which defined who Joe Browning was, something Jay had inherited from him, something that Joe would rely on in the days ahead as he continued to grope for answers and try to make sense of this. Joe Browning was a supreme pragmatist. As an engineer and a man, he looked for blacks and whites. Anything mottled finally made him nervous. If there was one finite thing that could explain Jay's flight, he would discover it. In his view of the world, a man he had known for nearly twenty-four years, no matter how complex a character, just didn't

81

pick up and leave in such a fashion unless he had done something wrong.

SEVENTEEN

AGAINST LOUIS JENKINS'S wishes that the authorities not be informed, at least not until after the graduation ceremony on Sunday, Nancy decided to contact them on Saturday evening. The Maryland State Police officer who came to call that night was Sergeant William E. Boone, a tall, ramrod-straight figure with a poker face that belied a droll sense of humor, and a way of speaking like the rat-a-tat-tat of a police blotter: *Name is William E. Boone. Family has lived, fornicated, and died right here in Charles County. No reason to live anywhere else or for anybody to know anything more. President Carsey's disappearance biggest thing to happen around these parts since John Wilkes Booth fled here from Washington after shooting Lincoln. What else?*

Plenty, it would seem. What about the college? Any money embezzled or books doctored? This was Joe Browning's greatest concern. *As long as things are going your way, no one usually comes creeping around with a magnifying glass. When they aren't, you can expect a pack of carnivorous, tight-lipped accountants to be lined up around the block.* Joe knew how much Jay loved wheeling and dealing and turning everything that he could to his advantage (after all, he had had an excellent teacher). If, for instance, the state's community college presidents were going to have a meeting, Jay would see to it that they go to some resort, not some sterile conference room in a hotel in Baltimore. Another time, when Jay was quite involved in consulting about "international education," he told one of his colleagues that he might be sending him to Nigeria to help a school set up a computer program, and might want him to stop in Paris to do some additional work on the way there, and in London on the way back. The man thought Jay was just having a big joke at his expense; even though Jay had pulled rabbit after rabbit out of his hat in Charles County, the notion of Tommy Sexton journeying to the heart of Africa seemed both exotic and preposterous, most of all to Sexton. But off he went.

"I'm sure Jay was bored shitless and tired of being harangued," Joe said. And while he also felt pretty sure that Jay didn't walk out the door with any cash, "it would surprise me if Jay didn't know that if he cut and run the first thing they'd do is check the books. They're not going to go back five years. They're going to go back a year. And knowing Jay, I'm sure he kept them clean as a hound's tooth."

He had. A scrupulous audit showed nothing irregular.

Well, then, how about another woman?

Joe Browning was surprised that Nancy hadn't raised that with him over the phone, and wondered if her ego simply wouldn't allow her to consider it. As it turned out, he was the only one surprised. The thought of Jay covertly taking up, let alone taking off, with someone else struck everyone as being as ridiculous as Tommy Sexton's trip to Nigeria. Why, Nancy had him on such a short leash that Evelyn Hungerford calculated he would only have had about fifteen minutes a day for that sort of thing, if that.

The most they came up with on that angle was a woman who worked at one of the branch campuses. She had been missing for a couple of days, but later came back; she and her husband had

had a marital spat and she had gone to her parents' house. End of speculation.

There was still the question of the Naval Ordnance Station. When Jay left there in 1965 to become president of the college, he didn't sever his ties completely. In fact, it was Joe Browning who recommended that Jay be kept on as a consultant and given a half-time contract. Jay had developed such an expertise in long-range guns that Browning considered him the base's "corporate memory" in that area, and so Jay continued to supervise Operation Gunfighter, a project he had initiated. He also added courses to the college's curriculum that benefited NOS, and organized seminars and symposiums.

Nonetheless, Joe was always jittery about the arrangement, even though it had been his idea, because he felt it would become obvious to both the base and the college that Jay didn't have half his time to devote to it. To complicate matters further, the Navy had been conducting an investigation at NOS prior to Jay's leaving, an investigation that stemmed from a tip that the base was not producing as much as its records alleged it was. Could Jay have somehow been involved in that? Could his financial situation have become so tenuous that he had been skimming, or could he have gotten hold of classified information and be planning to sell it? Had he, in effect, become a spy?

On the surface, it seemed a farfetched notion. Since his clearance at NOS was never more than SECRET, it would have been fairly difficult for him to gain access to classified information. But there was another factor: the sense, from people as different as John Sine and Jay's sister, that Jay may have worked for the CIA, that the nature of the consulting work he did—and the many places he traveled—might have been a smokescreen, in part, for work he was doing for the agency, possibly as a courier. Not even Joe Browning, who claimed to have had dealings with the CIA, would completely discount the idea—that either something had gone awry with the agency or that Jay had been "turned" by the

Russians—because of Jay's unerring ability "to pull a cloak around himself."

That, however, was not Sergeant Boone's problem to solve. As someone entrusted with the solemn purpose of upholding the law, he had two—and only two—things he needed to establish: Had Jay committed a crime? Or was he the possible victim of foul play? If the answers, to the extent the police were able to determine them, were negative, then Jay Carsey, or any other adult for that matter, was free to go wherever he chose. That he took personal money; that he took out a loan that Nancy didn't know about; that the note he left her did not give her power of attorney; the thorny question of whether he committed a moral crime by leaving—some would say abandoning—wife, work, and friends in the way he had: all of this was, and remains, beyond the purview of such figures as William E. Boone.

"I hope you realize," he said, eyes shielded by the inscrutable sunglasses so many state police officers seem to favor, "that if I had picked up and done this, nobody outside of my family would care. It wouldn't make the papers or nothing. But since Jay Carsey was who he was, we had to do everything that we could.

"Now, it's not unlikely for us to get one or two calls a month from a husband saying his wife has left, or the other way around. A wife would come into the barracks and say her husband is missing. He left for work at six the morning before, it's now noon of the following day, she doesn't know where he is, his car is still sitting in the parking lot in D.C. where he always parks it. Well, you do a little checking around and come back to her and ask, 'Does your husband have any friends he may have gone with?' She gets highly indignant, says, 'Absolutely not. The thought of such a thing. How could you think that?' Well, then you check around some more, check at his office, and you find out that some lady is missing. Hell, I had one man come into the barracks and he wanted to fight me, he got so mad that I implied his wife may have gone off with a male friend. The next morning he called me, very apologetic, and said that yeah, some lady had called him and her husband was missing and was sure he was with the guy's wife. So, hell, that's commonplace."

Based on the notes Jay had left Nancy, Boone's quarter of a century in law enforcement told him that Jay had probably left of his own volition. Nonetheless, Boone proceeded with his investigation. The audit at the college and the fact that no one else seemed to be missing from the immediate area reinforced his initial instinct. After Nancy mentioned Australia as a possible destination, Boone discovered that Immigration records only your entrance into a country, not your exit from America. In the case of Australia, there are four places you can enter, and Boone planned to go through the local congressman in an effort to get the cooperation of the Australian Embassy. He sent telexes to the police departments in Houston and San Diego (Nancy told him how much she and Jay had enjoyed their stays at the plush Hotel del Coronado, just offshore), and he entered Jay's name into the National Crime Information Center computer, just in case he was wanted for something that no one knew about. Since Jay had parked the college car at National Airport, Boone asked all the airlines to begin checking their records, even though he had no idea whether Jay used his real name or not, whether he had used a disguise, or even whether he flew from National at all. His parking the car there could easily have been some elaborate ruse, as thought out as everything else seemed to be. And since Jay said that he would use his credit cards for a few days, then throw them out, the companies in question were notified. If Nancy had to wait for the bills to arrive in the mail, as opposed to instantly finding out when a telling receipt came in, valuable time could be lost—if it hadn't been already.

EIGHTEEN

I F THERE WAS ONE THING that Jay and John Sine could always agree on, it was their open dislike of graduation; they even had a secret pact to make sure the ceremony never went past an hour. For seventeen years, they had handled it together and now John not only had to handle it alone (as Jay's p.s., in the most immediate sense, had asked him to), he was faced with the unenviable task of telling the faculty what only a handful of them knew.

First, though, John needed to talk with the commencement speaker. So he took Sam Massie, the head of the state board of community colleges, into his office and said, "Sam, I think there is something you ought to know. Jay has flown the coop. He left last Wednesday and there has been no word from him since. He sent Louis a letter of resignation. I am going to tell the faculty, but I'm not going to say anything about it at the ceremony."

Sam Massie said nothing at first; he just smiled. Then, looking nonplussed, he simply said, "These things happen. Let's get this thing on and do it."

And so they did. At the college's indoor pool, the faculty was lining up. It was a hot, muggy, rain-threatening day outside, as Gordon Barnes had told Jay it would be, and even more sweltering inside. The bizarre nature of what Jay had done was heightened, for an instant in John's mind, by the absurd sight of the faculty in full academic regalia alongside a pool.

"All right, now listen up," John said, as if he were a football coach urging his team to go out and have a good game, "President Carsey is not going to be here. We don't know where he is. I don't have any more details than that, so there's no sense in asking me." John was telling the truth. He didn't even know, at that point, that Nancy had contacted the state police. "Let's just go upstairs to the gym and act as if nothing has happened. We don't want anything to detract from the ceremony."

One of the faculty members who had learned of Jay's departure was Josephine Williams, an associate dean and English teacher. For the past three days she had been trying to make sense of what happened. She had always liked Jay, liked his charm, his wit and his intelligence, his refreshingly unorthodox way of doing things (an irony not lost on her now). She felt sorry that this was the way he chose to leave, a way she felt was less an act of cowardice than that of a man who was both weak and sick.

But Jay was not the only one Josephine Williams, a woman with fierce institutional loyalty, was feeling sorry for. "When you strike that kind of blow at this size community," she said, acknowledging Jay's importance to both the college and the county, "which for all its strengths and weaknesses had been a pretty coherent whole for a long, long time, then you strike a very brutal blow, and I was sorry for that, too. And then, I suppose, as a sort of ancillary, I was sorry for myself, because when that happens it's like someone dying in the family, you lose the part of your life which that person shared. You lose that part of your history, and I was saddened by that."

She was also extremely angry and, not surprisingly, chose to frame Jay's departure and her reaction to it in mostly literary terms. Troubled by the fascination she discovered people had, "people who were as educated as he was," with what Jay had done, she suspected that it didn't just stop with fascination; that these same people actually entertained the notion, consciously or unconsciously, of doing the same thing, and looked upon Jay as some sort of hero. He might be a hero, Josephine thought, but not the kind she admired. "He is heroic in the terms that the post–World War II French understood. What he did is perfectly existential and, to my mind, amoral. He served himself. There's something of Beckett in him and there's something of Sartre and something of Camus. I just think it's a wonderful irony that this real American engineer could turn out to be a quintessential twentieth-century postwar hero."

The fact remained, though, that she knew something was wrong. She knew Jay had been losing his grip, and like John, knew he had been drinking heavily. For all Jay's apparent concern about having to lay people off, it was really John who had to deliver the bad news, even though Jay was the target of everyone's unhappiness. She knew Jay was fed up with the board, because he would repeatedly say, "Jo, I don't have to put up with this. I could go back to Texas and pump gas"—the same thing, essentially, he had told John from time to time. And there was something else, something peculiar, at least peculiar for him. One by one, within the month before Jay left, he had taken all the associate deans to lunch and asked for their opinions on how to revamp things at the college. His unexpected invitation struck each of the deans the same way: since Jay usually sought no one else's counsel but his own, why was he doing this? Was he, as Josephine Williams suspected in hindsight, just going through the motions, or was he just trying to say goodbye?

Amorality and existentialism aside, though, Williams did not entirely rule out suicide. She knew someone who had almost committed suicide, and when she talked to that friend afterward, genuinely seeking to understand, the friend explained that a suicidal person doesn't see other options—like calling somebody. All the person can see is a tunnel which gets continually darker and deeper, so dark and deep, in fact, that he can't see a helping hand, even if there is one. Williams had found that helpful at the time, especially since "the guilt you can generate on your own is pretty good stuff," but she was not totally convinced—just as she was not totally convinced that Jay couldn't have found a better, more considerate way of doing this.

So as Josephine Williams filed into the gymnasium to greet the graduating class of 1982, it was amorality and existentialism that she found herself coming back to.

STEVE MAXWELL WAS also in the gym that Sunday. A physics teacher at the college, as well as a former NOS employee who had been involved with Operation Gunfighter, Maxwell had been a civilian for quite some time; but you wouldn't know it from his crewcut, his insistence on calling two in the afternoon fourteen hundred hours, or the way in which he viewed Jay's marriage to Nancy.

"It was ridiculous the way she ran him," he said. "But I figured he had signed on for the duration. Frankly, I think Jay was a little naïve when it came to the distribution of duties in a marriage." And, frankly, Maxwell was feeling a little foolish himself when John Sine delivered the news that Sunday. Just ten days earlier, he and Jay had been having a drink at a local bar, and Jay was telling him how he had won, that the battle was over. Maxwell took Jay's comment to mean the budget battles at the college. They had come up with solutions—albeit unpleasant ones—and the worst *was* over. But now, Maxwell realized, Jay had probably been saying goodbye, and he was feeling irritated with himself for not being more perceptive. "He was a little edgy and looked beat," Maxwell recalled. "It was hot that day. In fact, I got up and had them turn the air conditioner on. And we were just sitting there, drinking cold beer or cold Scotch, I forget which, and there was something on his mind and I could tell right away. But I guess I was just too selfish to try and draw him out.

"What really pisses me off though," he added, "is that he left before I had the chance to tell him what a really good guy I always thought he was. And what really makes me sad is when I think of what could have been. He and Nancy were a pair of chargers, and I really thought he was headed for the Cabinet."

As soon as Maxwell got home from graduation, he called Nancy and invited her to come over—partly to assuage his guilt and partly out of concern for her. She declined, telling him what she had told everyone else: she had been by the phone since Thursday and, until Jay called, there she would remain.

NINETEEN

NANCY WANTED TO make the call herself, even though Lamberth Carsey and Virginia Foster had offered to make it for her. She hadn't wanted to phone Jay's parents right away, because they were old and she didn't want to worry them unnecessarily. But since three days had passed and she hadn't heard from him, she hoped maybe they had—or had at least received a letter that was more enlightening than hers had been.

Just as Homer went to pick up the phone that Sunday morning, there was a knock on the door. Four people from the local Baptist church, dressed in their Sunday best. Virginia had gotten Nancy to agree that Homer and Bea should not receive the news alone, so she had contacted the preacher and he had arranged for these people to lend some moral support. Whatever Homer did, it seemed, he couldn't get away from religious folk.

At first, all Homer could tell was that it was Nancy. He couldn't make out what she was saying because she was crying so much and saying how much she loved Jay and how he had left her with no money and she didn't know why and she was sure he'd come back. He finally figured out what she was talking about, and all he could say was that they hadn't heard a thing, that they couldn't believe Julian would do anything like that, and that if they heard anything, anything at all, they would let her know.

Well, they did get a phone call later, but it wasn't from Jay. Virginia called them and spoke with Bea for a good long while, trying to explain how things can build up in a person and that people, even people like Jay, can go crazy. Virginia was delicate in her approach, a different one than she had taken with Susie; since she knew her sister did not brook much criticism of her pride and joy, she chose her words carefully.

And so, apparently, had Jay. In the Monday morning mail, after a sleepless night, Bea and Homer got their letter. Postmarked the same day as all the others, it had made its way to the Lone Star State slowly, to the house Jay had lived in for ten years, where his room was still intact, frozen in time. By not using a zip code, it seemed Jay wanted to delay, as long as possible, the upset he knew his letter would cause:

Mom & Dad—

I hate to provide you such pain in your later years but I have done as much as I wish and am disappearing. I always was afraid I had most of Ernest in me.

Immediately change your will to leave your assets to Susie and/or the boys.

Love,
Julian

It was one thing for Nancy to say it, quite another for them to read it. Bea had had a mild stroke not long before, and this news was not likely to improve her recovery from it. Over and over she would say to Homer, "I'm just sick about this," and he knew that, other than bridge, she would now have nothing to look forward to, that it would simply take all of her will to survive. If he had not been enough for her in sixty years, he was unlikely to fill that void in her life now. Everything that Jay had done, from the time he was a little booger (as Homer liked to call him) in Texas to his adult life in Maryland, had been a source of pride to both of them. They had kept every newspaper clipping, every memento, every photograph —many of which Jay had dutifully sent them—that spoke of his accomplishments. Scrapbooks abounded in their modest home, and were often brought out when the bridge ladies came to call.

Whenever Jay invited them to visit, they had made the long drive east, and Bea, especially, took vicarious pleasure in the way he and Nancy lived. Green's Inheritance was more than just a house to her. It symbolized a way of life that she felt she had been wrongly denied, but one that her Julian was compensating for. That was what made the fatalistic message of his note, on a card that had an ink drawing of the house on the front, so hard for her to comprehend— and, by its mention of her younger brother Ernest, so puzzling.

Ernest was the ne'er-do-well of the Nance family. He had always been hell-bent on adventure, a dashing, rakish figure who became a bombardier in World War II and came to stay with Homer and Bea in Rusk shortly afterward. He was allergic to responsibility of any kind, and everything he tried usually failed. He had a bar in Houston for a while, but wound up drinking more of the booze on hand than the customers did. He would take off for stretches of time, not let his wife (who eventually divorced him) know where he was, then come back drunk more often than not. But one time he didn't, and he later called to say he was in St. Louis, planning to marry someone else. He did, but died shortly afterward, penniless and alcoholic to the end.

So the fact of Jay's mentioning Ernest, whom he barely knew, made no sense. Was Jay really saying that he had always longed to be "a wild boy," which was Homer's view of Ernest—or was he carefully trying to ease his mother's pain by giving her something to cling to? If so, it didn't work. Her health began to deteriorate, and she and Homer even decided they would not discuss this embarrassing matter with anybody that they knew, other than family.

In a letter to Nancy not long after that, Bea wrote: "We have cried until we can't so now always come up with the same question—why? I don't know of anyone that had more to live for. You had such a full life—travel, beautiful home, good educations, and lots of friends. Julian is the last person in the world that I would have thought of doing such a thing.

"Has your lawyer been able to come up with any answers?" she continued. "I hope so. I hope that you can sleep. We can't."

Bea's letter notwithstanding, it didn't prevent Homer (like Joe Browning) from considering what Jay must have done wrong that prompted his actions and resulted in what Homer would come to call "this hideaway business." The origin for this suspicion came from his never being able to understand where Jay got all the money to do the things he and Nancy did.

"I thought maybe he'd taken a little," Homer said. "Hell, that's the same state where that Spiro Agnew fellow got in trouble. And there was always construction work going on at that college Julian ran, lots of money passing, you know. I just figured it was a way of life up there, so damn much corruption, giving contracts to your friends and so forth."

As for Jay's marriage to Nancy, Homer went over it and over it in his mind. On the surface, he thought they were ideally suited to each other, "being in the same line of work and all." At a big party Jay and Nancy had while the Carseys were visiting once, a party attended by a lot of "important people from Washington," Homer had an opportunity to watch Nancy operate as a hostess, an experience he would never forget. "I'll tell you," he recalled, "that was some fancy crowd, and she could butter up those boogers better than anybody I ever saw. She was just great at PR, and I know that helped Julian a lot, because he was always having to raise money and what not."

But there were things that troubled him. Given his own feeling about outward displays of affection, the fact that Jay and Nancy were like him and Bea in that regard was not one of them. No, what troubled him was the feeling both he and Bea had that Nancy was always on, always a little too gushy around them, as if they too were people to be charmed and won over. But her "insincerity" and even the exotic outfits she often wore ("Gosh darn, I thought she was weirdly dressed, not at all what an *ordinary* person would wear") did not trouble him as much as something that happened once in Baltimore.

Jay and Nancy had recently returned from one of their typical fifteen-countries-in-twenty-one-days trips and were waiting for a number of things they had purchased to arrive at the port there. Since Homer and Bea happened to be visiting, they went along for the ride. "I couldn't believe the amount of things they had bought," he said, "especially since Marchoza was just littered with stuff already. Hell, Julian had spent more for a new ramp to the water than a good automobile would cost. Anyway, up at the port, I looked at the stuff and said to Nancy, 'I seen everything here but a shrunken head,' and goddamn if she didn't turn around and show me that too.

"I never did say anything to Julian about the cost of all those purchases, but I could never understand why he didn't put his foot down about all that. Still can't."

Nor could he understand why Nancy and Jay had never had a child, especially since "they could have produced a genius or something."

But beyond his attempts to understand (including his realization that "Julian's time was not his own, because he was always doing what he was supposed to do"), beyond his own feelings of guilt that he may have let Jay down as a father, lay an unmistakable anger and disappointment, blended with pragmatism. "This was an insane thing for him to do," he said, cutting the air with his hands as if he were still a bandleader. "If he ever returns from his 'tour,' how is he ever going to get a reference? He'll never be able to get another job. Nobody wants a president who just hops up and runs off. If he had just established a firm hand with Nancy about money, this would not have happened. And if he had just resigned orthodoxly, he would have a clean slate. That's what I'd ask him, if I knew where the hell he was: why didn't you go through traditional channels and do it right?"

Once again, there it was: the question of whether what Jay did, because it is *not* within "traditional channels," because it challenges our notion of what is acceptable behavior, is an insane, irrational thing to do.

Perhaps John Sine was right. As more days passed, the former English and philosophy major found himself wondering if people were asking themselves the wrong question. Instead of trying to analyze why Jay did it, perhaps the real question was, why don't people do it more often?

TWENTY

THE DAY AFTER GRADUATION Katharyn Jones, as much to keep busy as anything else, began to clear out Jay's office. In box after box, she packed books, personal files, a framed photograph of Nancy, the wooden statue of Don Quixote, and the many other things that marked Jay's tenure at the college, mementos of a life, she was now reluctantly conceding, she hadn't really known at all.

The office was modestly furnished and small, much smaller than John Sine's, but Katharyn had never found that strange. She thought it perfectly in keeping with Jay's propensity for being low-key, almost as if he needed to constantly remind others that he had lived in a trailer once, that Green's Inheritance was an aberration, just another role he played so well, and that this little office was who, underneath, he truly was.

Moving around the office with the slow, careful motion of an undertaker, Katharyn found herself looking out the window, seeing all the buildings that were there because he had been. She felt the texture of the clean shirt and jacket that he always kept on a hanger, another reminder, at least on the surface, of how far he had come from the shy, gawky twenty-three-year-old who had arrived at the

Naval Ordnance Station (where she too had worked) nearly a quarter of a century before.

Through all the years that followed, she never lost that first impression, had always liked how down-to-earth he seemed, how unpushy he was compared with many of the other engineers Joe Browning had hired. And even though she was now feeling let down (she hadn't received a farewell letter and was taking it personally), she was still giving him the benefit of the doubt. He always had time for her, he never forgot her birthday, he always brought her back a gift from his travels. The idea that he might possibly have been unhappy with Nancy did not occur to her. She knew that Nancy could be domineering, but she also observed that it never seemed to bother Jay, that he always referred to her, genuinely not patronizingly, as "my good wife."

She knew the last year had been difficult for him, and she wondered if he felt a particular county commissioner had been out to get him. It was no secret that Loretta Nimmerichter was his bête noire. In fact, she was the first to ask if Jay had stolen any money, and she was supposed to have met with Jay the day before he vanished—to arrange a date for the dedication of the new arts center that he had pushed long and hard for. When he got to her office, though, she wasn't there. So he came back to the college and told Katharyn, who couldn't believe that she had stood him up, "Well, that's okay." Shortly thereafter he went home.

And now, six days later, one disturbing thought, more than any other, kept recurring to her: if somebody as nice and kind and thoughtful as Jay Carsey could do this, anyone could.

PEOPLE TELL THEMSELVES stories in order to live, Joan Didion wrote. And in these "stories," people, being human and imperfect, recall certain things accurately, while others emerge, in the telling, far from the way they happened, emerge in the way the teller of the tale wants—or needs—them to.

To a large extent, nobody's "story" fit that definition better than

Dom Monetta's, because nobody, with the exception of Nancy, had more reason to be both straightforward and blind. The relationship between a mentor and a protégé is always a tricky one. Sooner or later, the mentor will usually do something to disappoint his protégé, or the protégé will surpass the mentor's own accomplishments.

As Dom drove to Green's Inheritance the morning after he arrived back from New Mexico, he was struggling with this, and struggling with the fact that he, like Joe Browning, Homer, and others, did not feel Jay had done this in the proper way. He was sad and he was disappointed. To him, Jay was a child of the universe, a Gary Cooper type for whom good things seemed to come naturally, someone whose life with Nancy symbolized upper-middle-class prosperity, what everybody should strive for. Dom believed strongly in models, and theirs was the one on which he had firmly based his own aspirations, to rise from the Bronx and become head of the class. If the Carseys hadn't "made it," he didn't know who had. So what had happened? he kept asking himself as he arrived at the house that had always been a second home to him.

Bob Straus had told him Nancy was badly traumatized, and that hadn't changed. He told Nancy what Jay's note had said—about taking care of her "for a while"—and that bolstered her spirits a bit, because she took it as confirmation that he would eventually return from wherever he was. But Dom was not so sure, though he didn't say that to Nancy, at least not at first. Once Dom saw Jay's notes and listened to the tape, he realized, much to his surprise, how carefully planned Jay's departure had been. While Dom gives himself credit (with some justification) for being a perceptive person, he never saw this as an avenue Jay would choose to change his life. Like Katharyn Jones, he felt that Jay was a kind, considerate, generous individual, and people like that didn't do things like this.

But maybe that was one of the problems, Dom thought. Jay was "Uncle Jay" for a reason. He not only allowed other people to use him as a crutch, he encouraged it, and that was particularly true of his relationship with Nancy. Dom could understand why nearly everyone who knew them had the impression that Nancy controlled Jay, that she took far more than she gave. After all, didn't he cater to her every whim and apparently love doing so? Yes, he did—or had—but if you believe Dom Monetta, there was a reason for that, one that was both simple and complicated. The simple one was that he not only loved pleasing Nancy, but saw that as his function as a husband. She had given him (and Dom) something neither of them would have acquired on their own—"high pizzazz," in Dom's words—and Jay in turn played his role beautifully, as he had every other one he had assumed.

The complicated reason—the one that hardly anyone saw, and that Nancy only fully came to understand later—was that Jay, in showing his "gratitude" by doing all the things he did for her, running here, there, and everywhere, was subtly exercising a form of control over her, a most lethal kind, the kind that made her as dependent on him as a junkie is on a pusher. She could have been much more independent than she was, but he made it so easy for her not to be. When you are more indulged than Cleopatra, as Nancy claimed she was, when you are told that you are not to concern yourself about money, as Nancy claimed she was, is it any wonder that Nancy was reeling?

Maybe not. But Dom got the distinct impression that Jay and Nancy had had "heated discussions" about their "interpersonal dynamic" (phrases like this are a staple of Monetta's vast arsenal of language), and that the possibility of separation had been raised. He claimed that Nancy told him that. And there seemed to be supporting evidence in the note Jay sent her, in the line that read *I'm leaving because I know you can't.*

For her part, Nancy didn't deny that "something to that effect" might have been in Jay's letter, but was vehement that there were no discussions of the kind Dom claimed took place. "On my death-bed, on my life bed, on my whatever," she bristled, "never did Jay say anything about me leaving, him leaving, or divorce. It was *never* broached. It never occurred to me that he would even consider it. The life we had was one that I thought he wanted. He lived it. We lived it. And when it was no longer what he wanted, he should have been able to talk to me. If he had such a fear of disappointing me, then why did he do it this way, why did he hurt me so badly? He obviously wasn't as strong as I perceived him as being. If he had only come to me," she said quietly, "that would have made such a world of difference. It could have spared us all so much grief."

If Nancy was telling the truth, then why did Dom insist on believing otherwise? Because he needed, as Marilyn Southwell said, something to cling to. He was not the only one of the Carseys' friends to feel that surely Jay must have given Nancy some warning of what might happen, but he was the only one to insist, on a few different occasions, that they had discussed this. On some level, he *must* believe that; if he didn't, then he was admitting that he didn't know Jay at all.

What he did admit, though, was that he didn't look for faults in his friends. So when Nancy told him about Jay's drinking, it forced him to focus on something he hadn't paid any attention to before: that there were a number of times in the past year when Jay had come to Dom's apartment in the early morning and had rooted around in the refrigerator for an open bottle of wine. And when Katharyn Jones came by the house and mentioned that Jay had canceled more meetings than normal during the same period, Dom had to concede, after thinking about it, that she was right.

If the drinking and the meetings were pieces to the puzzle of why Jay left that Dom had missed, the issue of Nancy's wanting a child was not. Jay had spoken to Dom about his lack of desire to have one, and Dom was not unsympathetic. He had children of his own and loved them very much, but he knew, even before his painful divorce, how difficult parent-child relationships could be, how "the benefits only outweigh the costs in the long term." It wasn't like having a horse in the barn which, if you tire of it, "you can always ship back to Kentucky." No, it wasn't like that all, and that was why Dom felt that Jay's going through the medical tests at Johns Hopkins was not only typical of his trying to appease Nancy, but wrong.

News travels like wildfire in a place like "Chuck County." In fact, Nancy's announcement in 1977 that she was leaving her job to start a family made its way around the area nearly as quickly as the report that Jay had vanished. To say that people were surprised—and worried—is an understatement. Some felt that Jay already had a child in Nancy. Others feared, like Dom, that she wanted a child for the wrong reasons—a "possession" that she didn't have. There was also the question of Nancy's age (forty) and, in Evelyn Hungerford's mind, the cynical notion that they'd better spend more time in bed than she and others had the impression they did, and the same worry about Nancy's capacity to nurture that Dorothy Artes had. From the moment Jay left, Evelyn was haunted by the memory of Nancy's lying on a couch in the Hungerfords' living room, Jay behind her, stroking her head, with no return of affection on Nancy's part.

Regardless of everyone's concerns, before long there was another bulletin: the Carseys were having tests. And shortly after that, the disclosure by Nancy that it was *Jay's* problem, not hers: he had a low sperm count. And then, a new communiqué: *they* would adopt.

When Nancy made up her mind about something, people had learned it was easier to give in than try and match wills. But to everyone's amazement, Jay made it clear he wasn't having any of it. When a friend of the Carseys' phoned to let them know of a possible child for adoption, Jay responded as if the friend were pushing an unwanted magazine subscription. And when Louis Jenkins and his wife came over to play bridge one time, carrying a red-haired Cabbage Patch Doll in their arms, their good intentions sorely backfired.

For someone like Dom Monetta, the whole notion of child-as-acquisition was not an example of his being overly cynical. Far from it, coming from someone as passionately committed to prosperity as he was.

But how much, one asks, knowing that the question is subjective and unanswerable, is enough? Dom was involved enough in Jay's financial life—as someone who hired Jay on consulting jobs—to know that Nancy was "always ten percent above whatever financial level they were at, no matter what level. So if Jay was making a million dollars a year, or even ten million, Nancy would always find a way to acquire bigger and bigger things. If Jay made ten billion dollars a year, she would be refitting the battleship *New Jersey* and making it a private yacht." And lest anyone think he had gone soft on materialism, he added, "Understand, that's not criticism. Jay got caught up in the whirlwind and he played that game infinitely well for a long, long time."

Odd, it would seem, for someone who intrinsically didn't care about money. But what Dom didn't know was this: apparently Jay had not only come to feel that the acquiring had to stop, he had even talked to Nancy about getting rid of some of the things they had. "He said we should begin to think about what we want to do with all this stuff," she confessed, "and I asked if he had any plan in mind. I was resistant to the idea of tearing everything apart until we knew what we were going to do with it. I mean, saying 'divest' is one thing, but how?"

According to Nancy, their discussion couldn't even be called that; it was no more than "a casual mention." He had no specific plan to offer and, in his typical nonconfrontational way, didn't pursue the matter further.

Not pushing Nancy about the disposal of some of their worldly goods was one thing, leaving in the way he had quite another. For Dom, as for others, Jay had committed social suicide. But Dom was not one to have his feelings, or anything else, grouped with others'. His relationship with Jay was unique and special; it was his. As was the deep and lingering disillusionment that evolved from his initial sadness and disappointment. Jay had literally brought him into the social and professional world (just as Jay had been brought along by people like Bob Straus and Nancy), and had departed from it so suddenly that Dom felt as abandoned as an orphan.

"My attraction to Jay," he explained, "was that he was constant, he was steady, he was *there*. He was intelligent, supportive, had a whole lot of answers. He had a willingness to help me understand the nature of Southern Maryland and the nature of NOS, and he helped soften my normally abrasive manner. It's in his soul to be that generous. That's why he was called Uncle Jay.

"But," he continued, "he is a classic WASP male in that he has been socialized to be unwilling to share his true feelings—lockjaw, dignified, quiet in the face of adversity."

Fine, but aren't there a bunch of people in that category who don't flee, who find a way, somehow, to articulate their feelings?

Not really, he said. "They take other courses of action. They either commit suicide, actually, or they wind up with a classic morbidity marriage and don't even sleep in the same room as the woman they're married to. Or they find an external pursuit and then become workaholics and they put their entire world into their job. Or they conveniently schedule themselves for a heart attack or stroke and they die in a socially acceptable way. Or they create a mental process where they get themselves cancer and die that way. Or they smoke or drink themselves into lung or liver cancer. Or they find some little honey who they can see twice a week and they unload to her.

"But they all kind of go the same way because they can't express what they're feeling."

Is it really as grim as all that?

No, Dom said. Most of them finally grow up.

Or maybe, in Jay's case, they try to return to who they were—to at least recover some notion of what that was—before things like expectations and being a good boy and pleasing others and playing roles first pulled them in and then, in time, wore them down and threatened to snuff them out. Perhaps all Jay wanted, like Huckleberry Finn, was "to go somewheres," to have a change. Evelyn Hungerford remarked that everyone always said that "Uncle Jay was going to have a crown in heaven." Perhaps that was exactly what he *didn't* want, even if the idea had seemed appealing for a long time. By leaving in the way that he had, he had made a statement to which there could be no response. On its face, it was an extremely hostile thing to do—as wicked, in its own way, as Miss Watson felt Huck's desires were, especially since they would only land him in "the bad place."

But Huck was a boy and Jay Carsey was a forty-seven-year-old man, with a wife and an institution that had put its trust in him and friends who loved him (though many wondered if they had made it clear enough to him how much), and what he had done had shaken each of them. They were concerned for him, they were concerned for Nancy, and they were concerned for themselves, wondering what impact Jay's leaving might have on their respective spouses, and on the way their children viewed the world.

TWENTY-ONE

THOUGH THE NEWS came a week after Jay had left, the time in between had seemed an eternity.

Jay had flown to Houston.

The first piece of telling evidence was a bill sent directly to Nancy from the Houston Oaks, a hotel in the Westin chain which is located next to a fancy shopping area called the Galleria. He had used his American Express card, she discovered, to pay for his room on Wednesday night, the nineteenth, the day that he had left, and this bill represented a charge that was received too late to be recorded with the others when he checked out the next day.

Well, Nancy thought to herself as she phoned Sergeant Boone, I wasn't too far off in thinking that he might go to Texas.

Though Boone had already concluded that Jay left of his own free will, he didn't tell Nancy that. But he was able to confirm the following: Jay had boarded Pan Am Flight 991; it had made one stop in New Orleans before arriving at Houston International Airport; he had used his own name, charging the one-way ticket to American Express; and he had flown first-class. Before leaving, he had signed in at Pan Am's Clipper Club, had a few drinks, and appeared to be alone. An employee named Kitty Stevenson remembered him and not much else.

Once Boone knew all this, there was no reason—actually, no justification—for the state police to be involved any further. Boone finally told Nancy this, and she seemed to understand.

But naturally she didn't stop there. She was just getting started, alerting Dom Monetta and Joe Browning immediately, and recontacting Lamberth Carsey.

"Nancy," Lamberth said, "if there is one man in Houston who can find out if Jay is still here, it's Clyde Wilson."

CLYDE WILSON IS ONE of the most famous private investigators in the country. When you meet him and shake his huge hand, you feel as if you are grasping the entire state of Texas in your smaller palm, and that he is someone who has seen things and been places you would never want to experience or go. In a state where crimes seem to occur even more often than oil shooting forth from the ground, Wilson and his group of operatives, as he refers to them, are usually called on (by people of means) to go further than the police might—or can.

The fact that Nancy hadn't contacted the authorities immediately did not surprise Wilson. In his forty years of experience, he had found that the more prominent the individual in question, the more embarrassing it is to the ones who are seeking information about (or action against) him. Situations like Jay's were hardly unknown to Wilson. His agency alone receives about twenty cases a year. (Of the roughly 65,000 *reported* cases of Missing Persons entered into FBI computers each year, about 20 percent are adults. Like the reasons for such an act, precise figures not only remain elusive, they defy generalization.) The first thing Wilson does is to check the jails and the hospitals, both in the area from where the person has vanished and to where he is thought to have headed. Even if there was evidence that Jay had flown to Houston under his own name, the possibility that he had returned to the Washington area using a different one, trying to confuse anybody who might be on his trail, could not be ruled out.

If the reason to check the hospitals seems an obvious one and the jails less so, that is because people tend to forget the shame factor, Wilson said, the willingness some people have to stay behind bars for a day or two, incommunicado, rather than call a loved one and admit they were arrested for driving while intoxicated. The fear of value judgment, of what it might do to one's "reputation," can never be underestimated.

Half of the calls Wilson gets tend to be ones where he discovers the person has left with somebody. In the case of a prominent Houston attorney, Wilson, not the police, got a call from the man's wife a full two days after he disappeared. Unlike Nancy, she hadn't received a letter, only phone calls from his law office saying he had depositions scheduled and where the hell was he?

Registered under an assumed name in a low-rent motel just off Highway 59, Wilson discovered. "He had had a few drinks, gone to a party, had shacked up with a woman. He'd been loyal to his wife for thirty-some-odd years." The woman was long gone by the time Wilson arrived, but the man's conscience was bothering him —so much so that this "devout Christian" was contemplating suicide. "He was going to slash his wrists. In fact, the story to us was that he was going to draw a nice warm bath and had already gone out and bought a razor." He never used it and was persuaded to go home.

In Wilson's experience, half the disappearances he encounters are carefully planned, the other half are wild and impulsive, and, contrary to what people generally think, not just carried out by men. In Jay's case, from talking with Nancy and Lamberth and from learning about the notes and tape, Wilson felt fairly sure that this was as plotted out as a bank robbery. But that didn't mean that Jay, like that lawyer, wasn't holed up in a motel somewhere, ready to do himself in.

The most Wilson got from Nancy was this: Jay had been depressed, probably because of the financial problems at the college, had been drinking heavily, and took about $15,000 with him (she later discovered it was more). She also told him that Jay had an uncle who was an alcoholic and had also disappeared. She didn't tell him about his various physical ailments or the trouble he was having sleeping (though Wilson gleaned that from the note she read to him), but she did tell him something that she hadn't mentioned to anyone else: Jay's "diminishing interest in sex."

She also asked Wilson if he would contact a man named Carl Schwing, who lived in Galveston and whom Nancy thought Jay might contact. Schwing had worked at the community college for a number of years as the director of a pollution-abatement program. Started by Jay a year after he became president, the program was deemed so innovative and so important that it virtually became the model for every other program in the country. Of all the feathers in Jay's cap, this was possibly his greatest achievement as president: it served the community's needs, it focused a large and proud spotlight on a pioneering effort, and it garnered an enormous amount of money from federal grants and other sources. When Carl Schwing left the college in 1980, it was the only time, Steve Maxwell recalled, that he ever saw Jay rattled. "Schwing knew where the money was and how to get it."

But he didn't know where Jay was.

EVERY HOTEL AND MOTEL in the Houston area was contacted. Jay's bill from the Houston Oaks showed he had made no calls, leaving open the possibility, of course, that he had used a pay phone.

But he was still, apparently, using his real name.

There was a J.N. Carsey staying at a Howard Johnson's. Wilson drove there with no expectations. He had made this kind of trip many times over many years for many different reasons. Sometimes he would find a body, freshly dead, or someone consumed with grief, or someone who just wanted to talk. Informed that Jay had turned forty-seven less than a week before he left, Wilson reminded himself that both men and women of that age or older "can reach a point where they can't cope, life is closing in on them, they haven't found what they were looking for and life is passing them by in their own mind—they haven't found the happiness, the love, the affection, the rewards that they wanted. Whether it's monetary or sexual or whatever it is they're looking for, they just have not found it. If they have children, they're tired of them.

"They just want to start another life under another name. Oftentimes when you find these people and talk to them, sit down and ask them why they did this, you find that they don't really know. They can't give you any logical explanation for why they left. They just left. They just flat wanted to get away. Things had built up and the pressure was too much."

One of the many things Wilson then tries to do is persuade the person to at least phone the ones he has left and say he is all right. Sometimes Wilson can persuade the person to "go back and try again," and sometimes he can persuade the individual (or couple) to seek psychiatric help.

But many times none of this works. The person not only refuses to make contact, but is upset and angered that he has been discovered. All Wilson is able to ask then—something that every person he has ever found has been willing to do—is for the individual to pose for a photograph. The person will do that, provided he has assurance that Wilson will not divulge his location. "Oftentimes their loved ones are displeased with us because we've made that promise," he said, "but the fact is we're powerless. All we can say is, 'Thank you for your cooperation. We had a job to do, we've done it, and you are all right.' "

With Jay, Clyde Wilson never had that opportunity. Though there was indeed a J.N. Carsey at a Howard Johnson's in Houston, he was not Nancy's husband.

TWENTY-TWO

J OE BROWNING AND Dom Mo-
netta began spending hours on
the telephone with each other, racking their brains and feeling as
unsuccessful as Clyde Wilson was. They had promised Nancy that
they would aid in the search effort, but instead of seeing themselves
as a pair of determined gumshoes, they likened their situation to
two German shepherds chasing a Volkswagen: even if they found
Jay, what could they do with him?

Joe Browning came close. While Dom was checking some hotels
in Sydney and Nancy was sending a snapshot of Jay in a turtleneck
to friends in Texas, California, Mexico, and Australia, Joe phoned
the Hotel del Coronado in San Diego and learned that Jay had
made a reservation there . . . but canceled it.

He did go to San Diego though. Nancy received four nights'
worth of American Express receipts from the Westgate Hotel,
beginning on Thursday, the twentieth; he'd had a lavish meal at
a restaurant they had been to together. That meant he had stayed
only the one night in Houston—the one she knew about. While
there, however, he was busy, making a number of purchases,
including a Pierre Cardin suit. He had warned Nancy that he

was going to use their credit cards for a few days and he had. Since the cards were in both their names, she could have canceled them. But because she thought he would either come back or the cards would provide important clues as to where he was, she didn't. What she hadn't counted on, what both angered and befuddled her, was the amount and nature of the charges—charges she was liable for.

Evelyn Hungerford was as angry about this as Nancy, remarking that "Here I was, worrying about him like a mother would a son, worrying that this poor man might be lying dead out there somewhere, and then he charges some fancy suit. It just doesn't make sense. He *never* cared about clothes."

And probably still didn't, the suit becoming a paradoxical symbol, a statement almost, of the acquisitiveness he had apparently wanted to stop.

ONCE NANCY CONTACTED the state police, it was only a matter of time before the press reported the story—another vehicle, Nancy hoped, to let Jay know how much she wanted him to come home. Failing that, she told anyone who asked that she would "go to him, wherever he is."

Letters began to arrive for her—from people she and Jay knew together, from former students of hers, from childhood friends, even from total strangers.

Trevor Carpenter, who went with John Sine to pick up the college car at the airport, wrote of his confidence that her "intelligence and charm" would enable her to continue leading "a productive and exciting life."

A relative of Nancy's wrote that Jay's disappearance was an unpleasant reminder of the time her husband had taken their two children and vanished for three months. "Of course," she added, "I know none of the particulars in your case, but I do know that although the ensuing 1 1/2 years were the most difficult of my life,

112

they were also the start of a spiritual and emotional growth that I might have conveniently put off forever."

One of the teachers under Nancy when she was a principal wrote that she had "read once that with life's mishaps, men tend to blame circumstances, while women tend to blame themselves. I hope you're not doing that. Although it's been a few years since I've seen you, Jay *always* gave the impression that he very much liked all the things you both did and the life you led. . . . I believe that one day Jay will . . . realize how much he had in a creative, interesting wife who loved him."

A fiercely religious woman, unknown to Nancy, wrote to say that if Nancy did not know Christ, she should instantly "open [her] heart and ask Him to come into your Life." In addition, Nancy should "read the Gospel of John" and take comfort in knowing that she was in the nightly prayers of one Lula B. Harrison.

A letter from the president of another community college in Maryland urged Nancy to call him if she happened to be in Baltimore. "As you know," he intimated innocently, "I love to be seen in the company of a good-looking redhead."

An older couple named Jynx and Bert Adams, who played golf every other Wednesday with the Carseys at the local country club, sent Nancy a thousand dollars "to do with as you see fit." Not only had they played the Wednesday before Jay left, but they distinctly recalled Jay's saying that he was planning to buy Nancy a new lavender golf bag. In their note to her, they said "we only wish we could wave the magic wand that would bring Jay back—healthy and happy."

Letter after letter pointed out to Nancy that she was "a survivor" . . . that everyone shared her pain ("Jay's and your sorrows are part of the human condition and we have all known both") . . . that they knew words were inadequate to express how they felt . . . that if she didn't come to Captiva in the autumn it wouldn't be the same without her . . . that, above all, she should not lose hope.

. . .

SHE WAS TRYING, but it was becoming increasingly harder to do. No more receipts arrived from American Express, or from anywhere else for that matter. The few scraps of information she had gotten seemed more a cruel form of now-you-see-me-now-you-don't taunting than anything else. And Dom and Joe, who had urged Jay a year before to leave the college and essentially change his life, were now giving her a similar message, the same one Spencer Matthews had: forget Jay, find a job, and get on with your life.

She knew they, like everyone else, were just trying to be helpful, but what they were suggesting was impossible. She wanted her husband back, longed for their life to revert to what it was before everything changed. Since she couldn't ever recall his verbalizing that he was unhappy, she couldn't come to terms with the reality of what had happened, couldn't stop thinking that she and Jay had been different, had been an exception, had somehow been immune to the myriad things that can befall other people—but not them. Day after day, she would sit in the house, much too big now for one, and look at the hundreds of pictures they had accumulated over the years of all the places, near and far away, they had been —from Bethany Beach in Delaware to the Greek islands, from Kenya, Russia, Denmark, Mexico (on Nancy's fortieth birthday), and China, to the Reagans' Inaugural Ball just up the road in 1981; and of all the people who had found their way into the photographs and into their lives, be they friends like the Hungerfords, the Matthewses, Billy and Jane Zantzinger, and Bob and Peggy Schaumburg, or public figures like General William Westmoreland, Paul Nitze, and the governor of Maryland.

"In nearly every picture I looked at," she recalled, opening the photo album, "there were Jay and Nancy, Jay and Nancy, Jay and Nancy. And I just sat there and thought, Well, I may not have had all of him, but I certainly had a big, big piece. And even though I had seen him shut out others, even Dom, who would sometimes call the house and I would lie and say Jay was not here when I knew he didn't want to talk with anyone, when things were going so badly at the college, when he was having so much trouble dealing with no longer being Mr. Wonderful, no longer being Joy Boy, which he had been from the time he was a high school valedictorian . . . I just never thought he would bring down this kind of iron door on me.

"Part of the really deep pain of trying to understand and cope with this," she went on, "is that I could have seen him walking away from the college or walking away from people. But when he could X me out . . . I mean, all those years he had led me to believe I was so special to him. When did I become unspecial?"

When did I become unspecial? Though it seemed more a plaintive note than a question to which Nancy truly expected an answer, it didn't stop her from scrutinizing each photograph, looking for something, anything, that might provide an explanation, serve as a clue, a foreshadowing, of what he would later do; nor did it stop her from walking through every room of the house and trying to do the same.

But to Nancy each room was a symbol of their happiness, a tangible sign that they had made it in Reagan's America, had indeed made it well before it became Reagan's America, even though his policy toward money for education had made life difficult for people like Jay. She could never see the house the way many of their friends saw it—as more ostentatious than comfortable—because the house was Nancy, and she was the house, in the same way Jay's old trailer and small office were extensions of him. Even though she had told the *Baltimore Sun*, which published a long article about Green's Inheritance in 1976, that she wanted to "make this Jay and Nancy's house" when they bought it, she never corrected any of her friends when they referred to it solely as "Nancy's house." The reason: "I decorated it. Jay didn't care how it was decorated." When they first saw it, though, it was in a state of disrepair; and it was Jay, she said, who saw its possibilities and told her, "You can do something with that house, Nance, I know you can."

She could and did. And even though she would reluctantly concede that it was "not a good house for Jay because he couldn't fix anything," the experience of walking through it now was not all that different from peering at the photographs, each purchase a poignant reminder of the years they had spent together.

When Nancy looked at the rich green of the fringe-pocketed pool table in the game room, she recalled how much Jay loved to play, to apply chalk to the cue stick and then, an instant later, hear the crack of one ball against the next; and she smiled at the memory of how much trouble it was to get the table up to the third floor, how happy they were when they did, and how much pleasure it gave their friends and their "adopted" nephews and nieces.

In the room next to it, the one with an entire wall of masks, she laughed at how she and Jay would always conspire to put a guest who had had too much to drink in there to sleep it off, only to awaken and cry out in horror. (In truth, the room had such an ominous feeling that children would not stay overnight in it; the Carseys' maid was so spooked by it, and by the various skeletons scattered around the house in general, that she told one and all she wouldn't spend one second in the house, if she hadn't needed the money; and a television cameraman, an experienced veteran who had been on the frontlines covering wars in Central America and the Middle East, felt so uneasy in the mask room that he refused his producer's request to shoot footage of it.)

Walking into the formal dining room, with a French tapestry hanging at one end, and a carved, enameled Chinese screen covering another wall, Nancy stared at the one thing that loomed over everything else, the thing that immediately became a conversation piece when it was unveiled: a huge, tantalizing painting of Nancy, wearing an elegant, low-cut gown, looking for all the world like some baroness.

But as she wove her way past a Guatemalan marimba with

hanging gourds, a pair of temple dogs from Katmandu, an oil lamp from Ceylon, framed mirrors from Morocco, and Spanish armor, walking over Turkish, Persian, and Pakistani rugs, she came to a room that perhaps had more meaning than any other. It was a guest room, done in a quaint colonial style replete with spinning wheel, chamber pot, and sawdust dolls in an old baby buggy. There was a canopy bed, girly and frilly, and on top of it, its head resting on the pillow, was the red-haired Cabbage Patch Doll Nancy had been given.

At first glance, the room seemed so perfect for a child that it was hard to believe that no child lived in it, yet no child did. Nevertheless, there the doll was, somehow transcending itself, becoming Nancy as an innocent child again in Indiana, or, in another light, a defiant though illusory symbol of her having gotten what she wanted, of determined fantasy triumphing over the letdown of reality.

But strive as she had to create the aura of a "perfect life"—with a wonderful husband and a wonderful house and a "child" that was perfect because it never misbehaved—the fact that she was now alone, that one huge part of the mosaic had fallen out and might never be replaced, was more than she could bear.

The letters told her not to blame herself, and for the longest time she didn't. For the longest time, at least publicly, she insisted it was Jay's problem, that once he came to his senses he would be back, would return to being "the rational Uncle Jay that we all knew." After all, he had only asked both Dom and Ed Loeliger to look after her "for a while"—not forever. And after all, as recently as February, they had begun looking for an apartment to buy in Washington. Why would he encourage that, she asked herself, if he knew what he was planning to do?

But privately, at times when she wasn't being looked after by friends, invited to dinner at the country club or to parties or to play golf as if nothing had changed, at those moments when the loneliness was devastating—that was when she began to look inward, to worry that she had put Jay on too much of a pedestal and that "he didn't know how to come down," to consider that "maybe he knew how much I depended on him and he resented it," to ask herself if "perhaps I frightened him with all this optimistic talk" about how the summer would solve everything.

But when she wondered if she had possibly put too much pressure on him about having a baby, her question about that would always be countered by another: how can you be guilty of relentlessly pushing for something that you truly want? Like so much else about their relationship, when it came to communication, Nancy could never get Jay to articulate his objections. "I *wanted* to have a child," she said, "and the most I could ever get him to say was that he didn't want a twenty-year obligation. I suggested counseling, but he refused."

Maybe, she said, reiterating something she had said to Lamberth, his physical problems were much greater than anyone realized. "But maybe that's rationalization on my part. Maybe I want to think that's why he felt he had to leave, because it's just impossible to truly understand. I mean, there have been hours and hours of conversation devoted just to this. I don't think Jay realized how many people liked him so much and that, if there were a physical problem [other than the ones she knew about], we would have helped to care for him. I mean, you just can't project yourself into another person's skin and brain."

The letters said it would be nice if there was a book with answers that Nancy could turn to, and she obsessively began to read everything she could find or that friends recommended. But when Joe Browning recommended that *she* seek counseling, she said she would if she could, but that she couldn't afford it.

Her response was partly a convenient excuse, partly legitimate. Jay's leaving had put her in a financial bind. Since the note he left her, the one leaving her all the assets *and* the liabilities, had been neither witnessed nor notarized, she was not free to dispose of things as she wished. (That she didn't want to was another matter.) In order to gain trusteeship of their estate in the eyes of Maryland law, she would have to file for a "limited divorce." Once she did that, she would be able to sell things (like their time-sharing units in Florida, or a condominium they had on South Padre Island in Texas), but she would still be accountable for them. In other words, even in his absence and until seven years passed (when he could be declared legally dead, unless he came forward), Jay was entitled to his share of their estate. Unless a court could be satisfied that the note was a binding contract, he was, ironically enough, still in control.

The question of whether his failure to legitimize the note was deliberate and malicious, or whether it was an innocent oversight, was troubling to everyone, not just Nancy. If his departure was as carefully planned as it appeared, if he really meant to allow Nancy to get on with her life and not drag her down with him (as his other note had said), then why wouldn't he have made this a priority on his checklist of Things To Do Before I Leave?

Nancy's answer was that she was sure he thought "the message of the note would be enough." Others, though, viewed it more cynically, feeling that Jay had dealt with enough lawyers in his professional life to know better, that he was too calculating and precise an individual (his training as a chemical engineer too deeply ingrained within him) to have slipped up, that he needed a contingency plan, a way back, if he didn't find what he was looking for.

Whatever the real reason, Nancy could only depend for so long on the kindness of friendly bankers, the hospitality of friends, and some income she received from her family's farm.

That, at least, was what everybody thought.

One of the reasons she gave her friends for speaking with reporters and going on television was her desire to get a message to Jay, to tell him, "If you must be away alone, I understand that, but please do clean up our packaging, because it would be very helpful to me in becoming Nancy Stevens Carsey again, as opposed to always being Mrs. Jay Carsey." After all, she too was Dr. Carsey, she reminded everyone, a respected educator with advanced degrees who had "relegated Dr. Nancy to being Mrs. Jay for many years."

In other words, she seemed to be saying, she was going to have to get a job. Or so everybody thought.

Out of all the self-examination Nancy claimed she had done and was continuing to do, she didn't finally think there were any answers, at least not any satisfactory ones. And as time went on, she came to feel that it wasn't very healthy for her to go on dwelling about how she might have contributed to what happened. But in lamenting to a male friend of hers and Jay's that she didn't understand how she could have been married to Jay for fourteen years and not known this sort of impulse was inside him, that there must have been "some little box inside him which I couldn't enter," the friend told her, "Nancy, my wife doesn't know half of what is inside me."

He delivered the remark so casually that it not only caused Nancy to shudder, but to wonder how Jay's leaving *was* being viewed by others. While one part of her was convinced that "if Jay had stayed and weathered it, then he would have been a hero," another part asked wistfully: "Who's to say? Maybe he's a hero now to some people."

TWENTY-THREE

ONCE THE COMMENT WAS MADE nobody was quite sure how to take it, but it must have been viewed with a certain degree of seriousness because it sure changed the way husbands and wives behaved toward each other for quite some time. It wasn't Nancy's speculation about Jay's possibly being a hero in the eyes of some, but it just as well might have been. It came out one night as a group of men were sitting around the bar at the Hawthorne Country Club, men who were friends and acquaintances of Jay's, men who often traded talk about their golf game and how it had gone to hell, or engaged in the sort of joshing and randy jokes and tall tales that can enliven a slow summer evening in a small town.

But on that evening in 1982, they were not doing any of those things. They were partaking instead in the "hours and hours of conversation" Nancy had spoken about, trying to size up, in their own minds, what Jay's leaving meant, trying to weigh its import. Among them were a state representative, a realtor, an insurance salesman, a car dealer—men with wives and children and mortgages, figures of responsibility. Men who seemed to be open books and men, like Jay, who probably weren't. Some of them had clearly prospered and were living within their means; some had not and were living well beyond them. To an outsider wandering into the bar, these men, mostly in their forties and fifties, could have been gathered together in any number of places in any number of towns across the country on that humid evening, speaking their minds. But as with any group, men or women, that sits around and chews the fat, a consensus about *anything* can be hard to find. There are exceptions, of course, and that night turned out to be one of them.

"You know, fellas, I was just thinking," one of them said above the quiet clinking of ice in their glasses. "If only Jay had chartered a plane, we all could have gone."

IT WAS INEVITABLE. Sooner or later, somebody was bound to openly express what a number of people had either privately thought, or tried to block from their mind. Word of Mike Sprague's comment buzzed around Southern Maryland in no time. The notion—the fantasy—of just walking out of your life was not the kind of thing a person blithely brought up at the dinner table or mentioned in polite conversation. For the ones such an act would affect, it was the ultimate fear, and there wasn't one person, if he was being honest with himself, who hadn't, in the agonizing time since Jay had departed, mouthed to himself the time-worn but apt cliché, *There but for the grace of God go I.*

But there was more to the Sprague remark than the taboo chord it had struck. Without realizing it, he was reminding everyone that, even in his absence, Jay was still the one they looked to, still the one they expected to lead the way.

WHEN KAREN SPRAGUE heard what Mike had told the men at the club she laughed.

"I'd be right there helping him pack," she said, flashing a smile that could light up a room. "But he'd be back in two weeks."

Was she really that confident? Or was she ignoring the fact that all over the county husbands and wives had been jolted into looking at each other in odd and different ways, almost as if they had become strangers? And all over the county, everyone had been making a great effort to be sweeter to each other, ordinary meals had become exotic overnight, families began doing more things together. Given that Karen had been one of the women so incredulous of the way Jay catered to Nancy that she often kidded Mike, when they were about to embark on a trip, "Could you please put all the bags in the car, Uncle Jay, and then could you go to the grocery store and then . . . ?", did she really now feel that she knew him well enough to say that, that he wouldn't "pull a Jay"—the parlance eventually given to their friend's act?

"What I'm trying to say," she explained, leaning her angelic face forward, "is that if Jay had been married to me, it never would have gotten to that point. I feel I would have known if something was wrong, and we would have talked about it. And if I knew he was planning to do this, I would have said—and I *know* Nancy would have said—'Come on, Jay, let's take a vacation.' We would have talked him out of it, and he probably knew that."

As well as anyone, Karen Sprague understood how complicated the web of reasons no doubt was for Jay to do this. And because of that, she refused to make any value judgment. If she had been able to get one message to him a few months after he left, this would be it:

"Gee, Jay, I'm sorry you couldn't cope. But I don't think of you as an ogre, or anything like that. We've been taking care of Nancy, as I guess you knew we would. Wherever you are, I'd hate to think that you're ill. I just hope you're happy . . . that you're under a pineapple tree somewhere."

TWENTY-FOUR

THERE WERE NO PINEAPPLE trees where Jay was, but there was an abundance of warm weather, the kind he enjoyed.

"I figured I had five days before anything would really start to happen," he explained one day. The delivery was slow and deceptively relaxed, the voice belonging distinctly to a Texan, all those years in the East not having changed it a bit, though what they had done to him was a different matter. "I had planned to leave on Tuesday, but things got complicated and I couldn't get away." Besides, he felt, leaving on Wednesday was better, because Nancy would get her letter the next day, and he was pretty certain that she wouldn't do anything at first, that she wouldn't believe it, that there would be a lot of confusion. By the time it began to sink in that he might not be coming back, it would be the weekend and, he figured, "nobody could do anything anyway, especially with graduation on Sunday."

As in any story of considerable complexity, any story dealing with the unpredictable elements of human behavior, with the question of *why* people do what they do, no one clue or detail exists to make what Jay did nice, neat, and black-and-white explainable, to make it less threatening, to enable one to sit back and smugly say, "Aha, I get it, I see"—at least not with any certainty.

Because Jay's leaving was a confluence of so many factors, it becomes difficult to know exactly where to start. But, as it happens, a tent revival meeting, held every summer in a vacant lot across the way from Jay's family home in Rusk, Texas, seems as good a place as any.

JAY WAS ONLY two when the family moved to Rusk in 1937, but by the time he snuck into the revival meeting about eight years later, drawn there by all the shouting and carrying on, he brought some of his father's skepticism about religion with him. But neither that skepticism, nor his hearing about *Elmer Gantry* (Sinclair Lewis's novel about fundamentalist religion run amok), detracted in any way from the fascination Jay had with what he saw—the ability of one person to hold hundreds in thrall, to persuade them that he could do whatever he said he could do, that he was practically God himself, and to have them sighing and moaning and spiraling forward with rolled, bulging eyes into ecstasy. Between the snakes, the fire and brimstone, and all the funny speaking in tongues, this whole spectacle was more exciting (and scarier) than all the tales the ten-year-old boy had heard about his father's circus life put together.

And since it was Texas, that meant it was drought-dry much of the time, and so it was hardly surprising that rainmakers would come through places like Rusk and Ballinger, offering their own special brand of charm and sharing with the preachers the only piece of common ground necessary to both their vocations—the messianic ability to attract disciples and make them believe.

And though dreams were not hard to sell in such dreamless places as these, that didn't matter. Nor did it matter that Jay had never seen a rainmaker face to face. He grew up with the mysterious lore and legend of them, and that was good enough—in some ways even better.

Even though the war was on and wages were frozen, Jay recalled his childhood years in Rusk as idyllic, a time in which "there were no crises. We ate, had a garden in the back, and listened to the radio. We weren't poor—everybody was basically lower-middle-class—but we had no contingency money. We didn't travel—I spent summers picking cotton at my uncle's farm—we didn't go out and buy conspicuous consumption things, but we had enough money for penny-ante poker. We had a house and we had books, but we didn't own a quarter of a million dollars' worth of jewelry or a hundred thousand dollars' worth of collectibles from Kenya."

All of that may be true (even though his thinly veiled reference to Nancy's jewelry and their collectibles is exaggerated), but what is also true is that the household Jay recalled "was not the kind of place where you hugged your mother and all that sort of stuff. My parents were not openly affectionate, but, I've got to tell you, neither were anybody else's I knew. You intuitively knew as a small child that there was a great deal of strong feelings between families, but you never saw it overtly. In a place like Turkey, for instance, everybody you meet kisses you on both cheeks. That simply wasn't done in East Texas. Emotions were *private*."

Jay paused for a few seconds, the lay preacher in him clearly wanting to make sure that one understood how important that form of expression (or the lack thereof) was to him, then said, less emphatically, "It's what I call 'personal distance.' "

To the best of his knowledge, a single parent was unheard of in either Rusk or Bryan. But even though nobody got divorced, he conceded that "a lot of people who stayed together probably shouldn't have"—a category that could easily have included his own parents. "Personal distance" certainly seemed an appropriate shorthand term for a marriage Jay came to perceive as having "no tension," a household in which Jay would sit, night after night, and say to himself, "Yeah, Mom's playing bridge, Dad's gone into isolation."

"You see," he explained, "it's not dollars, it's lifestyle. In order to be in the country-club set, she had to provide the lifestyle through playing bridge. Dad, on the other hand, is a totally nonsocial animal, and became more and more so.

"But," he said, determined not to leave the wrong impression, "they did nothing for me that wasn't great. They fed me, clothed me, gave me a place to sleep. There was never any abuse of me at all."

For the most part, that was true—with one telling exception. Rusk, like many towns at that time, was entirely segregated. Blacks lived in "nigger town," whites only saw them on the main streets on Saturdays, and even then, it was tacitly understood that a black person would step into the street and pretend he didn't exist if a white person crossed his path on the sidewalk. Well, one day, a black laborer suddenly appeared at the front door of the Carseys' house and asked if he could use the bathroom. Since Bea was in the garden, Jay let him in. As it happened, Bea saw the man leaving the house, came rushing in the back door, and asked Jay what was going on. No sooner had Jay told her than he watched his mother become another person. "She went totally berserk and whipped me," he recalled, "then she spent the next two hours scrubbing the entire bathroom." When Bea's "persecution of Susie" occurred years after that, Jay at least had an unwelcome framework from which to view and rationalize it. His suppressed anger—not to mention the fear and recoil such behavior created in him—was a different matter.

Prejudice and persecution, though, were not the only things Jay received a harsh lesson about while growing up. At the tender age of eight, he was introduced to madness. Since the Carseys could not afford a babysitter and Bea's feet were firmly planted under the bridge table, Homer would often take Jay with him to the state mental hospital, where Homer had organized a small group of patients to play instruments for the weekly dance that would be held there. As with the revival meeting, Jay once again witnessed people screaming and yelling. But in this instance, many of them were not free to move forward and be healed and taken into the Lord's good graces; in this instance many were in straitjackets, banging their heads against the barred windows, seeking their own form of release. As for the ones who were not constrained, Jay would never forget how garishly dressed all the women were, how their lipstick would spread further and further from their lips as the evening wore on, and how, when one of them suddenly stopped in the middle of a waltz and dramatically removed everything but her slip, two attendants appeared within seconds and took her away.

Given all that he had seen and heard by the time he was thirteen, when the family moved to Bryan and he began to take responsibility for Susie, it is hardly surprising that Jay would say he was always old for his age in the way he thought.

IT IS VIRTUALLY impossible for Jay to think about the time he spent in Bryan without thinking about Homer, without stating unequivocally that "my singular admiration for my dad comes from his taking a job at the newspaper there so that I could go to college at A&M."

That may be true, but at the time Jay concealed the devastation he felt when his father discouraged him from pursuing a career in journalism and music. As Homer knew well (and others would come to), Jay was very good at concealing things, and it was only years later that he told a friend how much he "wanted to play that damn cornet" and lamented, "How do you tell a kid that he ain't worth a damn in something he really likes?" Nevertheless, the admiration he spoke of had its roots in the fact that Jay was always a planner, that "the decisions I seemed to make at a very young age were very goal-oriented. I had no doubt that

I was going to get out of high school, go to college, and leave Texas."

However loaded down with rationalization that statement might be, he was in fact very much the cool, precise engineer long before he ever studied to become one. He kept careful records of movies he had seen and books he had read, and when he tired of his own company and decided that he needed "a personality outlet," he got involved with the Methodist church. "It was a great place to develop certain kinds of skills," he said, "and I was very diabolical about that." But, as it turned out, Jay's role-playing had its occasional limits. One time he was singing a hymn with the choir and wound up veering drastically off-key. Whether it was out of embarrassment or being reminded of the absurdity of doing something he didn't believe in, he suddenly got up before the service was over and walked out the back door of the church. And though he would later sing in a choir again in Anniston, when it served his purposes with Jessica Ross to do so, he never went back to the church in Bryan, despite the pastor's repeated attempts to persuade him.

As for Nelda Bruns and Jean McDonald, who bird-dogged his every move both in church and out, Jay was aware that the same personal distance that marked his parents' marriage was precisely what made him appealing to them, though he chose to view it as the first sign of how "emotionally shallow" a person he was. It was a view of himself that he would continue to hold—until, years later, something happened to change all that.

At Texas A&M he felt special, "being in this isolated, elite system, being *able* to get a college degree. Now, I didn't feel any sense of elitism like the Prince of Waloo, but I knew that I had something that was unusual. I was a WASP, born in the Depression, with a college degree.

"So you move on to the next step. You say, 'Well, let's make a lot of money and become powerful and arrogant.' It's awfully nice to stand up and be stroked, a real ego satisfaction comes with that."

But before he could move on to the next step, the Texas Legislature passed a bill that required everyone in college to take a course in Texas history, a requirement that infuriated Jay at the time. He was all prepared to graduate in June of 1957—and this was the reason he couldn't. "They could get away with that in the Fifties," he recalled with bitterness, "because you had *no* sense of protest. What were you going to do, go out and march on the university? They'd have said, 'Well, fuck, we just won't give you a degree.' "

He may have been bitter about it, but ever since he had had his first "moment of truth"—the poisoning incident of two years before—he felt, and would continue to feel, lucky to have his degree, lucky to have his commission, and, most important, lucky to be alive. And for all his somewhat sugarcoated talk about what an idyllic childhood he'd had, the fact is that the personal distance he had witnessed between his parents (as well as the building resentment he had toward his mother for her treatment of Susie) greatly affected his relationship with them.

"Once I left home," he would say with distinct pride, "I left home. I wrote faithfully, but I was not a go-back-home-for-Christmas person. I didn't have any close, extended family relationship. That just wasn't me." Pausing for a reflective moment or two, he then said, "I guess there's a pattern."

TWENTY-FIVE

"N ow, ANNISTON," Jay said, "now that was a very significant period for me. I had left Texas and never planned to go back. I was in the cusp—Korea was over and Vietnam hadn't started— I was breaking away from home, and really dove into the female thing. It was the first time I really started to seek women out and it changed a portion of my sense of ability to do certain things that had a tremendous impact on me from that time on."

Breaking up someone's engagement seems an odd way of sensing one's power, but that was the way Jay viewed his successful effort to win over Jessica Ross.

"She was the first significant woman in my life," he claimed. "I'd had some women in Bryan and I'd had some women in College Station, but it wasn't the same thing in the sense that the women were there and I wasn't seeking them out. I'd met them in church or I'd gone to school with them. But in Anniston I broke through a new layer of understanding about the thing—seeing a woman I liked and going after her—and I was amazed at how successful I could be. I had never really thought through the process in my mind and, I'll tell you, I developed in that period of time one hell of a lot of optimism."

However "diabolical" he felt his role was in the courting of Jessica Ross, however much guilt he felt about his not eventually marrying her, it was that very optimism that would continue to mark his outlook on the world.

IF YOU WANT responsibility and you want it early and you want to do something besides make soap powder, then this is the place to be.

This was the essential recruiting pitch made to young engineers by the Naval Ordnance Station, and it was precisely the sort of rallying cry Jay Carsey was listening for. In thinking back to the beginning of his life in Indian Head, he recalled that "I was in the right place at the right time, a period in which defense and what was going on in the Navy was the hottest thing happening." And quite apart from feeling that he would "almost throw up at the idea of living in a town like Bryan or Rusk, that the only place any action could possibly be was in Washington, New York, Paris, or London," the ever-present pragmatist in him figured that a government job would pay him enough to live on *and* pay his way for a master's—the thing he had hoped to achieve at Harvard.

Dom Monetta's feeling that Jay was a child of the universe, someone to whom good things always seemed to happen, was only partly correct. Jay *was* in the right place at the right time, but to suggest that he always just "fell into" good fortune would be misleading. Even though his timing (which he attributed to fate) was usually impeccable, it was always surpassed by an element of calculation that came to him naturally, that can't really be learned, the kind that led Dorothy Artes to remark that in the more than sixty years she had lived in Indian Head *no one* was able to gauge more quickly—and less obviously—who was important and who was not than Jay Carsey.

"I don't know what it is that motivates one," he said, considering the suggestion that he may have been determined to succeed, at least in the American sense, because his father had not. "The truth is, I had no skills. I have no art. I'm mechanically illiterate, musically illiterate, and I hate manual labor—always have. So what do you do? You go get a bunch of degrees.

"When I started at Indian Head," he said, "I was either going to make a million dollars, which by the way I came close to making, or I was going to become president of something. Was going to do *something*."

Like any good engineer, one of the first things he did was to quietly and carefully survey the area and community he was soon to make his reputation in. He discovered that the bedrock of Southern Maryland was the families who had sailed over from England on the *Ark* and the *Dove* in 1634 and hoped to recreate an English social order based on manors, complete with landlords and tenants. And even though this master-slave system eventually dissipated, the elitism that attended it, the feeling of being privileged that was different from but not dissimilar to Jay's own, did not.

"It didn't matter if you couldn't read, couldn't write, or couldn't speak," he said. "It didn't matter if you were eccentric or even if you had no money. The *only* thing that mattered is that you were to the manner born. It's family and family is *everything*. If you're a Mudd [as in Dr. Mudd, who treated John Wilkes Booth] or a Jenkins, no matter what you do, you'll always be a Mudd or a Jenkins."

It was a wall of protection, Jay learned to his amazement, that even ensured one against charges of murder.

"I had a professor working for me at the college from a well-known local family. He was a very quiet, unobtrusive guy. His family goes back for hundreds of years. He married a total idiot of a woman—a drug addict. She was everything that Southern Maryland hated. But he married her, so that was accepted. So she got involved with a drug pusher in the area who was an outsider—Lebanese. They went through a big scandal. So one day, the husband walked in with his pistol and shot the guy in the head. Evidently, after the guy dropped to the floor—I love this part of the story—he shot him a second time. That, to me, was the key to the whole murder.

"Now, I'm serious about this story. Everybody in Southern Maryland said, 'Good riddance, that son of a bitch was worthless, the wife was worthless, he should have shot her.' We had put him 'on leave' for a year while the furor was going on because I had no choice as president of the college. So what happens? They slapped him on the wrist and gave him a year's probation where he had to report to somebody. We reinstated him, and everybody sat around and applauded because he had got rid of this evil vermin."

Even though this wall of protection didn't, in Jay's opinion, begin to erode until a mere two years before he left, it remained steadfast (if not above the law) in its feeling about all the other elements that came to comprise Southern Maryland during the time Jay lived there. "Professionals like myself were allowed to enter because of position. But," he said, more serious than joking, "if you were non-Anglo, a special meeting would have to be set up. And even if you were a WASP or a WASC [White Anglo-Saxon Catholic], you can move in, but it still has to be done with skill and talent, because there are unwritten rules."

As for the nouveau riche, they could eventually enter because of money, but the fact remained: regardless of whether you were a professional or wealthy or a suburbanite whose job was in Washington, you might live in Southern Maryland, you might work in Southern Maryland, but you would never be *from* Southern Maryland.

Though this class system was completely alien to the young Texan, he hid whatever feeling of inferiority he had about his background behind a steely yet charming determination to pierce this seemingly closed world, a world that he found far more captivating than offputting. It was almost as if he said to himself, *Okay, Jay, so you didn't grow up with sterling silver and crystal and an elegant cherry-wood table with more than one fork, knife, and spoon by your plate at any one time. And you didn't have your own horse to ride, or stylish clothes, or go to an elite Eastern prep school that might have smoothed and gilded a path for you to Harvard or Yale and into the powerful Old Boy network, fueled with blue blood, that would afford you the life that you not only wanted to have, but one that you felt your birthright entitled you to. . . . On the other hand, you're an optimist, a believer in fate, a child of the Depression. How many young men of your age almost died when they were twenty, or didn't get a military commission and had to participate in active combat?*

Besides, you're smart, people like you, always have. Why, Nelda and Jean were around the house so much Dad thought they had taken up residence there, and Gary so idolized you it was uncomfortable and embarrassing. Sure, you like time for yourself, but you're too gregarious to be a total hermit and, anyway, if there's one thing you know how to do it's communicate . . . maybe not emotionally, not in any intimate way, but you speak well, and you should, having watched those fire-and-brimstone preachers and trying to emulate them when you taught Sunday School at the Methodist church in Bryan. You know how to bring people around to your way of thinking, and there's probably not that many people, Harvard and Yale included, who have the raw ability and the instinct to do that. There are some things money can't buy and you, who were always told that you were old for your age, have always known that. Still, it sure would be nice to have some and you're willing to work hard to get it. Mother always felt that Dad didn't have enough to give her the status she wanted, aside from those early days when he had all his bands, when money was real, as he never tired of saying, and before you came along. So maybe, being life's great gift to her and all, you can do something to change that. . . .

And so he did, not only rising quickly at NOS and impressing Joe Browning as someone with leadership potential, as someone who could go out and "sell" a place that was a geographic backwater, but in becoming a person of consequence in the community as well. No sooner had he arrived, it seemed, than people were remarking about that quiet, laid-back, *eligible* Texan who was teaching swimming to youngsters and taking such an active role in the Red Cross and the Boy Scouts and somehow still finding time to be a lay preacher on Sundays.

But if anyone had the notion that he spent the night before his sermons toiling away on them in his little trailer or in standing before a mirror and reciting them aloud, Jay would have been the last person to tamper with that impression. Truth is, those Saturday nights in question would usually consist of long, boisterous bouts of drinking beer and shooting pool and playing the slots, of hanging out with guys like John Budzinski, Jay Thornburg (a.k.a. "Jay II"), and Bob Schaumburg, or of his continuing practice of the "gamesmanship of seduction." But when Sunday morning came, even if he was short of sleep, Jay would find a clean white shirt and tie and, leaving his skepticism behind, drive the back roads of Charles and St. Mary's counties in his new Corvette, stopping at churches in such tiny, speck-on-the-map towns as Pisgah and Ironsides to warn the parishioners of the evils of drink and premarital sex in the same way that his grandfather had cautioned his father all those years before, but one that would have made Elmer Gantry beam with pride.

Jay's aforementioned cronies would always laugh at the irony of all this, but their amusement was mixed with respect. Of the three, Bob Schaumburg became the closest one to Jay—or so Schaumburg thought. He was with Jay and John Sine the day Jay first saw Nancy at the Officers' Club and shot out of his chair. He asked Jay to be best man at his wedding (to a woman Jay had gone out with once or twice), and Jay asked him to be Susie's godfather. They both had spent time with Lois Sorenson, and Bob had a role in *The Rainmaker*. If there was only one thing that this group of outsiders (Schaumburg was from New York, Thornburg from Kansas, Budzinski from Michigan) had in common with the landed gentry, it was a certain incestuous quality that was hard to avoid in a place as small as Southern Maryland—and understandable given the long hours and lethal nature of the work they were doing, work that made each of them—especially after an explosion killed a number of their friends—rudely aware of his own mortality at such a young, immortal age.

Never given much to tears, Jay cried when word reached him that day. But the fact that he *hadn't* been killed only underscored the optimism about his own destiny he so strongly felt.

"I REMEMBER HIS inviting me to go to a dinner party at one of the officers' homes, and I wore my one good dress and I managed all right, but I remember thinking that he was really looking for someone much more sophisticated than myself, and that I didn't fit the bill.

"Maybe that sounds very cold," Peggy Schaumburg said, "but that's the way I felt."

Peggy Schaumburg's instincts were right. Jay wasn't looking for some sweet local girl who might feel inadequate in the kind of fast company he was hoping to travel in. And even though he wasn't specifically looking for anyone in any permanent sense, Marilyn Southwell came close.

Depending on the circumstances, it can be amusing how the mere mention of someone's name can change a person's demeanor, as if one had opened a door that the person had not only closed long ago but had intended to stay shut. Two words, *Marilyn Southwell*, and suddenly it was Camelot all over again for Jay and he was a full-fledged Kennedy acolyte, a young man whose buoyancy matched the president's own, who wanted to do something for his country, and who could remember exactly where he was that November day in 1963 when his source of inspiration was extinguished.

"Now Marilyn Southwell was a very unusual woman," he said, brightening, once he regained his composure. "She was ahead of her time. You've got to remember, this was the early Sixties, before women's lib actually, and she was already listening to a different drummer. She was a strong woman, and I enjoy being around someone like that. What she did was take an East Texas kid and sort of show him some other kinds of worlds. She took me and did some of what I think I badly needed, and that was polishing."

Jay would have been content to leave it at that, to mercifully put the Southwell file back where it belonged, but that would have left the story somewhat incomplete. Pressed on the matter, he admitted that it was "an intense relationship, an exciting, blooming affair, but with absolutely no sense on either of our parts that it had any place to go."

If Jay ultimately found the circle Marilyn moved in too daunting, if on some level it ironically made him feel as inadequate as Peggy Schaumburg had, he wouldn't say. What he would say—and this seemed a direct contradiction of the independent streak he purportedly admired in Marilyn—was that he soon realized that "she was looking for somebody with money and I wasn't it."

To some extent, that was rationalization on his part, something at which he is quite adept. Despite his claim that "neither of us was emotionally involved," the truth is that Marilyn hurt him and he wasn't used to that. He was used to being the one whose actions resulted in someone else's pain, be it the frustration Nelda Bruns and Jean McDonald felt at his elusiveness, or the deception Jessica Ross felt when he didn't propose, or the rejection that Lois Sorenson would come to feel.

The hurt that Marilyn inflicted had nothing to do with sexual incompatibility; if it had, he could have eventually accepted that. No, what happened with Marilyn cut much deeper. It had to do with his inability to play a role with her, and, more important, with his inability to measure up—at least in her eyes. To her mind, if a person had an abundance of drive and talent, then how could that person be satisfied to merely be a big fish in a small pond? This whole notion of being a Pillar of the Community struck her as ridiculous and, in Jay's case, hypocritical as well. Not only that, but she said so, said that he was only paying lip service to his desire to be part of a world she was aspiring to herself.

Why else, she wondered, would he not rent an apartment in Washington and seem to be content to go on living in a trailer in as provincial a place as Indian Head? If, ultimately, he was happy just sitting at the counter of Charlie's Diner, listening to her recount details of who was at what party, of what Senator so-and-so said to Mrs. X, of what the vote was likely to be on an important bill in the House that week, then why would he often call her at odd hours to say how lonely he was, how unfulfilled he felt, this seemingly self-contained, self-sufficient fellow?

And why did he think she would be impressed when he phoned her in 1965 to let her know that he was going to become president of the community college, the youngest one in the country? Did he really expect her to say, "Hey, that's great, Jay, you've really made it, really arrived," when she was thinking just the opposite, that it was like becoming a town manager? Apparently, he didn't, because he said, "You know, Marilyn, the one thing I can always count on with you is that you will rain on my parade."

Their interchange was partly in jest, consistent with the good-natured bantering that they often indulged in, that they both required. But it was also serious. While Jay was very much his own man, a rugged individualist with an agenda of his own, he was also (especially when it came to Marilyn) attuned to what others thought. In keeping Marilyn posted as to what he was doing, it was almost as if he was looking to her to keep him honest, as if he needed her to prick his balloon of self-importance and help him keep his life in perspective. The more she chided him and withheld her approval, the more he sought it.

But no one expression of disapproval on her part hurt him more than her feelings about the child he had had out of wedlock. In warning him that the guilt from not staying in contact with that child would stick with him always, Marilyn was simply reinforcing something he already felt, but which was also an interesting indicator of the nonconfrontational way he dealt with things, fitting "the pattern" of someone who was emotionally shallow, of someone who, for the most part, cut himself off from Texas once he left, who defiantly prided himself on living in "the here and now."

But there were contradictions. Whether it was out of natural curiosity or something else, he returned to Bryan in 1962 for his tenth high school reunion (only to find so many people who were either selling shoes or had let their physical appearance change beyond recognition that he considers that day one of the worst, most depressing of his life). On the way there, he stopped in Fort Worth to see Jean McDonald, with whom, it turns out, he had not lost touch. And, as it happens, he hadn't lost touch with Jessica Ross either. In Chicago on business for NOS, he had gone to see her and her husband, a doctor she married not long after Jay had broken things off.

Why would Jay do any of these things, maintain these ties to the past, if he was wholeheartedly dedicated to living in the present?

"You're overshooting the airport," he said, an analogy he liked to use if he thought someone was missing his point. "I am not, as I said before, a come-backer. When my father retired from the paper in Bryan, he *never* went back there, never went back to find out how anybody was doing, wasn't even curious. Now, it's true that I had a tendency while I was a bachelor to keep up with the women who had been in my past. I never cut that off. Why do it? But goddamnit, don't keep confusing where I am now with where I was when I was twenty-five years old. It's the cast of thousands, I'm trying to tell you, that I don't care about."

Fine, but isn't a child a little different from one mere member of a horde of people, a link that is impossible to break?

"Look," he said, "I wasn't one hundred percent sure that it was my kid. But I paid financial support for a while, discharged what I thought was my liability for being ninety percent sure. Now, that's probably a disturbing symptom, that I can walk away in the sense of having no emotional concern about it, but that's what

I did. Anyway, it belongs to somebody else in the mind of the law."

And who might that possibly be? Nelda Bruns and Gary Goodwin suggest that it would be Jean McDonald, if it was anyone, that there was always a little bit of doubt in their minds whether the actor she married was indeed the father of her son. Jay's sister recalled how she and Jay went swimming with Jean and her son once, and that Jay was so good about playing with the boy. For her part, though, Jean McDonald emphatically claimed that Patrick was not Jay's son.

So what if there was no child, what if it was all some expedient myth Jay created partly to explain why he didn't want a child with Nancy; partly to confirm that (given the later problem of a low sperm count) he was, at least at one time, capable of procreating one; partly to reinforce (with Marilyn and others) his self-image of being emotionally shallow, loath to make a lasting commitment and, in this instance, callous?

He had told Marilyn, according to her, that if he had been forced to marry the woman in question, he "would never have left Texas and would never have become a person." If that was true, doesn't it seem odd that neither Nelda nor Gary nor Jean nor Susie seems to know anything definitive about this child?

"Look," Jay said, "I'm going to protect certain things. And unless you are able—and I don't think you will be, because I'm going to clog it up enough—I'm determined to take those things to the grave with me."

TWENTY-SIX

"DOODIE! HEY, Dooooodie!"
How often Jay had heard
his only sister's voice call out to him to come and play with her,
to read to her, to be the whole wide world to her. And how
curious that neither of them realized, then or now, that the word
Susie had created because she couldn't pronounce Julian stood for
two things—his name and his responsibility.

Just as he told Nancy once that he had "weaned his parents
early" so that they wouldn't expect too much from him once
he moved away, he said he essentially did the same thing with
Susie, but not without acknowledging (reluctantly) his role in
her life.

When Susie came to stay with Jay in his trailer during the
summer of 1963, the invitation he extended had little to do with
her being his sister and everything to do, he claimed, with his
being someone "who responds to cries for help.

"My mother sort of persecuted her and it upset me because
I hate persecution. Flushing catechisms—or whatever you call
those things—down the toilet and what not—my reaction to
that is *bullshit*. I'm a Carsey in the sense that I've got—at least
I think I do—absolutely no prejudice in my soul. So I went to

142

mass with her, I could care less about mass, never been before in my life, and helped her to convert. Big deal. She's got a lot of *joie de vivre* to her and I enjoy that in a person. She was somebody that I thought could do something. So buying her a car—which by the way turned out to be worthless—and paying for her to go to nursing school, which cost practically nothing, I'd have done that for somebody else even if it hadn't been my sister."

But it was his sister and that's what made his talking about her now as if she were a total stranger so unsettling. He admitted that he was more than a brother to her, that she was more like his child than his sibling. But having said that, why did he feel compelled not only to downplay his importance to her, but to focus instead on how he had walked away from her after that day at Marchoza in 1968? As with the child out of wedlock, he seemed to have an almost masochistic need to cast himself in the worst possible light, speaking of that day in a way that was eerily similar, using phrases like "dispensing my obligation" and "my commitment was over."

"I won't deny," he said, "that Nancy rejected my sister as part of her desire to reject everything in my past. But I will also admit that it wasn't all Nancy's fault. I put distance there, too. As I've said, the blood-relation family thing doesn't excite me. As far as I was concerned, I'd done what I thought was important for her, she was married, and we had a great arrangement. I said, 'If you get in trouble, if the world comes to an end, give me a call.'" And if it doesn't, Jay thought to himself, sure that Susie would understand, don't.

She understood all right, painful as it was, but when he was informed that Susie felt she "lost" him that day, he acted so baffled that all he could manage to do was reiterate that she was married, had a child, and was leading a life far different from the one he and Nancy had—and to ask, in a way that appeared to indicate the toll that his parenting of her took on him, "What on earth was she trying to find?"

. . .

THE SAME QUESTION, actually, could be more legitimately asked of him than of Susie, whose expression of emotion and sadness, at least, seemed a lot clearer than the ambivalence and mixed signals that emanated from him and defined his persona.

If Jay was, on one level, the status-seeking owner of a red Corvette with one blue eye on Marilyn Southwell's Washington, he certainly balanced it dramatically by the trailer in which he lived (using the oven, for economic reasons, to dry his clothes), a way of life that not only symbolized his modest upbringing but was one in which he felt most comfortable. Like most people, he wanted success— to have his name on the lips of countless admirers—but he appeared to want it on terms, *his*, that the community found amusing and never tired of talking about. He even said to a friend once, "You know, I bet that I am the only college president in the country who lives in a trailer."

But what many viewed as eccentricity became, years later, one of the key symbols they returned to when they sat around trying to figure out where—and why—that college president had gone.

TWENTY-SEVEN

"I'LL BET YOU twenty-five dollars that you will get married before I do, Joe. In fact, I'm so sure of it that I'll even write it down so we'll remember."

Jay was sitting at the bar of Joe Ann Joe's, drinking Schlitz (his favorite) and smoking a pipe, when he made that wager with Joe Miller in 1962. Three years older than Jay, Joe was his soulmate, their views closely aligned on everything from matrimony and religion to the joys of Virginia ham and the game of seek-and-search. Joe had a Porsche and the two of them, these two bachelors, were a familiar sight as they dragged up and down Indian Head Highway, whooping it up.

At Joe Ann Joe's, Jay would often sit at the bar by himself, reading the *New Yorker*, talking with tobacco farmers, and telling anyone who would listen that Tchaikovsky was the finest composer who had ever lived. And when he was hungry, he would just walk to the back of the bar, where Joe and his parents lived and where Ann Miller, who considered Jay a member of the family, was more than happy to provide him with a home-cooked meal.

Though Jay was friendly with all the engineers he worked with at the plant, he found in Joe Miller someone who didn't suffer from "the Marty complex," who had the same fear and concern about settling into a monogamous relationship that he did, and who became the closest thing Jay had at that time to a confidant.

"He was, I would say, someone who knew himself pretty well," Miller said, "knew his danger areas, that sort of thing. He knew that he was a paradox—the Corvette and the no-more-than-adequate way he dressed; the lay preacher and his lack of faith; the small-town Texan who wanted to get a Ph.D.; the college president who lived in a trailer—and he enjoyed this capacity for extremes.

"I do think we were confidants," Miller said, though hastened to add what others had said over and over—that Jay could be extremely cryptic in what he told you. But there was one point in particular about which he was perfectly lucid. "It came up once when we were talking about marriage," Miller said, "and I remember him saying—actually, I'll never forget him saying—how he felt compatibility was much more important than being in love."

It was soon after Jay made that comment that he met Nancy.

STRIKINGLY ATTRACTIVE . . . *gregarious . . . forceful individual . . . more talent in her bones than any person I have ever met.* These were only some of the things that Jay felt about Nancy once he recovered from his initial shock of seeing her at the Officers' Club. He could have added *but married*, but if Jessica Ross's engagement hadn't stopped him, why should a marriage Nancy wanted to escape from?

"My sense of that marriage," Jay said, "was that Gordon wasn't ambitious enough for her. Part of the reason I believe she married him was that her father's illness had wiped them out and her mother was having money problems. Anyway, Gordon was a great guy. I liked him. But he would have been quite happy staying right there and being an officer and doing the explosives thing and traveling a lot. That would be my shallow analysis. Everybody is more complicated, and he was, too.

"Anyway, the way it started was very platonic, but there was certainly a chemistry there. She was not just a pretty woman. She was an unusual, vibrant, extraordinary person. And there was a compatibility factor—I used to make speeches about compatibility factors—that I found appealing. We were both WASPs, Depression kids, college-educated. She was popular in high school, valedictorian of her class, and so was I. She played tennis and golf, I played tennis and golf; she played pinochle and bridge and I did too. Come to think of it, she played as good a game of duplicate bridge as anyone I know. We both enjoyed theater and museums and going out to eat. . . . But there was still this business with her husband and my feelings of guilt about that. I will admit that I had messed around with some married women before, but this was the first situation, in the plain old phrase of it, where I had cuckolded the husband, and I had broken my classic rule: 'don't litter in the playpen'—don't have an affair in the same area you live in.

"Now my own personal opinion—and everybody can deny this—is that Gordon was never innocent about what was going on, and probably wanted out of the marriage also. But nobody, I think, gets cuckolded without resenting it."

Jay was right in thinking that Gordon wanted out of the marriage as much as Nancy did, but since there was no surface bitterness among all of them, Gordon and Nancy even went so far as to "celebrate" their separation, and Jay tagged along. On the day before Gordon was to leave for an atoll in the Pacific, where he was going to work in underwater demolition, he and Nancy sold some land they had planned to build a house on (when Nancy received her share five thousand dollars she turned to Jay and exclaimed, "I already bought myself a mink coat") and then went to Vince and Evelyn Hungerford's to play bridge. After a good time and far too many drinks, Gordon announced that he wanted to drive Nancy home, a final farewell.

He shouldn't have, because, moments later, his Triumph skidded off Indian Head Highway, turned over twice, and Nancy was thrown from the vehicle. When she regained consciousness, an ambulance was taking her to the hospital. Instead of being thankful that she was being administered to quickly, she was obsessed with the notion that she didn't, under any circumstances and no matter what her injuries turned out to be, want to stay at the hospital, that she wanted to be returned to the Hungerfords', where she was sure that Evelyn's father, a doctor, would come and take care of her.

As many already knew, when Nancy made her mind up about something, she was not an easy person to say no to. Her wish, despite cracked ribs and a fractured skull, was granted.

But there was something Gordon knew that no one else did. Delaying his departure, and visiting her as much as Jay would and often at the same time (a scenario so ideal Nancy couldn't have scripted it better), Gordon knew why the hospital was the last place Nancy wanted to be. The car accident was the reliving of a nightmare for her. The day before her high school graduation, and shortly before her father died, Nancy and her mother were driving out to the family's farm when a car hit them head-on and, once again, Nancy was thrown clear. But on that occasion, she slipped into a coma and it was feared she would die. A special graduation ceremony was held for her in the hospital, the details of which she later read about in the newspaper when she regained consciousness and was recovering from a fractured skull. So when her father died not long after that, Gordon was not surprised that she didn't want to go to the funeral home.

Had Jay known that at the time, given his healthy respect for fate and coincidence (no matter how morbid), he probably would have added *we both had had near-fatal brushes with death* to his compatibility list . . . and amended it later when he discovered that whenever the subject of death arose—specifically his view that once you're gone, you're gone, finis, kaput, there is nothing else—it touched on Nancy's greatest fear, making her so upset and angry that she couldn't even discuss it with him. Nonetheless, it was her father's death, Jay felt, that forced her to acquire the very strength of character that drew him to her.

But there was another item that belonged on the compatibility list, something whose nature had none of the surface qualities Jay had mentioned, whose dynamic was far more deadly. It was something that worked for them for a good long while, that satisfied both their needs—until it gradually tore Jay apart.

TWENTY-EIGHT

HOW OFTEN, over a glass of wine, in a moonlit bedroom, or just dancing cheek to cheek, does a couple, of long standing or short, remark to each other—as poignantly as they can, as clichéd as it sounds, as if it had never been said before—that timing is everything. It might sound corny, but in the case of Jay Carsey's meeting Nancy Brumfield, it was certainly true. Had Nancy come into Jay's life a few years earlier, say around the time he first got acquainted with Marilyn Southwell, he might not have been ready for her. At any rate, he seemed ready for her now—partly because she embodied much of what he had liked about Marilyn, and partly because he was ready for a new challenge and Nancy seemed the perfect person to help him meet it.

As always, he was being more pragmatic—more "selfish," he said—than emotional. Nonetheless, Nancy simply *was* the most exciting, unusual woman in Southern Maryland. Everyone knew it—especially she. Even people who never tired of saying how narcissistic she was were willing to concede that point without much protest. They might not want to live with her, they said, but they would never equate her with the words dull and ordinary. Considering what Jay was about to do—essentially create something out of nothing—he needed the element of pizzazz that Dom Monetta had talked about.

"At that point in time," Jay recalled, "I was still working for Indian Head, but they had me uptown, doing all sorts of stuff for the Navy, and I was tired of the Department of Defense. I'd been in seven years and I felt it was like being in the military. The excitement at the beginning of Polaris had worn off, and I was getting restless. I figured if I stayed in for twelve years, I might as well stay twenty and do the whole retirement bit. So I started to interview around, at places like McKinsey [a private consulting firm]. I had been teaching math part-time at the community college for a few years, and suddenly the president of the college decided to become the county's superintendent of schools. So the job was open, and John Sine applied for it as the only full-time professor. We knew each other from *The Rainmaker*, and from playing golf and tennis together. Anyway, John knew that one of the board members was a good friend of mine, a guy I knew from Indian Head, and he asked me to put in a good word for him. Now, you're probably thinking that *I* wanted the job, and I'm telling you that I didn't want the job, never even *thought* of the job. I mean, there's no way that anybody would want a president of a college who had never even taken an education course. I did have my master's in engineering administration at that point, but I was twenty-nine years old and didn't know p from q about education. . . .

"So I go along and tell George Dyson that I think John would make a great president—one of the few pure things I have ever done in my life, by the way—and he looks at me and says, 'Why don't you take the job?' 'George, you're absolutely crazy,' I tell him. 'I'm not an educator, I'm an administrator,' and he says, 'That's what we want. We've had educators. We need somebody to take this college and go with it.' "

They had the right guy.

ONCE AGAIN, JAY heard words that he could dance to. "You had something you wanted to achieve and you were the driving force to get it achieved," Jay said. "The money available wasn't anywhere near Polaris, but you didn't have to worry about it. The college was holding night classes in a local high school, then we moved to some buildings on an abandoned Nike missile site, and then, in 1968, to the place where it is today.

"I started out with one hundred and seventy-three acres of bare ground and cornfields, and I built the fucker. I want to tell you that's a very exhilarating thing, a lot of fun to be in at the inception stage. That's why I find Genesis to be a more exciting book than Deuteronomy. If I wanted to build another building, I went into my state congressman or my county commissioners and *sold* the concept. I was a salesman and I had a sellable article. I could assess what had to be done and then go out and get it done. The process was very planned out. I developed a strategy, tactics for selling the plan—it's like any other kind of business, except it's public sector instead of private. And if you are able to internalize the goals, as I was, then you don't have to be told that what you've done is great, because you've already had the adrenaline effect of the achievement.

"There was probably nothing I enjoyed more than being a bit of a con artist for the institution. If I could con the county commissioners out of an extra fifteen thousand, fifty thousand, or even a hundred million dollars they didn't really want to give me, I felt a great deal of satisfaction in doing that. On the other hand, I am a terrible process-and-procedure person. John ran the college;

I did the politics. So we're talking about a Camelot period of about fourteen years, a time of total pleasure and no pain and agony, a great world in terms of lack of supervision and a total ability to do whatever I wanted to do."

Many people, in looking back at their accomplishments, would doubtless stop there, choosing to let the record—*their* version of it, at any rate—show what they would like it to show; to let certain myths—the myths that most people point to as models for their lives, as ways of explaining their motivations—remain lofty and glowing, pristine and untarnished. And though there were elements of his life that Jay warned he would make deliberately vague, his tenure as president of the college was not one of them.

"When I came into the community college business in 1965, the timing was *perfect*. I was in the right place at the right time. Now, I could let my ego get in the way and tell you that Charles County *needed* a community college, that it was the best thing that ever happened to the county, that it wouldn't be there if I hadn't used my particular skills. I'm not saying that some of that isn't true, but it's also ludicrous to say that it wasn't the time and the place. [Admiral Hyman G.] Rickover could talk about the Polaris missile and say, 'God, that was my baby,' but it had to be the right place, the right time, the right people.

"The growth of community colleges nationwide, not just in Maryland, was '65 to '75. During that period there was a new community college *every week*—fifty a year for ten years. By '75 I had been at it for that long. I was a guru in the field. It was like Elvis Presley. You say, why was Elvis Presley so great? 'Louisiana Hayride,' 1955. He was in the right place at the right time with a decent voice. As for me, it's not so much talent, skill, and aggressiveness and all this bullshit that you go through with leadership and charisma. It has something to do with it. But it's the luck of the draw. I would have had to have been an ass to screw it up."

Perhaps. But hidden beneath the admirably modest (in truth,

too modest) surface of his comments, hidden behind triumph after triumph, lay a feeling of fraudulence that was always with him, that he never rid himself of, that partly explained his uneasiness with the role of rainmaker and father-figure that he, to a large extent, created and perpetuated . . . and which eventually did him in.

JAY FOUND OUT soon enough that pizzazz had a price. He got a preview of it when Nancy announced that she had gotten herself a mink coat, even though he hadn't had to pay for it. He learned quickly that living in a trailer was not Nancy's idea of how a young couple should live—certainly not one that was clearly destined for better things. Whatever Jay found charming about the paradox was lost on her. When she and Gordon first moved to Indian Head they had lived in one and she hated it; and when her mother and step-father considered getting one Nancy argued vehemently and was able to dissuade them. As far as she was concerned, even if you tried to stretch the point and call it a mobile home, it was still a trailer. In any case, Nancy had decided to leave Indian Head Elementary and teach in Prince George's County, so they took an apartment there. (Jay held on to the trailer, though, as much for symbolic reasons as sentimental ones.)

If sprucing Jay up was one of the main priorities on Nancy's list of things she needed to do, so was her desire, stemming as much from insecurity as anything else, to start from square one with him. In fact, her need to possess him was so great that she threw away all the letters he had received from any woman he had ever been involved with. "She wanted me to reject everything that had preceded her," Jay said, "parents, sister, former girlfriends. But as I've said, I didn't totally blame her, because it was in my nature to do so anyway," unaware that he was reversing his position on past relationships. (The only woman Nancy truly seemed threatened by was Marilyn, who was married by this point. Of the role she might have played in shaping Jay's life, Nancy would later concede, grudgingly, that "she probably got him ready for me," nothing more.)

But Nancy's possessiveness didn't stop there. It extended to the guys he used to pal around with at NOS, who had formed a group called the Duffers that played golf on Saturday mornings. They would have liked Jay to be a regular, but he wasn't; even on the infrequent occasions he was able to slip away and play with them, Nancy always wanted to know when he would be back, and would tell anyone who came to pick Jay up not to keep him away too long. That she was a golfer herself and knew that the time it took to play eighteen holes could vary wildly didn't matter. What's more—and this was what never ceased to amaze people who observed them as a couple—Nancy's possessiveness didn't seem to matter to Jay. There was hardly any time for it to matter to him.

"The social world that Nancy created for us," Jay said, "didn't just consist of Charles County. We had Prince George's, we had Annapolis, we had Washington, we had Baltimore. Wherever Nancy goes, she attracts people. She drives the style. So in a weekend we didn't just have one or two things to go to. We might have as many as *twenty-five* things to go to, and Nancy, bless her heart, would see to it that we would go to all of them. Parties and entertaining and eating out—this is the stuff that makes her heart beat. And traveling—she is the greatest traveler in the world, and she enthused me with a desire to do it. We were absolutely lockstep as a couple, living an upwardly mobile lifestyle, young college president become King of England, that sort of stuff. Hell, I must have put two hundred thousand miles on our Mercedes in one year alone! I was thirty-some years old and *I* loved it . . . I wasn't just along for the ride. It's a hell of a lot of fun to be a high roller in the express lane. . . ."

If all that he said was true, that this was the kind of life he dreamed about when he promised himself that he would leave Texas, that Nancy was the perfect person to smooth his rough edges, then what made Jay call Joe Miller one day in March of 1968 and say that it was very important that they have lunch?

Nancy's divorce from Gordon had come through shortly before that (Maryland law stated that a couple had to wait two years from the time they were legally separated), and everyone assumed that Jay and Nancy would get married. After all, even though it was 1968 and the country was becoming less judgmental about unmarried people living together, Jay was a college president in a small, conservative community. It's not that people didn't have affairs in Southern Maryland, but the high profile that Jay and Nancy had by this point—Mr. and Mrs. Education—did not lend itself to their living together permanently in their current arrangement.

Jay was in a state of high anxiety when he phoned Joe Miller that day. Even though Joe had left the area when Joe Ann Joe's closed five years before, he and Jay had remained close. Since he was working in Washington for the Department of Commerce and Jay often had business in town, they would see each other every few months, Jay often dropping by his office unannounced. But on this particular day, wanting to make sure that Joe was free, Jay phoned ahead of time, asking if they could meet at Wearly's, a restaurant near Union Station. Joe had no idea what Jay wanted to talk with him about, no inkling as to why it was so urgent that they meet, but he felt that Jay knew him well enough that he could count on Joe to help in whatever way possible, if indeed help was required.

It was—primarily in the form of advice.

"Look, Joe," Jay began, once he ordered a drink, "you're somebody, and I hope you know this, that I've always felt I could talk to, that I could trust. Nancy and I are thinking about getting married, everybody is *expecting* us to get married, and I don't think I want to go through with it. It's not that I'm not crazy about her, or anything like that. But I'm scared shitless and I'm feeling that I just want to drop back and punt."

It was plain to Joe Miller that his friend had more to say, so he just sat there, giving Jay time to sort out his thoughts and begin again.

"I also ought to tell you that I've already gotten a postal box here in town. I am thinking of leaving Southern Maryland and living here in Washington. As you know, I've been very successful in getting the new campus built and all that, but it's one thing to get something built and another to manage it, and it's beginning to dawn on me how much more my time will be tied up than it is already. So I guess what I'm asking, Joe, is that if I decide not to live here, could I rely on you to get my mail to me and protect my whereabouts?"

Since Joe was still unmarried himself, Jay was sure that Joe would be sympathetic to the conflict he felt. On the other hand, in a lighter vein, Jay thought Joe might persuade him to go ahead with the marriage so that he could collect on the twenty-five-dollar bet they had made at Joe Ann Joe's a number of years before.

Both things, in fact, passed through Joe's mind, as did the feeling that without Nancy, Jay would tend to have a somewhat dull life, but that with her "on the ticket" he would achieve more than he might on his own. And, of course, there was also Jay's whole spiel about compatibility. Joe could hardly forget about that. But when he finally began to speak, he didn't specifically mention any of these things.

"My response," Joe said, "will be tempered by my eleventh-generation-Virginia breeding of responsibility. Robert E. Lee said that 'Duty is the sublimest emotion,' and it seems to me you have a sense of responsibility to Nancy—"

"Well," Jay broke in, "that's something I'll just have to reckon with."

"Let me finish," Joe said gently. "And your responsibility toward the community is, as you say, only going to increase, with the Kiwanis and Lions clubs and so forth, and it will be a lot easier to have a wife to do this with. But if you're asking me to cover for you, should you decide to walk away from everything, my answer is yes, of course, I'll do whatever I can to help."

The two friends sat and reminisced for a while. When Joe eventually did suggest that Nancy was providing him with some of the things he didn't have, Jay didn't deny that, but he said that living with Nancy had made him realize just how binding a relationship it would continue to be, that she was a very clinging person who didn't let him get too far away from her, and that she would always be the lead partner, because it was simply her nature to be "the center of the universe in her world."

When Joe went back to his office that afternoon, he had no sense of what Jay would decide.

"FOR TWO WEEKS before that lunch," Jay recalled, "I agonized over what I should do. I remember thinking that I didn't have any assets or any money of any consequence. I was making less as a president than I had as an engineer, even though I was still consulting for Indian Head. I wasn't exactly wealthy, but I wasn't broke. As far as Nancy, I had led her along to a certain extent, so obviously I felt some sense of guilt about that. But I also felt that she had her own hidden agenda—a marriage she wanted to get out of, and a lifestyle she wanted to get into—and I think she saw me as a direction to do that. Now some of that may be Rationalization 101, but I think there's a lot of truth to it.

"Anyway, we had already made wedding plans, her mother and stepfather were planning to come, all the teachers in the school where Nancy was principal were getting excited. And my parents hadn't met Nancy yet, but they thought we already *were* married. Still, you would think that I would have had the guts to talk to Nancy about my misgivings, to just come out and say, 'I don't want to do this,' but I couldn't do it, and *there* is the fatal flaw in my character."

But in arranging the lunch that day, Jay was behaving like a person who seriously contemplates suicide, but doesn't really want to go through with it. While he could say that "it's so indicative of me, that I sat there and let Joe talk me out of it," he immediately countered that by saying that he was glad Joe did, glad because he had no idea what he would have done, or where he would have gone.

Nancy, of course, never learned about Jay's lunch with Joe Miller. Since the only other person Jay tried to contact that day wasn't home, he never got the "second opinion" that Marilyn Southwell would have given him, one that he could have guessed at anyway. Jay was right to trust Joe Miller. He never told anyone about that lunch, about the delicate subject Jay had raised with him, until he was asked about it twenty years later—and only then because the course that Jay's life had followed made him feel that it was appropriate to reveal it.

TWENTY-NINE

CUMBERLAND, MARYLAND, lies just south of the Mason-Dixon Line in the western part of the state. The first time Jay Carsey and Nancy Brumfield found reason to go there together was on April 3, 1968. Jay would have been content to be married by a justice of the peace, but he agreed to a Methodist church. Nancy would have preferred the kind of big blowout she and Gordon had

had, but she settled for a quiet ceremony with just family—hers. (Jay didn't bother to invite his parents, because it would have meant admitting to his mother that he had been living in sin.)

They had chosen Cumberland for practical reasons, not romantic ones. It was closer to Indiana, so that Nancy's mother and stepfather wouldn't have so far to travel. And it was far enough away from Southern Maryland that they could use that as the reason they weren't inviting anybody, thereby offending no one. They chose April because it was a good time for Jay to be away from the college (by this point in his brief tenure, he had already arranged a two-month sabbatical every third year, which he would usually combine with his normal vacation time) and Nancy from her school; and it was a wonderful time, they felt, to take themselves to Morocco, Spain, and Portugal for a honeymoon.

Before leaving on their trip (this was "the event of consequence," Jay said, not the wedding itself), they had a reception for their friends at the Officers' Club, the place they had first met. Everybody drank to their good health and happiness, and before the party was over, one of the guests took Nancy aside and offered her some blunt but well-meaning advice.

"Now you can really push him," Steve Maxwell said. "You can play Josephine and get him in the Cabinet."

"JAY TOOK TO foreign travel like a duck takes to water," Nancy said, and she was right. Europe opened his eyes even wider than they were when he first left Texas and came to Washington, and he took as active a role in planning their subsequent trips as she did. Not only was he able to arrange these frequent sabbaticals, he had begun to make enough contacts around the world that he would often extend the length of the trips by combining business with pleasure, even though the business was sometimes connected to his various consulting ventures as well.

For their first trip to the Far East in 1970—a trip in which they changed their itinerary midstream and finished up with a cruise of the Greek islands—they spent a few days at a convention in Hawaii, then continued on to Japan from there.

Tokyo, Hong Kong, Cambodia ("Nancy claims Angkor Wat ruins are the greatest she has ever seen, and that covers most of the significant ruins of the world," she wrote in their third-person journal, alluding to the two summers of traveling she had done alone after her separation from Gordon), *Singapore, Bali, Bangkok* ("Nancy even had her picture taken with an enormous python around her neck. . . . Jay had some frustrations trying to get some of the goodies we bought shipped to the States, [but] we were able to do some more shopping before taking an afternoon flight to Ceylon"), *Ceylon* ("One of the gentlemen in the Ministry of Education whom we had met in Honolulu"—representatives of junior colleges from around the world had also attended the convention in Hawaii—"contacted us the first day and set up an educational trip to Kandy where we visited the Kandy University as well as a junior college. . . . Brass shopping was tremendous and we had quite a large shipment of brass and other things sent to us from there. Ceylonese food is basically curry, but is hot and spicy and much to our surprise, even the advantaged families eat the meals with their fingers!"), *Nepal* ("Katmandu is a remarkable area, full of temple lions, and we managed to eventually find a pair to have shipped home. Nancy also bought some furs. We had been asked to contact a Dr. Stough who is an educational adviser for AID [Agency for International Development] in Katmandu, and Tuesday evening he and his wife had a dinner party for us. We learned a great deal about the educational system in Nepal"), *India* ("Our timing in Agra was unbelievably fortunate. It was one of the five days during each month in which you can see the Taj Mahal by moonlight. We took a petti-cab there and had the experience of seeing that unbelievable edifice. . . . One of the interesting aspects about Kashmir is that while you're staying on your houseboat, salesmen paddle up to you on their boats and then bring their wares in and lay them on the rug to tempt you. Jay found this type of shopping a little more difficult to resist than shopping in the bazaars and markets. We did buy some interesting things—including too many suits for Jay and a delightful fur piece for Nancy"), *Iran* ("In Tehran, the Superintendent of the American Schools and his wife invited us to the American School, to dinner at their country club, and a late visit to their home. We found the Iranian caviar was much better than any we had ever tasted anyplace. . . . We were delighted to go to Isfahan because it gave us an opportunity to see 'old' Persia. Jay also got a chance to contrast the technical college there and the University in Tehran"), *Istanbul* ("We spent our anniversary [visiting] the famous Topkapi museum"), *Greece* ("We cruised to Patmos, where we rode the donkeys to the monastery on top of the island. . . . In Rhodes, we had an opportunity to visit the American school. . . . The night of the [ship] Captain's dinner we learned Saritaki dancing").

After a trip so breakneck and filled with enough adventure (they narrowly escaped a fire in their hotel in Hong Kong and arrived in Phnom Penh at the same time violence was beginning to break out) that it could even have provided Jules Verne with fresh material, the Carseys were met in Baltimore by Bob and Peggy Schaumburg and taken home.

As the Schaumburgs heard the tales of their friends' trip, looked at all the pictures they had taken, and eventually were shown all the things they had purchased, Peggy was understandably envious.

Whatever envy she felt, though, was far outweighed by something else—her realization that her first instinct all those years before had been correct, that Jay had indeed found what he had been looking for.

But hearing about their trip also reminded Peggy Schaumburg of another, much different one, the two-week sensitivity-training session the Carseys had gone to in Maine the previous summer.

She and Bob had agreed to meet Jay and Nancy on their return from that trip too, but were unprepared for Nancy's request.

"We need to be with people who love us," she said softly. "We need to be with people who love us."

THIRTY

WHEN THE CARSEYS bought a new Mercedes in 1970, none of their friends were surprised. After all, they had just returned from their trip to the Far and Middle East, their profile and circle seemed to reach new heights and widen every day, and they were about to buy an apartment in Washington to go along with Marchoza, their place on the Chesapeake. Nobody was quite sure how they were managing to pay for all this, but there wasn't a person they knew who was impolite enough to ask. Not wanting to draw attention to the amount of outside consulting Jay was doing (and possibly start people wondering how he could do that *and* be president), they would strongly imply that Nancy had a nest egg of "family money" and leave it at that.

But of all the reasons they had for buying the Mercedes, the best one turned out to be one they hadn't considered at all.

Jay was leaving the college one afternoon that summer, and was beginning to ascend a steep hill a mile or so away when he turned slightly to get his briefcase.

At the same moment, a state police car, going about seventy miles per hour in answer to a call, came over the hill and was heading straight for the Mercedes, which had drifted toward the wrong side of the narrow country road. By the time Jay looked up he couldn't avoid the collision. It was 1955 all over again, another moment of truth, another twist of fate.

"If I hadn't been in a Mercedes," Jay said, "I'd be a dead man. If I hadn't been thirty-five years old, I probably wouldn't have survived the accident. The head-on collision dropped the motor, but it did not come into the driver's seat. One of my legs just accordioned, and I hit the steering wheel and it really did a number on my chest. I mean, it was massively ridiculous. Blood was coming out of my mouth and eyes. I don't remember the rescue squad coming, but on the other hand, I remember being in the van and arriving at the hospital, yet don't recall getting to the hospital room."

Nancy was at school when she got the news. "I was at the hospital as much as they would let me," she said. "He had tubes running everywhere and I was terrified. I stayed with Evie and Vince during that time and I remember walking into their backyard and thinking, *God, what if I have to lose him? I can't live without this man.* I remember that so plainly. That I couldn't live without this man."

Jay had internal injuries, cracked ribs, and his leg was so severely damaged that it was feared he might never walk again. But after spending months in a wheelchair—months in which he recuperated at home and Nancy took good care of him, practically willing him back to health, months in which he was even able to turn his disability into a media event by gamely meeting his commitments in a specially equipped van—he did.

Once again, he felt lucky to be alive. As a gesture of gratitude to his continuing good fortune, he contacted Mercedes-Benz and said that if they ever needed someone to push their product in an ad, he'd be happy to oblige.

. . .

THAT WAS JAY, always happy to oblige, always eager to please. When Halloween rolled around, Jay would dress up and go to Nancy's school to entertain the kids. He would go to PTA meetings with her. When they returned from their trips, the two of them would show slides to the children and talk of their travels. When Jay said they were lockstep as a couple, he wasn't exaggerating. And he would do all this in addition to fulfilling his own considerable responsibilities each day.

To one teacher at District Heights Elementary, stunned by this attentiveness, theirs seemed "a fairy-tale romance," complete with Jay's monthly anniversary cards and presents, including a tank of kissing fish. It was a period in their lives when Nancy, a master of flattery, was always remarking to others (with Jay present) how sweet and thoughtful he was; apparently it worked, because it only spurred him on to do even more things. When they entered a golf tournament together, he wore lavender, just for her. And when he saw a suit of armor in Washington that he thought she would like, he was so excited that he set a new speed record in his effort to get the Iron Duke, as it came to be called, home to Marchoza.

Nancy's talent for making something out of nothing, for making something in her image—a talent that Jay possessed in a different way and which he first glimpsed at the apartment Nancy and Gordon had in Indian Head—continued to flower at Marchoza. Jay supplied the majority of the money, then stood back and watched Nancy go to work. When he spoke of her as having "more talent in her bones than any person I have ever met," this was one of the many talents he was in awe of. She lined the walls with barn wood, furnished the cottage with things from their travels and from her childhood, and transformed the adjoining greenhouse into a solarium. To top it off, they had privacy, a pier that extended one hundred and twenty feet, and a sailboat.

If they had found utopia on the water, their thinking went, why not also seek it in Washington? So ten years after Marilyn Southwell had urged him to do so, Jay Carsey found himself living in the nation's capital, directly across from the Kennedy Center in an apartment at Watergate South.

Given his mechanical deficiencies ("Screwing in a light bulb is about the extent of what I can do, and even that has some fright to it for me if anybody is watching"), Jay found the Watergate situation ideal. "Look, you have your car in an enclosed garage right downstairs, so you don't have to sweep the damn snow off the thing in the winter and try to get the fucker started, which *always* drove me crazy. Since you own the apartment you're not paying any rent. You pay the association a maintenance fee and you don't have to fix anything. One of the best restaurants in Washington is right in your lobby, and if you wanted dinner, you could call down and they brought it up. You've got a pool, a drugstore, a grocery store, a liquor store, and a dry cleaners. Shit, you don't have to go anywhere. If you go away, you just lock the door and walk away from it with no concern. Your mail is kept for you, there's a protected security system, and this was the beauty of the thing, I was writing it off against the corporation I had set up for all my consulting work. That Watergate life was perfect. What else did you need?"

The more apt question is what did Nancy need. They had a social life that often consisted of taking people out to dinner, to the Kennedy Center for a performance (they had their own box), and then back to the apartment for a nightcap, a social life that they both thrived on. But according to Jay, something was missing, and that something was a place in the same world that Marilyn had strived for during the Kennedy years, the invitation-only world of inside Washington. "Cracking the top social scene in Washington means being on an inside track that we weren't on," Jay said. "So Watergate was a disappointment to Nancy because she never made those inroads, and she partially blamed it on me: why wasn't I a U.S. senator, that sort of thing. And when you get into that scene, then you really are seeing people with tons of money. People who are not only wealthy but they show their wealth—the Georgetown home with all the talk about how much it cost—and that was a frustration to her."

It was not the only one. Her job as principal in one of the largest school districts in the country was becoming more and more stressful. She not only had desegregation, vandalism, and calls in the middle of the night to deal with, but a male hierarchy in which she had to use a lot of guile to get the things she wanted. The pressures began to affect Nancy to such a degree that she would often come home in a rage, crying that she couldn't continue. When her teachers heard her raise her voice and watched her throw pencils across the room, they felt she was merely doing it for dramatic effect. Their devotion to her—and her support of them—was so strong that even if they had been told she was unhappy, they wouldn't have wanted to believe it. But in fact, her unhappiness got so bad, worried Jay so much, that he did something almost completely out of character for him, something he hadn't done since he had that lunch in Washington with Joe Miller: he confided in someone else.

When he sauntered in to John Sine's office during one of these periods and sat down, John thought nothing of it. He had gotten used to looking up from his desk and seeing Jay drop by unannounced, either to report in cryptic fashion about some deal he had just put together or to ask a question or to simply cut up. They had the easy rapport of two men who had worked together a long time, who knew the degree to which they could count on each other. But as John soon found out, this particular visit had nothing to do with either college business or general gossip.

"I've got to get Nancy out of that job," Jay told his colleague. "It's just tearing her up."

He didn't say much beyond that, but that didn't surprise John. What surprised him was that Jay had said anything at all. In fact, John couldn't remember Jay's ever coming in to talk about his personal life.

As it turned out, Jay needn't have said anything.

One Saturday morning not long after that, John came over to Marchoza for an informal meeting with Jay. It was about nine o'clock or so, and Nancy was getting ready to go out and play golf. John could hear her in the next room, talking to herself, slowly becoming more and more agitated. She couldn't find her golf shoes, it seemed, and before John fully realized what was happening, Nancy began screaming at Jay, letting loose a barrage of words, John recalled, that "I'd never heard before." No sooner had she demanded that Jay stop what he was doing *immediately* and help her than she turned on John and said that he had a hell of a lot of nerve just sitting there when she needed assistance.

Never a great fan of Nancy's and, unlike Jay, not one to back away from a confrontation, John stood up and said, "Hey, lady, you've got a license to tell *him* what to do, but with me you've got nothing." Nancy backed away, but her ranting continued for another five minutes, until she found what she was looking for.

When John left Marchoza that day, still shaken by what had happened, he nonetheless had hope—hope that he would never have to witness anything like that again.

AS JAY'S LUCK would have it, Nancy was eligible for a year's sabbatical at half pay. Instead of their embarking on yet another trip, Jay encouraged her to use the time to finish getting her doctorate in education (with a special focus on human relations) at George Washington University, and she agreed. Since Jay had already gotten his (in public administration), the idea of their both being "Dr. Carsey" was irresistible to her.

What was far less tempting—what in fact was something that neither of them was pleased about—was the prospect of returning to Charles County to live. The county commissioners decided that they wanted their "president as resident," and told Jay that. Since everything had gone Jay's way during his tenure up to that point, what the commissioners didn't know (and wouldn't really find out until years later) was that Jay was someone who didn't like being told what to do. Because he was so good at masking his feelings, because he always gave the appearance of being so good-natured and accommodating, they couldn't be blamed for not sensing the unhappiness their decision caused. But Jay understood enough about the area's history (and its dread of outsiders) to know that the decision was a sound one—that the good citizens of the county did, after all, pay his salary—even if he didn't agree with it personally. At the same time, he understood the importance of getting something in return, he understood his wife, and knew the degree to which they had both gotten accustomed to a certain way of living. If they were going to return to Charles County, they would reenter in grand fashion, trumpets blaring, a generous housing and entertainment allowance included.

The first place they got interested in was next to the courthouse in historic Port Tobacco, one of the thirteen colonies' most active shipping ports . . . until the harbor silted up and disappeared. As do many old homes in the area, this one had a name—Chimney House—and was in splendid condition. That's what made it especially attractive to Jay, that you could just buy the place and start living there, without having "to spend tons and tons of money renovating it."

What happened with Chimney House is one of those long, complicated stories that anyone who has ever gone looking for a house can usually tell, the short version of which is, they had it, then they didn't. "That was a very traumatic period for Nancy," Jay recalled, "because she really had her heart set on that house. It wasn't traumatic for me, but I kind of wanted it for the wrong reasons."

Nancy recovered, however, when she saw Green's Inheritance, when she saw its possibilities. Unlike Chimney House, this was a house in desperate need of love and care, and, most of all, money. Though it was in good shape structurally and the roof was relatively new, it needed an almost complete restoration inside, needed someone like Nancy "to dive into it and do what she is probably as good at as one percent of the people in the United States," Jay said.

In order to buy this particular white elephant, Jay needed to put thirty thousand dollars down, and obtain a mortgage for another sixty. Even though he realized it was "a steal," what worried him was that it would require "at least sixty thousand more, knowing Nancy, to put that house into decent shape and furnish it." That meant doing something he did not want to do—selling Watergate, or Marchoza, or both.

There was another complication. The land surrounding the house consisted of 188 acres and the estate was asking $275,000 for everything. Since Jay clearly couldn't afford that, he did what *he* was as adept at as anybody around: he concocted a brilliant scheme. Together with Louis Jenkins and Carl Baldus, the real estate figure who was, conveniently enough, selling the estate, they formed a holding corporation (which Jay optimistically dubbed Camelot), and sold enough shares to complete the purchase. Because Jay sensed that the value of the land, being so close to Washington, would only skyrocket in price, the corporation carved up the acres into wooded lots, put roads in, and eventually sold these rustic dreams for what Jay called "a pretty penny."

The biggest winner—or so it seemed at the time—was Jay. He had his house *and* thirty-three acres of privacy. To those who had known him from the time he first came to Indian Head in 1958, he had sure come a long way from that trailer behind Dick Fuchs's service station.

THIRTY-ONE

WHEN NANCY RETURNED to work from her year off, she was transferred to a new school, one that was closer to Green's Inheritance than her previous school had been. That was especially fortunate for Jay, who was transporting Nancy back and forth as much as he humanly could. Even though she had a shiny new Triumph, Jay didn't seem to mind his role of chauffeur; in fact, *he* was often the one to suggest that he take her hither and yon. If friends wanted to snicker about his slavish catering to Nancy, that was fine with him. As far as he was concerned, he was merely doing what "any good husband" should.

But the location of the school didn't begin to ease the problems and the stress that had made Nancy's sabbatical year such a godsend. The kind of scene that John Sine had witnessed that day at Marchoza began to recur. Nancy would go into "pink funks" (as Jay called them) and he would have difficulty pulling her out of them. For someone who didn't recall "ever raising my voice and yelling and screaming at anything in my life—dogs, cats, chickens included"—it was a searing experience, one that left him unsure of what to do.

"Nancy can be, when she wants to be," he murmured, clearly

disturbed by the subject, "as verbally abusive as anybody I have ever met. That occasional situation—let's say it happened once a month, whatever—drove a great deal of anger into my soul. And I would rationalize like hell that she wasn't really doing it to me, that I just happened to be standing there. Ninety-nine percent of the time she was just lashing out at something that was bothering her—whether she was mad at her golf game, or the guys who cut the grass, or Evie, or the alarm system—which had *nothing* to do with the moment. To my mind, it doesn't make any difference. The punishment—and that is what would just drive me crazy sometimes—*never* fit the crime.

"I want to tell you that after that happens, time after time after time, I think it does something to you."

BUT IF IT was doing something to him in 1975, no one was aware of it, not even Nancy. Homer had said that Jay was "always so good at hiding his feelings," and Homer was right. Knowing that fighting back was not something he was capable of doing, feeling that even if he were it might only fuel her anger more, Jay reacted on the surface as everyone—including Nancy, especially Nancy—had come to expect: "Old, steady Uncle Jay, marching along down the stream," he would later say of himself. "If a bomb goes off next door, I'd say, 'Oh, let's solve the problem.' "

If confronting Nancy in particular and unpleasant things in general was one of his weaknesses, solving problems was always one of Jay's strengths. It was what made him valuable as an engineer, valuable as a consultant, and it was what he hoped would lead to fewer outbursts in his personal life.

Approaching the problem of Nancy's job as coolly and practically as he did most things, he thought it over, came up with what he felt was a viable solution, and sat down with Nancy to discuss it.

"Nance," he said, "I think you ought to quit. It's ridiculous for you to continue. We don't need the money, Uncle Sam is getting half of it anyway, and the damn thing just isn't fun anymore. Walk away from it and then decide what you want to do."

IT HAS BEEN said that when a woman has a baby, the father often feels excluded from the special bonding and nurturing that is unique to mother and child.

Up to that time, Jay and Nancy had been more to each other than just husband and wife. Time and again, they would play— or replay—roles that were familiar to them: Jay as father, Nancy as daughter—the rock she could cling to for stability, the person she could count on to adore her and keep the spotlight burning bright; Nancy as mother, Jay as son—the person he was determined to please, whose approval he needed every bit as much as she needed his attention. This was the deadly form of compatibility that made it possible for them to coexist, the item that Jay could not have put on his list because it was too deep in his unconscious for him to be fully aware of it.

To a certain extent, the birth of Green's Inheritance changed that. Whatever worries Jay had over the costs of renovating and furnishing Green's Inheritance were surpassed by the excitement of their new house. Nancy went about the remodeling with the zeal and ability that Jay so admired about her, and Jay just stood back and marveled at how quickly she managed to work her magic, his love for being present at the creation of things as strong as ever. No sooner had they moved in, it seemed, than the house became the showpiece that Nancy had in mind, that Nancy needed it to be if she were to become the grande dame of Southern Maryland. In fact, Green's Inheritance was such a magnet for people that it was hard to distinguish between the house and the woman who had created it, so intertwined were the two in people's minds.

It's not that Jay didn't continue doing Nancy's bidding, personally inviting by phone all the people that Nancy wanted to entertain, a number that would often exceed two hundred. And it's not that Nancy's emotional dependence on him wasn't as strong as ever, calling his office at regular intervals throughout the day (as she did the day he left) to check on where he was. It's just that the house became *her* child, and Jay seemed to slip further and further from the foreground, more relegated than ever to the role of provider and servant.

Jay provided, I enhanced was how Nancy looked at it, and she felt that Jay wanted it that way. He did, but it wasn't as black-and-white as Nancy made it seem. The providing was simply becoming harder and harder to do. Even though they had sold both their Watergate apartment and Marchoza, their holdings now included time-sharing units in Sanibel and Captiva (two neighboring places on the Gulf Coast of Florida), as well as a condominium in a Hilton hotel on South Padre Island in Texas. Jay was right to invest in real estate, but that didn't help when he was running short of liquid assets. For some reason, he paid cash for the time-share instead of assuming a mortgage; and when he consequently found he needed to borrow money, it was at a time when interest rates were around 15 percent. Yet on the rare occasions when Nancy asked if they could afford something (Evelyn Hungerford doesn't believe that Nancy ever did), Jay would tell her not to worry about it. Time and again, he seemed to allow his conviction about the many obligations of a good husband to make him blind to a worsening situation, to his own needs, and, ultimately, to his very survival. Reality, sadly, was something neither one of them had an easy time grappling with.

So with Jay offering no resistance at all, Nancy went on being Nancy, entertaining lavishly, extending the circle of people they knew wider and wider, buying more and more exotic things for the house (which meant they had to go on more and more trips to find them; not to Sears, of course, but to the farthest reaches of the globe). And Jay, far from being a silent partner, was actively encouraging some of it, almost as if he were bent on self-destruction. As with real estate, he felt sure that jewelry would be a good

173

investment, and Nancy was happy to oblige. He felt the same way about art, but this was trickier, because he had in mind a full-length portrait of Nancy, to be done by one of the Egelis, a family of painters who were gaining prominence in the state for doing the portraits of well-known Maryland people.

When Nancy began going back and forth to Annapolis for sittings and Jay was dutifully driving her, all of their friends assumed this was yet another example of something Nancy had pushed for and Jay had meekly gone along with.

They were wrong.

"We needed something on one wall of the dining room and I thought it would be fun to get a portrait of Nancy before she got much older. I also thought that the guy who did the portrait would probably become famous; he was quite young, and his dad and granddad were already famous portrait painters. In fact, after he did her portrait, he got a commission to do the governor's.

"You know," he went on, reflecting back, "it's like a lot of things in life. I personally enjoyed the experience, found it fascinating to watch the good ones operate."

His curious mixture of perpetually boyish enthusiasm and almost clinical detachment aside, the large painting not only served to reinforce Nancy's position as ruler of the house, but it eventually took on an importance that no one could have foreseen at the time it was hung.

ODD, ISN'T IT, the way society seems to demand an answer for practically everything a person does, every move a person makes, usually using that person's friends and colleagues as agents for ferreting out answers? When Nancy decided to leave her post as principal, she didn't tell her fellow teachers that she simply didn't find it fun anymore, that the money she was getting paid didn't begin to compensate for the anxiety she felt. And even though that was certainly at the core of it, it wasn't an "acceptable" enough answer to explain why she was stepping down when she was so clearly moving up. Not in America at any rate. So when Nancy was asked the Big Question, she replied that she was leaving to start a family.

While it was true that the child she had in Green's Inheritance occupied a great deal of her time and the life she and Jay had was very social, Nancy still found herself feeling left out whenever discussions turned to her friends' children—Southern Maryland's biggest export. Quite apart from Nancy's not liking to be left out of anything, this particular form of exclusion was painful. As "Aunt Nancy," she had done everything an aunt could do, especially one who was not even related to the children she came into contact with. And she had spent enough time with children in the classroom to know what they respond to, with the added bonus of Green's Inheritance being like a huge toy shop and funhouse rolled into one.

But for Nancy it was not the same as having her own child. She hadn't wanted to have a child with Gordon, and it was one of the reasons their marriage fell apart. But she was just over forty now and running out of time. . . .

In a story with an ample supply of versions, Jay claimed that for three to four years they made as "honest and clear-cut an effort to have a baby as you could make," that he was "willing to try until he was forty-five," that if it had happened earlier in their marriage it would have been fine with him ("I don't like kids, but I'm not as bad as W. C. Fields. I certainly would have been able to handle it if one came along"). But he later said that forty-five, as far as he was concerned, was way too late, that he didn't want to be lumbered with "a twenty-year commitment beginning at the age of thirty-eight."

What seemed closer to the truth, and something he didn't disagree with, was that he felt he had done more than his share of fathering in taking care of Susie, that that was even more of an inhibiting factor to him than whatever guilt he felt about the child he claimed to have had out of wedlock, a child that he, not surprisingly, never told Nancy about.

But even that explanation didn't come close enough. Like anyone who is far more complex than he or she might initially seem, especially one who vowed to "clog" certain things in order to resist full understanding and scrutiny, Jay resembled an onion that required delicate peeling.

"The kid thing was beginning to drive her crazy," Jay said, a classic understatement since Nancy was so public and outspoken about her desire *and* her frustration. That of course didn't help, only adding to Jay's feeling, slowly building, that the other ways in which he had tried to be a good partner didn't matter, that all that mattered was what he was doing now, not what he did yesterday. In his mind, on some crucial level he was failing as a husband, failing to satisfy Nancy's expectations of him, to fully measure up. If their life in Washington had finally fallen short for Nancy because he "wasn't JFK," it was not succeeding now because he was apparently incapable of doing what nearly any ordinary Joe could do—father a child.

"When she didn't get pregnant," Jay said, "she was insisting I go through the whole round of tests." That he agreed to do that was not surprising; if he hadn't, it would have meant a direct confrontation with Nancy, a prospect "I would go twenty miles out of my way to avoid."

But it went much deeper than that, as deep, perhaps, as the humiliation he felt when his low sperm count became common knowledge. Even though Evelyn Hungerford might have seemed cold and cynical when her first reaction to the news of Nancy's wanting a child was in the form of advice (begin by making love to each other), she was not far off the mark.

In saying that "we went through the motions" of trying to conceive, Jay was saying a lot more than he realized—at least initially. Even when Jay and Nancy first began seeing each other, the physical part of their relationship was fine, though hardly memorable.

Smoldering desire for each other was not on Jay's compatibility list —and neither of them seemed to feel it was anything to worry about.

But it became something to worry about, especially since Nancy was pressing so hard for a baby. "I think part of the sex-life problem was that I didn't really want to have a kid," Jay finally admitted. "I wanted to have a kid because she wanted to have a kid. I don't know any better way to put it."

With that kind of enthusiasm, it is hardly surprising that no child resulted.

THE NEXT BULLETIN that came forth from Green's Inheritance was brief and characteristic of Nancy's strong will: using the royal we, the news that *We will adopt* did not surprise people nearly so much as Jay's announcement that they most certainly wouldn't. It was the first time in anyone's memory—including Nancy's—that Jay had taken a position against her. If he had been passive with Nancy about having a child of their own, he was vehement in letting her know that he was not about "to raise somebody else's kid." Not only did the idea leave him "absolutely cold," but he even said that if she was hell-bent on doing it, she better start thinking about finding a different husband.

Startled by his response, Nancy suggested they seek counseling, to try and figure out why he was so adamant about it, but Jay refused. People came to *him* for help, not the other way around.

Whatever pride he felt, though, in finally standing up to Nancy and speaking his mind was mixed with, and overshadowed by, guilt—guilt that he "wasn't willing to satisfy what seemed to be a real genuine interest on her part about having a child."

That guilt, of course, didn't begin with his refusal to adopt, and it wouldn't end there. For all his talk about being a person who lived in the here-and-now and who was able to cut things off as easily as a remorseless executioner, he couldn't escape that feeling. In Jay's case, if he was to be believed, his truck with guilt would usually occur *after* he had done something, after he had a chance to reflect back on it, whether it was breaking off from Jessica Ross or, to a lesser degree, Lois Sorenson, walking away from the child out of wedlock, or cuckolding Gordy Brumfield.

But what seemed to distinguish Jay's guilt was his extraordinary willingness to accept blame for something, a capacity so great that it knew no boundaries, that was masochistic in the purest sense. Instead of saying he was sad that his physical relationship with Nancy couldn't have been better and accepting that its success depended on both partners, he didn't hesitate in traveling down martyr row, saying that "it was more my fault than hers," that for all the interest he seemed to display in sex he "might as well have been a monk."

"So you start looking at all sides of yourself," he explained, trying to relive that period and, without realizing it, echoing his parents' marriage. "Your teeth need straightening, your eyesight is beginning to go bad. Nancy wants you to be Clark Gable, and you're not. So you begin to feel that you're not ever going to be able to be what she wants you to be. The constant frustration of the expectations that she has. And when you have internalized that you can't live up to those expectations—at least my perception of them—you begin to feel inadequate in all areas. And I want to tell you, *that* is frustrating when you basically have a superiority complex. That turns and begins to get awfully tricky inside your psyche and you begin to really dislike yourself."

QUITE APART FROM the self-loathing Jay was beginning to feel, Nancy's upset about his position toward adoption manifested itself in more and more angry eruptions and constant needling. In front of John Sine (once again) she bemoaned the fact that Jay couldn't tie his tie as neatly as John could. In front of the Schaumburgs she chastised him for being so unhandy, unlike Bob who could fix anything.

Everyone knew that Nancy blamed Jay for not giving her what she wanted, but these same friends also expected that Nancy would either keep at him until she wore him down and an adopted child took up residence at Green's Inheritance—or that after an indeterminate period of sulking, she would become fixated on some new notion of what would add to their life.

As for the uncomfortable public scenes, they had experienced those before and, knowing how volatile Nancy could be, were sure they would witness them again. Unless, of course, Jay's startling new assertiveness, which friends had thought long overdue and secretly hoped for, continued.

THIRTY-TWO

JAY COULDN'T EXACTLY remember where the gun came from, but that didn't matter. He kept it hidden in the house because he felt he had to. Since Nancy's outbursts, as it happened, weren't always verbal in nature, the anger Jay felt she had driven into his soul had now turned to fear.

On two occasions she threatened him with a knife. He didn't want to go on living like that, but he didn't know what to do other than contain her as best he could. "These things tended to happen around the monthly cycle," he recalled, his words taking on a hushed tone, his whole body tensing up, "and it sometimes combined with alcohol. I don't know how else to say it, but sometimes she would just snap, and I want to make it *very* clear that when that happened, she became a different person."

THE GUN, IT turned out, had belonged to Gordon. How and why it had found its way to a drawer in Green's Inheritance was not as clear as Nancy's unsettling transformation. But Gordon had had his own reasons for owning it. The drama he had witnessed in college—the night Nancy had refused to get out of the car and he had to break the window—recurred in their marriage. Unlike Jay, though, Gordon fought back.

Nancy had received a present from a man who had always pined for her from a distance. It was a sharp metallic object, shaped like a fish and dangling from a chain. One time they were having an argument about something, and Nancy kept swinging the chain closer and closer to Gordon, until it was finally beginning to scrape him on the arm.

The next thing Nancy knew she was feeling the full impact of Gordon's fist against her face, a blow that sent her hurtling across the room.

Gordon tolerated a lot of things in his marriage to Nancy, but that kind of taunting was not one of them.

AT THE TIME that happened, Nancy told anyone who asked that she had fallen down and hurt herself, but Evelyn Hungerford, who never liked Gordon that much, eventually got Nancy to confess what had occurred.

As for the incidents Jay referred to, he never revealed them to anyone at the time.

His remark that Nancy "became a different person" not only

recalled the time his mother punished him for allowing a black man into their house in Rusk and the way she persecuted Susie; but it echoed something that Gordon would later say, in reflecting on his marriage to Nancy, about how she was the sort of woman it was dangerously easy to have a love-hate relationship with, wanting to spoil her forever one minute, on the verge of choking the life out of her the next.

When Jay was told of Dorothy Artes's feeling that Nancy had a Jekyll-and-Hyde personality, that she was the most giving teacher Dorothy had ever seen but couldn't (or wouldn't) allow that nurturing to extend to the men in her life, he sat in his chair for a few minutes, staring down at the floor.

Though he worked hard to convince you that he was not the sort of person ever to feel depressed, that he was not acquainted with feelings like that because he was an eternal optimist, then this moment was certainly a dramatic aberration for him. When he finally responded, his eyes suddenly looked very sad.

"You know," he said, willing to concede only so much, "what she says about Nancy as a teacher is true. She was the best fifth-grade teacher to ever come down the pike. So maybe you're talking to the wrong person. Maybe Dorothy Artes is your story."

OF COURSE DOROTHY Artes was *part* of the story, as was Evelyn Hungerford, as was Joe Browning, as were all the people who felt affected by what Jay had done. Sometimes it is the person at a certain remove from a situation who can see it more clearly than the one who is living it every day. In that sense, somebody like Dorothy Artes resembled a de Tocqueville, who could visit America as a foreigner and feel its texture in a way that a native could not.

Shifting gears when he became uncomfortable, trying to deflect attention from himself, was something Jay seemed to have a lifetime of practice in doing. So instead of being able to sit down with Nancy and articulate his unhappiness, this walking time bomb just continued pretending that everything was fine.

IF THE ONLY child Jay and Nancy were ever likely to have was Green's Inheritance, then Nancy was determined to nurture it as best she could. The more articles that appeared about the house (be they in the local paper or in the *Baltimore Sun* magazine), the more parties she seemed to give, expending a degree of energy that Jay could only describe as "absolutely manic," an energy that he felt she had inherited from her mother.

Not only were there more parties, but each one seemed to have more people than the one before, more people to marvel at what Nancy had wrought. The house became a fixture on the Charles County Garden Club tour and, being a landmark house, one of the elite group that made up the National Register of Historic Places. What began as an exciting proposition for Jay was turning into an awesome burden. Not only was his life becoming less and less his own—if there had been pockets of quiet time for himself before they bought Green's Inheritance, there was little, if any, of that now—the financing of that life was turning into a nightmare.

The oil and electricity bills alone—just the sheer process of keeping the place open for business, which was the function Jay saw it assuming—were astronomical. Never all that comfortable in the house to begin with, he began to take a hard look at all the things he and Nancy had acquired, and to realize that in a year's time there would be more, and in two years' time, more still.

As he wandered around the house, the significance of the items changed for him. Instead of magically transporting him back to all the places they had gone to purchase them, to all the good times they had shared, he began to wonder how on earth they could ever get rid of them, and to recall how much simpler his life had been when he had little money and lived modestly.

When he stared at the temple rubbings they had gotten in Cambodia, he realized that if they were ever to sell them, they needed the "right kind of buyer," that it was foolish to think "you could just walk out on the street in La Plata [the county seat] and say, "Would you like some Cambodian temple rubbings?" and have money in hand by nightfall.

As he stood in his bedroom he smirked and let out a sigh. He looked at the huge fountain and smiled when he thought of all the people who would pull him aside and ask how he was ever able to sleep, knowing they were too polite to also ask why a fountain was there to begin with, "something that people didn't understand *any* place, but Southern Maryland particularly."

Walking into the room where all the masks were reminded him that no child he knew was willing to stay in the house overnight, and it reminded him of all the trouble they had had with cleaning women, who might come once or twice, then offer some excuse as to why they couldn't return. Finally it dawned on Jay that they were "scared crapless of some of the stuff in that house." (They were also scared of Nancy. Laverne Price, who stayed the longest, was not only upset by Nancy's "nasty temper" and treatment of Jay, but felt that Nancy's demands on her were unreasonable. "When I first went there, I was ready to come home. It was bad enough that there were all those skeletons and masks—I kept every door locked to protect myself—but Mrs. Carsey tried to give me too much work to do in one day. I said I couldn't do it, but Dr. Carsey told me not to worry and just take my time. He was the nicest man, would always come get me and take me home.")

Looking in Nancy's closets was a sobering experience for Jay, made him realize how much of his married life he had devoted to just shopping with Nancy.

"Here we go again. You'd think that I would have been able

to sit down with Nancy and talk about my feeling that we needed to divest of some of this stuff," he said, his disgust with himself resurfacing, "but I couldn't. Oh, I hinted around—that we didn't need to sell the house and land, but we didn't need to keep it looking like the Smithsonian—but I want to tell you, and I know you won't believe me, that you didn't have *discussions* with Nancy.

"First of all, divesting of something presented a real psychological problem for her. She had *no* sense of divestment. *You don't get rid of it because you don't get rid of it. We own it and nobody else does.* That was the way she viewed things. The *only* divestment that she could understand was trading upward.

"Secondly, a conversation between us might have to do with how many people we were going to invite to our next party, or whatever plane hijacking might just have occurred. In fact, even when I said no way in hell did I want to adopt a kid, there was no real discussion about it. In the last ten years of our marriage, I can't think of one personal conversation we ever had. A discussion with Nancy always became a confrontation, and as I've told you, I would avoid that like the plague. I could confront bureaucratic things fairly well, but with Nancy I would always walk around the problem. That was my way of working with her, avoiding *all* conflicts."

ONCE AGAIN, JAY was holding himself almost entirely to blame. By avoiding direct conflicts with Nancy and continuing to supply the money for whatever it was she wanted (claiming that his "essential weakness" was not in taking Nancy places and doing things for her, but in lacking "the will and courage to tether her insatiable acquisitiveness"), he was trying, in his own quiet, desperate way, to assuage his own guilt—guilt not just for feeling that he couldn't measure up to Nancy's expectations, but deepened now with self-blame for a marriage that he was coming to feel should never have taken place.

"It goes back, I think, to that lunch with Joe Miller," he said, "and the fact that I was delightfully happy *not* being married. But I made a decision to marry Nancy and I had a great deal of fondness for her. The Russians have sixteen, seventeen, or twenty-five words for love and we've just got one. Nancy had an aura about her that I found exciting, but I'm not sure that there was an aura of love.

"The fact is, I went into that marriage for incredibly selfish reasons—not necessarily bad ones, evil ones, or wrong ones, but selfish ones—and I think when you do that, the marriage is doomed in the long run to failure. Certainly mine was a case. It was by no means unpleasant. It was the *way* the marriage environment became that I found unpleasant. I mean, once you've gone around the world three times, gone on every goddamn cruise ship, traveled first-class, stayed at the Plaza in New York and the Savoy in London—we never stayed anyplace else—once you've done that sort of thing, you've *done* it, and you acquire all this crap, you've got houses full of it . . . I don't know, it's very complicated. It may have something to do with youth. What once was very exciting, an addiction almost, began to get more and more exhausting, and I began to feel that what we had was a transient happiness, a fake happiness; I began to see the difference between wanting something and truly enjoying it.

"In those last four or five years especially"—the period of time Evelyn Hungerford would come to call the fatal Last Third of the Carseys' marriage—"I wasn't necessarily making Nancy happy. I think she was happy in the lifestyle, but the last couple of trips we took were very unsatisfactory to me—like Australia and New Zealand in three weeks, or taking a train from Vladivostok to Minsk in eight days. And, to tell you the truth, I wasn't completely convinced that the unhappiness wasn't on both sides.

"Our marriage was perfect on paper, but incomplete in emotion," he said, "and after a while you begin to ask yourself—at least I did—*what* you're in love with, or *what* you're attached to, or *what's* exciting you. . . . And I think that anybody that got deep down

185

inside our life would say it was a shallow marriage. Surfacewise, it was a whirlwind of excitement. But the one-on-one marriage was shallow, and I would take ninety percent of the blame for that, because I don't see how you can have a marriage that isn't shallow unless you have communication, and I don't know how I can stress it enough, I was a very poor communicator. We'd talk a lot, but we wouldn't communicate well.

"And when you go into those kinds of marriages and children don't come out of it, then the marriage has to hang on to some qualities that we just simply didn't have."

THIRTY-THREE

ONE MORNING IN MAY of 1978, the Carseys drove about seventy-five miles to a private school near Richmond, Virginia. One of their favorite "nieces," the Hungerfords' only daughter, Pamela, was being graduated from St. Margaret's and they had been invited to attend. But no sooner had they arrived and walked to where the ceremony was going to be held than Nancy realized she had forgotten something.

"Jay," she said, "I don't have my sunglasses. Would you go back and get them for me?"

Since Vince and Evelyn Hungerford had gotten used to

Nancy's asking Jay to do things for her, her request didn't seem unusual.

"Okay," he said, ever the obedient slave, "I'll be back as soon as I can."

The Hungerfords thought Jay was joking. Surely he wasn't going to drive all the way back to Green's Inheritance just to pick up an item that could be purchased locally. Going into Washington from Charles County to pick up potato salad was bad enough, but this was absurd.

Jay wasn't joking, but none of them—including Nancy—knew why.

"I WENT BACK to get those sunglasses for one very simple reason: so that I could have seventeen drinks along the way."

In saying that, Jay was probably exaggerating. Nevertheless, his need to be alone and drink had become so urgent that he was prepared to do almost anything, even become the object of his friends' amazed stares and silent ridicule, if it meant finding the time to "get a fix."

He had become that desperate. He had become one of the eighteen million—the eighteen million people in America who are considered alcoholics or "alcohol abusers." For someone who had always thought of himself as somehow being special, it was easy at first for Jay to ignore, to not accept, that he had become a statistic. It was easy because, for the longest time, he simply chose the route familiar to all who have traveled it, the dark route of denial.

"If you can't handle a hell of a lot of booze," Jay said, "you're not going to get on terribly well in a place like Southern Maryland. Understand, I don't mean that as a criticism of anyone there, but the lifestyle there really contributes to alcoholism. Drugs, at least when I was there, were a no-no, but booze was something else.

"Now you take Nancy, for instance. Nancy is a heavy drinker. And like most heavy drinkers, she eventually crashes. On the other hand, I was the one who always took all the drunks home. I guess it was kind of a macho thing, saying to myself that I could drink more than anybody else and still be the last one standing. I *never* had a hangover, *never* took an aspirin, *never* took a tranquilizer. I could drink three fifths of vodka in a twenty-four-hour period and *never* come up for air. Believe me, I'm not bragging about it. I wish it weren't true. I had a friend of mine in college who would drink one beer and crash, and I used to say, 'You're a lucky son of a bitch.' "

The period Jay was talking about began in 1977, around the time Nancy gave up her job and well before either his colleagues began to notice or Nancy did. "That was when my drinking really started to escalate, and I would say my consumption, based on champagne, beer, wine, hard booze, and everything else, was somewhere between one and two quarts a day, three-hundred-and-sixty-five days a year.

"To be perfectly honest, I didn't think I could continue in the life Nancy and I had and not drink. Let's just take an example. I'd go to six parties on a Saturday night. That was par for the course. You go in, stay an hour, have two or three scotch-and-waters, see everybody, leave. Now if you have three of those at each party, that's *eighteen* scotch-and-waters."

The way Jay looked at it, he was fine (relatively speaking) when he only drank on weekends and after five on weekdays, a routine that he came to think of as Point A, the routine of "a typical, fairly moderate to hard drinker." But when he found that he couldn't function, that he simply couldn't get through a weekday without having a tumbler of vodka when he got up in the morning, then another one at ten, and at two, and at four, he felt that he had not only reached but gone well beyond "the crossover point"—the point of no return where he sensed that if he kept on like that he was going to kill himself.

The next step in Jay's view was Point C, when you simply

couldn't understand *why* you were unable to go back to Point A. "I am an awfully stubborn individual and it was becoming important to me as a rational, intelligent person that I got back to A, not drinking during the weekdays, but I finally—and that was the hardest thing—I finally said to myself, I can't do it. I just can't do it. . . ."

GIVEN HIS POSITION (not to mention his pride and his secretive nature), the other thing he couldn't do was allow anyone to find out how crucial his need to drink had become. That would be a public admission of weakness, an admission that he could never make.

When he first bought Green's Inheritance, the thing he loved best was the privacy that the wooded land surrounding the house provided. Little did he know at the time one of the ways he would put that solitude to use.

Beyond the two brick pillars that mark the entrance to the property is a long driveway, lined with an array of beautiful, sturdy trees that lead all the way up to the house, trees that, each autumn, would rain down a shower of red and orange. And each autumn for the last three or four years that Jay lived at Green's Inheritance, he would lie in wait for those leaves to fall, for the moment that he could sneak down the drive, like a spy or any type of figure who was leading a secret life, and safely hide half-gallon containers of vodka and plastic glasses underneath them.

As he had with so many things in his life, he even began to view this as a ritualistic game, to wonder how long it would take people to find him out. Buying the vodka at different places in the area (in order not to arouse suspicion) became part of the game, as did the choice of vodka itself ("the drinker's drink," because, generally speaking, "you don't smell anything"). And, of course, the drinks he would slip into drawers at both Green's Inheritance and in Florida played their role in the scheme too. Even when Nancy later discovered some of them once or twice, Jay was so good at coming up with "explanations" why they were there, why she was being silly for even worrying, that their interchanges too not only became part of the deceit, but, knowing that she wanted to believe him, part of the control that he exerted over her—the control that virtually no one could see.

When Jay was told that someone said that "he didn't seem to drink any more than anyone else in Southern Maryland," he laughed the laugh of someone who knew that he had fooled a lot of people (with certain exceptions near the end), but who hadn't, hard as he tried, fooled himself.

Whatever protection those dead leaves provided as a wall between Jay and his friends, between Jay and Nancy, did not, alas, protect him from a self-disgust that grew with each drink. He found that his memory and thought processes became erratic. He would go to the grocery store and forget what he was supposed to buy. He would find himself recounting stories to people who had heard them before, something he had always prided himself on never doing. "The damn thing is," he said, "you *can't* remember. I didn't black out, I didn't lose control, had a great time, was good old Uncle Jay—but son of a bitch if I could bring back the whole day." In an effort to combat this dilemma, he would get up early in the morning and sit with the cat they had, gently stroking its head, trying to remember.

He began to lose interest in food ("Can you imagine, one of the great pleasures in life, and you find that you don't give a shit whether you eat or not, that you just eat to live . . ."), and to have trouble sleeping. His body was "beginning to yell and scream at me from time to time" and he discovered that he literally couldn't sit and read four pages in a row of anything.

The one thing he discovered he *could* do was his job (at least up until the last six months before he left). "It's amazing," he said, "but you *can* be an administrator and delegate and be loquacious and charismatic. The alcohol actually kind of inflames that. Decisions get made more quickly."

Perhaps, but you have to be alive to make them, and Jay was beginning to wonder how much longer he would be.

"You know, I find suicide the most alien thought God ever put on the face of the earth, but I was committing suicide by drinking as much as I was in an incremental way. I've seen a lot of fifty- and sixty-year-old alcoholics who aren't dead, but they are. Maybe your liver hasn't passed yet and your heart hasn't quit beating, but your brain cells are all gone, your will to function has all gone. You're just going through a very modest pace of existence, but you're really a dead person. It's death by the installment plan."

Nonetheless, he didn't seek help of any kind, not even in Washington where he probably wouldn't have been recognized if he had begun going to Alcoholics Anonymous meetings. While he said that he was too much "a loner and an egotist" to consider that, he also claimed, rather ironically, that he "didn't have the strength or willpower to go AA."

But those were not the real reasons. Jay's real objection to AA had to do with two things that had bothered him from the time he was an adolescent: the "religious aspect" and the "exhibitionism" of it. "As far as I'm concerned, it's the Masons and the Lions Club. I reject all those kinds of things. In that respect I've got a lot of my dad in me."

JAY DID DO something about his drinking problem, however, something that was even more bizarre than the hiding of bottles. So immersed had he become in the dangerous game he was playing that he began going to the Library of Congress on a regular basis, gathering together everything he could find about alcoholism. If his only purpose for making those trips was that he sincerely wanted to help himself, that would be understandable. But it wasn't. He also wanted to become "the world's greatest expert on the subject."

THIRTY-FOUR

STAYING ALIVE WAS ONE THING. Whether Jay *wanted* to go on making decisions as president of the college was quite another. By 1981 he had been in the job for more than fifteen years (twice as long as the national average for such a position), and Camelot was ending—not just at Charles County Community College, but at institutions around the country. Not only was enrollment declining at the same time operating costs were soaring, but federal money for education, which had begun to dry up under the Carter administration, became one of the prime targets of severe budget cuts in the world of Reaganomics. Even the Department of Education itself—the agency that Nancy, her sights always set high, hoped Jay would eventually head—was being threatened with extinction.

In the spring of that year, a young woman named Edie Kopp came to interview Jay for an article in *The Surveyor*, the school newspaper. Instead of finding Jay calm and relaxed, the qualities that nearly everyone associated with his persona, she found him irritable and almost hostile when she asked about the college's financial situation and how it was affecting him in particular—namely, how did he feel about the prospect of having his housing and entertaining allowance drastically reduced, of no longer having

EXIT THE RAINMAKER

the use of college maintenance workers to take care of the grounds at Green's Inheritance?

Since the second of her two questions dealt with something that was not generally known at the time, Jay was caught off guard and responded defensively. He basically said that in his humble opinion people in Charles County were unable to understand what they read in the local papers and that the interview was over. The "great scorn and disrespect" toward the citizenry that Edie felt Jay revealed by his remark not only shocked her at the time, but took a different form a few months later.

There was a festival at the National Colonial Farm, the Accokeek project on the Potomac that Jay had first gotten involved with through Bob Straus and whose foundation Jay was president of. Jay and Nancy arrived together, Edie recalled, but "he did not seem to be projecting the normal Jay Carsey image." Not only did she notice that Jay and Nancy were "pointedly not speaking to each other," but what seemed even more significant to her was his "look of ennui."

ENNUI. IT WAS a word he would use himself in looking back at that period of his life. He would find himself standing in the shower or just driving along or even bending down to tie his shoe when, suddenly without warning, the "end of the pike" would flash before his eyes.

Being the expert on long-range guns that he was, it seemed only fitting that he would begin to look back on his career as president and say to himself, *All right, Jay, now that you've already made a million pounds of cannon powder, what are you going to do—make another million?* Whatever excitement he had derived from his extraordinary skill in playing a role had turned into exhaustion. Knowing that he had been in the right place at the right time when he took over the presidency was not something that he could block from his thoughts now, not when he felt that, each day, he was losing the essence of who he was.

193

"The job had quit being total pleasure and became sort of pain and agony," he said, "and I had been blessed with fourteen years of no pain and agony, of lack of supervision and *total* ability to do whatever I wanted to do. It's a lot easier, I can assure you, to do a public-sector job when everything is going your way. But the whole nature of the damn job changed. It became more and more a legal game. I had gone from occasionally having drinks with Ed Digges, the college's lawyer, to feeling like I was living in his bedroom.

"The job is your role, and the role is your job. You're constantly a public person and you're identified that way. You *are* the college. Your image is the college. You *have* to be 'good old Jay Carsey.' I wish I had an answer for why some people love it so much and enjoy doing it so much, but I don't. I certainly enjoyed doing it for quite a long time, but the fact of the matter is I had run out of gimmicks, I had run out of scams, and found myself back in straight bureaucracy, boxed in to public-sector administration. I was forty-five years old and I sure as hell couldn't become the president of ITT."

Maybe not, but even if he began feeling that he "didn't want to wait around for the gold watch" (that the idea of "one more award, one more presentation, one more stroke, and a special plaque on your grave" made him feel nauseated), there was nothing to prevent him from becoming a consultant full-time, the very thing that Dom Monetta and Joe Browning were urging him to do.

Consulting had been extremely lucrative for Jay. There were some years that he made as much as a hundred thousand dollars from it alone—an amount that not even Monetta and Browning were fully aware of. Along with his college salary (forty-five thousand at the time he departed) and various perks, one would think that he was not exactly strapped for cash.

But he was. It wasn't just the all-cash purchase of the time-sharing units in Florida. And it wasn't just his borrowing of money when interest rates were exorbitant. It was, more than anything, a realization that *whatever* he made in a year, Nancy would find a way to spend above it.

For Jay, it was Catch-22, a predicament he had never had to face before. Here was a man who had never truly experienced failure, who had never, at least in his professional life, had to wonder when he woke up each morning whether he was in good seed or not, whether he would be smiled at or frowned upon that day. By his own admission and the testament of others, the sun had always shone on Julian Nance Carsey; and when rain was needed, he was always the one, time and again, to bring it.

But life goes in cycles, and nobody was more aware of that than he was. His pragmatic instincts were too finely honed for him to think that Camelot could last forever—and to think that he wouldn't have to face the harsh feeling of fraudulence that is often buried deep within people who are either unacquainted with failure or have experienced it briefly enough to know that it can visit again unannounced. Being a child of the Depression was something Jay always saw as a mark of character, not something to be ashamed of.

Nonetheless, he found himself wrestling with problems he had not had to deal with before, a situation on which the county commissioners were about to shine an uncomfortable spotlight, one that would focus on Jay in particular. For someone so used to having everything his way, this only added to the emotional maelstrom that was already affecting his personal life. The dilemma was clear: the more time he had to spend on college problems and restoring the institution's financial health, the less money he could make from consulting.

So what stopped Jay from just resigning, from shielding himself from the wrath and second-guessing he would eventually face from members of his faculty and from the community at large for not being able to come up with the perfect solution? After all, the thinking went, he had always delivered in the past, why should he fail now?

Well, for one thing, the idea of consulting full-time did not appeal to Jay. Even though he was extremely good at it, and even though it was crucial to the way of life he and Nancy had created (so crucial, in fact, that he said "it kept me alive an extra seven years"), he felt there was an element of prostitution to it that he couldn't abide, a hypocrisy to it that had begun to gnaw at him. Though he considered himself "a pretty good bureaucratic hustler" who always felt comfortable "selling the college," he said that he didn't feel comfortable being "a one-on-one hustler."

There was more to it, of course, and it had to do with the same resistance he had had about moving to Washington when Marilyn Southwell had urged him to all those years before. Even if David Riesman (the sociologist who has been observing and writing about college presidents for years) is right in saying that "there are no lonelier people in the world than college presidents," that "they have the illusion of power but they don't really have power," that "they have prominence without significance," that "the faculty views them as failed academics," and that, all in all, "it's an absolutely frightful job," it was a job that, as far as Jay was concerned, carried with it a visibility that consulting did not.

Besides, if Jay were to resign as president of the college *and* stay married to Nancy, he was going to have to do better than just make money as a Beltway Bandit. If he was confused about other things in his life, that was not one of them.

THIRTY-FIVE

I N THE AUTUMN OF 1980, just a few months before the problems at the college started to become pressing, Jay began going to New York on Wednesdays. On one such Wednesday, according to Jay, Nancy went shopping while he went to meet with someone in the New York City community college system, one of the organizations for whom he did consulting. He arranged to meet Nancy back at the Plaza late in the afternoon, but, as it happened, his appointment never took place (the person he was supposed to see had had to leave town on short notice) and he had a few hours to himself, something with which he was almost totally unfamiliar.

Since the day was so balmy and Central Park was directly across from the hotel, Jay decided to take a walk, perhaps even sit and read, things he rarely had the chance to do anymore. The last thing he was going to do was try to find Nancy at Saks Fifth Avenue or Bergdorf Goodman.

As he walked past couples in rowboats, past ice cream vendors and carts filled with hot dogs and knishes, past bicyclists whizzing by and elegant older women with their even more elegant dogs, he was reminded of how much he loved New York, of the time he had driven there with Marilyn Southwell once, and of the bridge tournament he had come to play in with Jean McDonald, who was living there then and trying to make it as an actress, unwilling to abandon her dream of becoming another Marilyn Monroe. And it made him think about his life in Maryland, not so much that it seemed too provincial by comparison but that it made him realize he had been in one place an awfully long time.

But there was one thing that he loved about New York more than any other, and that was the *New Yorker*. He had always loved everything about it, the cartoons, James Thurber, S. J. Perelman, and "The Talk of the Town." And since he was such a loyal and longtime subscriber, he enjoyed talking with anyone who shared his enthusiasm.

On this particular day, that person happened to be sitting on a park bench. She was alone, about thirty-five years old, with blond hair and a lithe figure. Though Jay didn't find her movie-star beautiful, he felt sufficiently drawn by her presence to sit down. Their ensuing conversation started innocently enough, about what a pretty day it was, and what she was reading in the current issue. He asked if she came to the park often and she said that she did, every day in fact, to jog. But wasn't that dangerous? he wondered, and she said that you couldn't dwell on things like that if you lived in New York, and besides, she only jogged during the day, when all the other runners at least offered some form of protection.

"I take it that you don't live in New York?" she said.

"No," Jay said, "I'm just here on business."

"What sort?"

"I'm in education," he said, without being more specific. "And you?"

"I'm a dancer with the New York City Ballet," she said.

It was the opening he'd been waiting for. He loved ballet, he said, seizing common ground, and immediately launched into a speech about how brilliant George Balanchine was, and how he couldn't imagine what the company and the ballet world in general would do when he retired.

As he had always been, Jay was lucky; he had struck the right note, all the while trying to conceal the wave of excitement that he had been feeling from the moment he saw her. Though he was in Central Park, he could just as easily have been in that little park in Anniston, Alabama, sweet-talking Jessica Ross about how much he would love to sing in the choir every Sunday.

If Dom Monetta had been in Central Park that day, he would have said that this chance encounter was proof positive that Jay was a child of the universe. But the fact is, twenty-two years had passed from that sweltering day in Anniston to this one, and a lot of things had changed. Jay was no longer a young, confident figure on his way up, but a man who was running out of time, in more ways than one.

All he could think about was that she might get up from the bench at any moment—and that he wanted to see her again. Having managed to establish that she had rehearsals in the morning, was free on weekday afternoons, and performed in the evenings—except of course when the company was out of town—he soon heard himself saying that he had to be in New York the following Wednesday and wondered if she could arrange for him to come to Lincoln Center and watch her rehearse.

Yes, as a matter of fact, she could, and quickly jotted down the name of the person he should see when he got to the theater at ten o'clock. As she got up to leave Jay decided to remain behind for a minute or two, to watch her depart, to make sure it wasn't a dream.

ON THE WAY back to Maryland the next day, Jay kept replaying the scene in his mind. He was amused that they had only exchanged first names, that he knew nothing about her background, and he was thrilled by the notion that he would see her again the next week.

But in his euphoria he had forgotten one thing—that ever since Nancy had stopped working, she went almost everywhere with him.

"I don't think anything except the atomic or nuclear bomb falling on the top of Green's Inheritance would have kept me away from New York," he said, unmistakable determination in his voice. "I had never done *anything* to make Nancy suspicious, and I always had this flock of reasons when I wanted to go someplace, although I hardly ever got away. That was one of the unusual things about our marriage; in fourteen years, I only spent a handful of nights away from Nancy.

"Anyway, you can't imagine the horrendous set of lies and charades that I had to play to get there. Boy oh boy, that was something else. But I pulled it off and went up there."

He caught an early-morning Metroliner from Union Station in Washington and took a taxi to Lincoln Center. Clutching the piece of paper Jean had given him as if it were his very salvation, he asked for the person whose name was on it. No sooner had Jay been escorted to the rehearsal than he focused on the reason he had come, the object of his newfound affection.

Jean stood about five feet four and had "an aura of sensuality" about her that seemed even more pronounced than the week before. She had told him that she was not a principal in the company and never would be, but Jay could not have cared less. Watching her move effortlessly across the stage, he was just happy to be there.

When the rehearsal ended, she came over and said that it would take her only a few minutes to change.

"Would you like to have lunch?" Jay said when she reemerged.

That would be nice, she said. Where did he have in mind?

He suggested the Russian Tea Room, a personal favorite of his and Nancy's.

"Well," Jean said, "I usually only eat salad, but that would be fine. I'd like to put a dress on, though."

Jean did not live in a conventional apartment, but at the posh St. Moritz Hotel on Central Park South. Jay found that strange at first, the pragmatist and former high school journalist in him wondering how she could afford to live there on a dancer's salary. Unless she had private means—or a patron, so to speak—it seemed impossible.

Over blini and caviar, neither of them probed the other's background. Each knew only what the other volunteered, a situation Jay found ideal. Jean was from the Midwest and had never married; at least that was the sense Jay had. He said that he was married but had no children, and did not specify what his job was or where he lived. The Washington area was all he would say. Circling each other like boxers in the first round of a fight, they talked about food (salads aside, ethnic food was what she liked best, Armenian in particular) and they talked about movies, they talked about theater, and they talked more about ballet.

What they didn't talk about, what they simply did, was walk back to the St. Moritz when lunch was over and begin an affair.

"I HAD AN emotional experience with her that I hadn't known I was capable of having," Jay said. "It was a revelation that there was something out there I wanted to look for. There was no doubt I was looking for a different kind of relationship with a woman. And I really wanted to fall in love, without having defined it. Not knowing necessarily what it was, but knowing what it wasn't. And I knew it wasn't in the marriage that I had. So it contributed not to a sense of frustration, but to a sense of depression, a sense of having missed things. . . .

"From the time I met Nancy until the time I left, I had done all this upwardly mobile stuff, had been a bureaucrat in the society of the Sixties. Women's lib had come along, there was a change in the sexual mores, but I had barely gotten past the missionary position. Hell, I hadn't really had any conversation with anybody who had done anything dramatic.

"So here I was, forty-five years old, and I could see that in twenty or thirty years I was going to tumble into a dark hole. You start thinking about—as everybody used to try to tell me—what a fantastic life you have had up till then, about all the things you've done. But once you start adding up what you *haven't* done, then you say, 'Well, the things I've done, I've done. I don't necessarily want to keep doing them—or do them again.' I could have been president of another college, might have been president of the University of Maryland. But then you say, 'What's the difference between that and what you're doing?' Damn good question.

"Work is a cruel word. We damn English, we're the poorest linguists in the world. It's doing something to make a living and hopefully enjoy, and something that you hope doesn't make you feel like you're cheating when you collect your paycheck."

All of which brought him back to Jean, to the point where he began to say to himself, *If I stay where I am, doing what I am, I'm not going to have another chance at this.*

THE AFFAIR WENT on for months, an affair that Jay found so idyllic and exhilarating it made him feel like a character in Ernest Hemingway's *A Moveable Feast.*

But he also found the mechanics of trying to get to New York exhausting. He was lying to Nancy, lying to Katharyn Jones, lying to everybody. Yet even though he felt guilty about what he was doing ("That's just the old Calvinist in me. An affair's not something that a college president is supposed to be having"), it didn't stop him from occasionally going to New York on Tuesday nights and staying at the Plaza—giving him more time to spend with Jean, and giving Nancy a phone number in the event she needed to reach him.

If there was one thing that remained constant about the affair, it was the fact that neither Jay nor Jean ever focused on anything but the present. They didn't show each other photographs, they never said anything about their parents, they merely lived for the time each week they could spend together. The one thing Jay did figure out was that Jean was able to live in the St. Moritz because somebody named Boris, somebody that was—or had been—connected with the ballet company, made it possible for her to do so.

But even that didn't bother Jay. Jealousy was an emotion that he claimed not to understand. Whereas others thought Nancy's excessive flirtatiousness would have given most husbands fits, Jay said it didn't bother him at all. He felt the same way about Boris. As long as he was able to be with Jean, nothing else mattered.

Given how strongly he felt about the relationship, how it had reawakened something in him that was either dormant or that he didn't even know was there, how it forced him to look at his marriage, there was still the question of why he didn't leave Nancy for her.

The discussion, he said, never came up—"there wasn't a 'what if' conversation that ever occurred because there wasn't any knowledge on either side about anything explicit." It was the sheer joy of the experience, Jay seemed to be saying, that was important, not whether there was any future for them together.

But there was more.

In September of 1981, nearly a year after he had first seen Jean in Central Park and their liaison began, Jay was planning to come up one Tuesday night. They had arranged to meet at the bar in the Oak Room of the Plaza as soon as he got in. But the Tuesday in question was one of those days when even the best-laid plans go awry. Not only did it seem more and more unlikely as the day wore on that he would be able to get away, but he found himself in such a "damn whirlwind bunch of fucking social events" he couldn't even get to a phone to let Jean know that he couldn't make it.

As Jay relived that sequence of events, a startling change came over him, a change that was different from the reaction of (mostly) pleasant surprise he had when asked about Marilyn Southwell or even from the shellshocked way he talked about Nancy's verbal and physical outbursts. At first, the change was barely noticeable. His body seemed to go taut and there was a slight quiver in his long frame.

"I felt bad about not being able to get there that night, even worse that I couldn't break away for a second to call and let her know. So I decided that I would go up early on Wednesday, as I usually did, though I had begun to change the day occasionally to fit either her schedule or mine, and to avoid suspicion. Anyway, I figured I would surprise her and show up at rehearsal and hope that she would forgive me for standing her up.

"So I get to Lincoln Center, go to see the guy who lets me in, he of course knows me by this time, though he doesn't know my name, and I say that I am here to see Jean."

Jay got up out of his chair and began to pace furiously back and forth: the only thing separating him from New York at that moment was geography.

"I don't know how long the guy looked at me, it seemed like an hour, before he said, 'You're here to see Jean?' as if I was asking him about someone he didn't know. 'Don't you know what happened to her?' "

No, Jay said, he didn't. He had just gotten into town.

"Well, for some reason she was out jogging in Central Park last night, about two in the morning, and was murdered."

Jay just stood there, unable to move. His face showed no emotion.

That was then. Now, as he relived it, his whole body was shaking. Unfamiliar tears streamed down his face. He pounded his hand on the table and struggled to catch his breath.

"I mean," he said, sobbing, "nobody in their right mind jogs in Central Park at two in the morning. But goddamnit, and this is what really tears me up, if I had gotten a call through, she might not have been out there. Or if I had gotten up there, if I hadn't gotten fucked up that night, she sure as hell wouldn't have been out there. Maybe she decided that week that two o'clock in the morning was the time to go jogging. I don't know what she decided."

For the first time, it seemed, fate had worked against him. It was another moment of truth, but it didn't contain the ending he wanted. To Jay, it hardly mattered whether Jean was stabbed or raped or shot at close range. All that mattered was that she was gone.

When he got the news, he did what he had done in the past, what his instincts told him to do: he fled.

Once back in Maryland, he refused to read the newspapers.

And he began to drink even more heavily.

"If you're a heavy drinker and something happens that is particularly traumatic," he said, "it's awfully easy to go to another magnitude of layer of drink. Instead of this tall a tumbler"—he gestured with his thumb and forefinger—"that tall a tumbler. It puts you in another state of memory lapse. Works on your memory bank a little bit more. You kind of forget."

He didn't.

THIRTY-SIX

When Anne Morrow Lindbergh wrote *Gift from the Sea* a good deal of her inspiration came from the time she had spent on the barrier islands of Sanibel and Captiva, joined at the hip off the west coast of Florida. Facing the Gulf of Mexico, they are as glorious as Jay found his affair with Jean to be. There are birds, every kind and everywhere: brown pelicans (not in the least bit bashful as they hold court on dock pilings); egrets that walk gracefully along roads, unperturbed by cars; red-shouldered hawks; roseate spoonbills; and anhingas that are funnier than most stand-up comics in the way they sun themselves after each time they dive for fish. And there are so many varieties of shells on the beach that most humans are often frozen in what has come to be called the Sanibel Stoop.

Someone who had been there once, someone unknown to the Carseys, had stood outside the cottage she was staying in one night, under a full moon, and thought to herself, This is significant. You should memorize this. This is peace.

And so, it seemed, it had been for Jay and Nancy, who had been coming to Sanibel-Captiva for more Novembers and Marches than they could even remember. Green's Inheritance was full of the magnificent shells that Nancy had collected there, not to mention the photographs of all the good times they had had, all the friends they had made.

But that particular November, the November of 1981, was different. The problems at the college had reached such a critical point that Jay wasn't sure that they should go, wasn't sure that such a move wouldn't be viewed as his defiantly thumbing his nose at the people who were paying his salary and as being insensitive to the situation in general—especially since Louis Jenkins had specifically asked Jay to let him know if he was going to be away for more than forty-eight hours. (He and Nancy would be gone so often that people joked it was a rare occasion when the president would pass through Charles County.)

But as anyone who had come to know Jay was well aware, he could be as stubborn as an armadillo. So, out of a basic, deep-rooted belief that he had worked hard for—and deserved—all the perks he had accumulated over the years, out of a streak of rugged Texas independence that made it hard for him to abide by the wishes of others (at least in his public life), and out of an understandable, though irrational, perception that he was personally being blamed for the college's changing fortunes, he decided they would go to Florida. He would commute back and forth as much as necessary, and hope that the board wouldn't discover that he was actually out of town. As they had about Nancy's portrait, close friends assumed that the decision to go to Florida was Nancy's, that she had selfishly insisted on it. But that wasn't true.

"If we hadn't gone to Florida," Jay said, "I would have been admitting to Nancy that the world had changed. I simply didn't want to do that."

Maybe not, but the world had changed, and November turned out to be one of the worst months of their marriage.

·   ·   ·

THE DISILLUSIONMENT THAT Jay had begun to feel well before Jean died had only intensified. Her death was significant, he felt, because it became a catalyst for pulling together the strands of discontent that he had managed to keep buried. "I began to find myself getting irritated at things that had only mildly aggravated me before. I don't just mean my job, but things that were going on all around me. I don't mean visibly irritated, I'm too good an actor for that, but I found myself looking at people that I had to have a good relationship with professionally or socially and I'd be sitting there and looking and talking to them and saying to myself, *This shit-ass, I don't really give a shit if I say another word to you*, not exactly in those words, but *What am I doing spending my time with somebody as dull as you are?* I started going through that mindset, all of a sudden looking at people in a different light and looking at things in a slightly different light."

And in doing so, he realized that no matter how tired he was of the role that he—and everyone else—had become accustomed to his playing, it would be impossible—or so he thought—for him to change the equation, for people ever to see him as other than the president of the college, the high priest they had always been able to turn to with *their* problems. And if that was true, he didn't see how he was ever going to meet another Jean, something that he desperately wanted to do.

"But I want to tell you," he said, "and I don't know how strongly I can say this and make you believe me: if the New York thing hadn't happened it wouldn't have made *any* difference. I'd have still done what I did. It wasn't what made me do it. I don't think I would ever, in hindsight, have left Nancy for Jean if that was the only reason. It was one of a string of things."

ON ONE PARTICULAR day that month in Florida, not long after Jim Simpson had been to visit, not long after Nancy had begun to find tumblers in odd places early in the morning and to confront Jay about them, not long after a trip they had made to Cape Canaveral to watch the space shuttle go up and attend a big blowout (where they met Robert Redford and danced in the rain), and just before he had to board another plane that would take him to yet another meeting back in Maryland, Jay was sitting on the beach while Nancy took a sailing class.

Finding time to be by himself had always been a problem for Jay, but it is likely that he never felt more grateful for the rare time alone than he did that morning. The sun was shining and the beach was filled with people gathering shells. As he looked out at the Gulf of Mexico, he knew that if he were suddenly to get into a boat and set sail he would eventually reach the state of his birth.

But Texas was far, far off in the distance and the things he began trying to confront that morning were much more immediate. He tried to fantasize going on a month's trip overseas with Nancy and not buying a thing, but as hard as he tried he simply couldn't do it, deciding that it would be "cruel and unusual punishment" for her. He looked around the beach and said to himself that as lovely as Sanibel and Captiva were, they were actually as clear a symptom as any of the problems in his marriage, that if no change of any kind was made, he would be coming to this place, every November and March, for year after year after year. But no sooner had he said that than he stopped short and reminded himself that he must be crazy to be thinking that way, that it's every man's *dream* to come to such a spot. Maybe so, he thought as he watched the light play off the shimmering waves, but the excitement of that dream had long since started to fade for him.

Once again, the chemical engineer in him began to methodically review and analyze his situation. When Nancy remarked after Jay left that there must have been some little box inside him that she could not enter, she could hardly have known that while she was off sailing, he was sitting on the beach with something similar in mind.

"I kind of put little boxes together," he explained, "and I said, Okay, I definitely want to do A—which meant leaving my marriage, leaving the job, leaving the whole lifestyle, and I definitely want to do B—which basically meant doing something entirely different, not having any idea what that might be, but trusting that fate would deal kindly with me, that whatever it was could only be better than what I would be leaving behind.

"Nancy and I were no longer in a position, politically or financially, for her to continue being a Perle Mesta. And I've got to tell you, I felt a great deal of guilt about her diffusing her many talents on just being that, because that is what she thought I wanted her to be. The mistake of Green's Inheritance was that it threw us into a sense of affluence that doesn't match the role of a college president. It was too damn ostentatious, and it made me very nervous. And I know that somebody's got to be J. Paul Getty, or even Joe Browning, bless his heart, putting his stocks and bonds in a box and looking at them every day, but I came to realize—probably always knew it—that I didn't.

"But of course there were many things I enjoyed doing, and I thought about them—weekly bridge, twenty hours of tennis, golf, Redskins games—and whether I would miss doing them. I was just asking the basic question and *not* judging it against something else, like running a bar or going to Australia, and my answer was no. Once you've hit six decent drives off the tee, why do you want to hit another six dozen?"

Just as he had already begun making lists in an effort to remember things he had done the day before, he began making a list of the people he felt it would be "emotionally anguishing to leave."

It didn't take long. Three people.

Dom Monetta
Joe Browning
John Sine

"So I sat there and I asked myself: *What's wrong with me? That's not normal. Am I so emotionally out of sync that I would come up with that small a list after all those years?* I thought I'd have a list of fifty people."

Not only was he astonished that it was so short, but it became "the bolt of lightning" that tipped him over to the decision he ultimately made.

"I think there comes a time when you make some decisions that seem very selfish to everybody and *are* selfish. I could have gone back to work for Indian Head full-time and made more money in terms of real salary. I could have consulted full-time, and I probably could have gotten into the political game, or been a professor at GW. But even if Nancy had wanted to be married to a professor, which she most certainly didn't, the fact is, and I can't stress this enough, *I had done what I wanted to do.*

"I felt as if I was dying inside. I was becoming dull, commonplace. Not that I'm not dull now, but in terms of my own perception I was just on a treadmill. I didn't know whether Nancy was driving me harder or I was driving myself against some concept of what I should be, or both. I decided I wanted to do something else with my life and I didn't want to go through the wrenching session I would have if I had left in a conventional way. If I had told Nancy what I wanted to do, I would have wasted a year out of my life, and I didn't want to go through the confrontation and agony of that. Besides, I would have had eight hundred and fifty-two other people trying to talk me out of it. I sure as hell was not going to do what I did in 1968 when I had lunch with Joe Miller. I was not going to talk to *anybody* about what I was planning, because it was a very clean-cut decision in my mind—a *perfect* decision actually—and any way I sort through a rationale for doing it differently, I still say it wouldn't have worked. I did what I wanted to do the *only* way I, Julian Nance Carsey, could see of getting it done."

But as far as he was concerned, then and now, it was the *making* of the decision that day in Florida, *not* his actual leaving six months later, that was the hard part, the thing that required the most courage.

"Look, let's face it, not too many people would make that decision in my position at that time in life. If someone was standing on the road outside of Green's Inheritance, somebody who didn't know anything about my life, they would say, 'Good God, how could anybody leave that kind of a world? What does he lack? He could have a better backhand, or maybe have four tickets to the Redskins instead of two, but how could it get any better?'

"I was living everyone's version of the American dream. To do what I decided to do, to leave all that behind, is to go against the very mores of society."

FOR SOMEONE WHO, time and time again, had always done what was expected of him, who had always played the role of Mr. Good and Responsible, he left the beach that day with a surprisingly low degree of guilt and a decided spring in his step. If the life he had been living was irrecoverably American, his decision to light out was far more universal.

He had always said that he was a terrible process-and-procedure person whose real excitement came at the beginning of things, who thought Genesis the most intriguing book of all. But he couldn't possibly have imagined, until that moment, how accurate that self-assessment was. Sure, he had walked out the back door of the church that Sunday in Bryan, and he had severed relationships more abruptly and less graciously than was necessary, and he had even contemplated fleeing just before his marriage to Nancy. But this was different. In those instances, he had never reached a point of true desperation. In those instances, such notions as tumbling into a black hole did not cross his mind. He had had his brushes with death, but fate, he was convinced, had pulled him through. And it was fate that he was counting on once more to give him a new beginning, even though he hadn't a clue as to what or where it would be.

If the haunting image of a clear run to the grave without any change of any consequence kept flashing before his eyes, who is to say that his vision was blurred, that his thinking was misguided?

THIRTY-SEVEN

FOR SOMEONE USED to playing roles, the one Jay would have to play over the next six months would be his greatest test: having to pretend that everything was normal while he went about attending to the details that would enable him to leave. Instead of always holding the lantern, this was one time when he was more than eager to be chopping the wood.

Feeling like da Vinci's *Mona Lisa*, he kept an inscrutable smile on his face as he slowly and secretly began to transfer money to a bank account at American Security in Washington, an account he had had from the time he first came to Indian Head, an account that Nancy never knew about. He decided that he wasn't going to take anything—such as a car or money from the college—that stood even the remotest chance of showing up later on a computer. Being a fugitive held no interest for him. And he decided that he was not going to take anything of personal value, such as Nancy's jewelry. He just wanted to take enough "walking-around, maintenance money," he said, "to give me a chance to survive for a while."

Since the majority of his and Nancy's money was tied up in real estate and personal property, he had to be fairly calculating about all this, but not excessively so. After all, Nancy knew relatively little about their finances—another element of his control.

Coming to the conclusion that he needed about a thousand dollars a month to live on (and wanting to buy as much time as possible), he not only pulled out money that he had put aside for retirement, but he got Nancy to sign over her retirement money as well, telling her it was important for tax reasons that she have an Individual Retirement Account. After taking out two loans that she also didn't know about, he had accumulated about twenty-eight thousand dollars, enough to keep him going for more than two years.

In his ongoing effort to keep up appearances, he discussed planting a big garden with Nancy and he even agreed to begin looking for an apartment in Washington. But as good an actor as Jay claimed to be, the flaws in his daily performance began to be noticed.

Even in Florida that November, Jim Simpson wasn't the only one who felt that Jay was not his usual self. Evelyn Hungerford (who also had a time-share there) could see that he was drinking more than usual and didn't look well, but she blamed it on pressures at the college and on Nancy for insisting they come down in the first place. And when the Carseys spent Thanksgiving with Karen and Mike Sprague in Port St. Lucie, Karen noticed that Jay hardly said a word, that he just sat there, staring into space.

Once he got back, he and Tommy Sexton were driving to a meeting in a neighboring county when Jay said something that

Sexton found as surprising as the time Jay sent him to Nigeria. Never having heard Jay remark on personal matters before, at least not to him, Sexton was taken aback when Jay suddenly said that he was sorry he had ever purchased Green's Inheritance. "I'll tell you," he said, "*that* was a big mistake. I'd sell it tomorrow if Nancy would."

Jay's problems at the college only grew worse, and they involved more than just the budget. The board had, of course, discovered that Jay had gone to Florida, and they were not pleased that he had defied their wishes. After all, the members as well as the county commissioners felt he served at their pleasure and would do well to remember that—especially when things were so rocky. But Jay did not apologize graciously or back away meekly. He basically said that he had come through before, and that he would come through again. Fine, they said, they wanted him to, they had complete faith in him, but they reminded him that they meant what they said about his not being away for more than forty-eight hours without notice, and they wondered if he could somehow prevail upon Nancy not to come to any more board meetings. Even though the meetings were open to the public, some of the members were upset at the casual way she walked in and out, the tight designer jeans she wore, and the imperious way she often acted, as if the meetings had been scheduled just for her.

Jay said he would talk to her, but he had said something similar to John Sine a few months before about a different matter and it hadn't helped. In September, at the beginning of that school year, the year that would turn out to be Jay's last, John had arranged a welcome-back dinner at the country club for administration and faculty members and had decided that spouses would not be invited. Not once, but three times, Jay approached John and asked if it would be all right for Nancy to come. And each time, John, whom Jay could always count on to be firm and straightforward with him, said no, absolutely not. Even though John knew how much discomfort this was causing Jay, knew how Nancy hated being excluded from anything, he felt it would be wrong to make an exception—especially since cost-cutting was supposed to be the order of the day.

When Jay came into John's office a fourth time, it was not to ask again if Nancy could attend, or even to insist, as president, that she be there. He simply wanted to ask if John could phone her himself and explain the situation.

"Look," John said, "I can't believe we're still discussing this. Nancy is *your* wife, not mine. And you have to tell her that she can't come."

But when the evening in question rolled around, Jay walked into Hawthorne Country Club with Nancy. No sooner had they gone into the bar and begun to mix with the faculty than Nancy loudly informed one and all that she wouldn't be joining them for dinner because "John told Jay I wasn't invited." So when everyone went in to eat, Nancy remained behind—at first. Five minutes later, though, she stood at the entrance to the dining room, asking Jay to have one person after another come over and keep her company. And not long after that, she waltzed into the room, front and center, and said that Jay had given her permission to visit with everybody.

For John, whose initial fury had become bemusement, it not only brought back that scene at Marchoza over a decade before and others since, but it was a final confirmation of something that both perplexed and saddened him: the realization that Jay seemed totally emasculated by Nancy, that he could no longer act or function within the environment that the two of them had created. "It was as though the whole thing," John said later, "their whole life together, had left him without sinew, without the things he needed to move his arms and legs, to form the thoughts coming out of his mouth. It was as if he didn't speak the language of reality."

Jay became more and more reliant on John. Instead of sensing that it might be unwise to raise the subject of Nancy with John again, Jay actually asked him if he would help Nancy with the work she was doing for the Accokeek Foundation, work that Jay had arranged and which Bob Straus strongly felt was not getting done, the issue that blew up not long after that when Nancy stormed into the Accokeek board meeting and demanded that Jay resign.

"No way," John said, more in disbelief than anger, "I won't do it. The people she has been working with tell me that she won't do anything they say. Besides, I don't think she wants to do the work anyway."

Though Jay didn't press it further, his behavior became increasingly troubling to John and others at the college. He either canceled meetings without explanation (if he didn't drive over to mill around with Buddy Sprague at his liquor store or wander off by himself to drink, he would go home in the afternoon to take a nap) or, when he did have them, he seemed to become more and more indecisive as to what the solutions to the problems should be.

Jay didn't remember that he canceled meetings and he didn't remember coming home occasionally for a nap, but he did recall doing little, if any, work during those last few months—other than continuing to pick up empty vodka bottles in the woods and stuff them into large green garbage bags.

"I was just putting in time," he admitted. "Mentally I was through. I appeared at the office each morning and cleaned out my In basket. Why should I be doing any planning when I wasn't going to be there? If there was a really tough, messy problem to solve, I just ignored it and walked away.

"I finally got exhausted from keeping up the facade, from trying to be the same old Jay. I can't tell you the tension of those last two months, which had nothing to do with tension per se. It's just like if you were planning a heist."

. . .

SINCE HE ALREADY had the majority of his getaway money put aside, the tension primarily had to do with timing and execution. He was so consumed with this that with each passing day there was less and less of him there. Ever since that liberating morning on the beach in Florida, it was only a question of when. Nothing else mattered. He would walk the floors at night, unable to sleep. When he and Nancy would go somewhere he would practically ask for a drink at the same time he said hello. When they went to the party where Nancy tripped and fell as she entered, he was not only too tired to help her up, he didn't want to. Yes, his back bothered him. Yes, he was concerned about his eyesight. Yes, a friend's recent death in a plane crash only reinforced to him how fragile life was. Of course he didn't like getting angry phone calls at home, personally blaming him for the layoffs that the college needed to make. And of course he knew that a few observant people at the college had begun to notice how much he was drinking (they would have to have been blind, he said, not to be aware).

But did he think that anyone had *any* inkling of what he was planning to do? Absolutely not. Not Edie Kopp, who saw him and Nancy at a local art show opening six weeks before he left, offered him some punch, and he half-jokingly asked her for a panacea instead. Not Bob Straus, who had noticed how puffy and bloated his face had become and who had come right out and warned him that his drinking would eventually kill him. Not Louis Jenkins, whom he told how much he longed to watch Monday Night Football at home. Not John Sine, who felt he was "blotto" on more than one occasion. Not Buddy Sprague, who felt, as all his friends did, that Jay would overcome his problems at the college and triumph as he always had. And most of all, not Nancy, who felt sure that the summer would bring him—and them—the peace they needed, the rest that would enable Jay to keep them both living in the manner she was sure they both loved.

No, the way Jay saw it, even if the facade had begun to crumble, even if his friends and colleagues chose to view his various slips as cries for help, even if they knew that what he was about to do was not without precedent, he felt confident that the most they might expect was that he would either resign from the college or ask for a divorce. The writer Ambrose Bierce might follow Pancho Villa into Mexico in 1913 and never return, and Judge Joseph F. Crater, immersed in political scandal, might vanish from New York City and drop off the face of the earth on a hot August evening in 1930, but "pulling a Crater" was something that you read about strangers doing, not people you knew, and certainly not someone like Julian Nance Carsey, college president, dutiful husband, and everyone's favorite uncle. If there was one thing everyone could count on, it was that.

And that, of course, is what made Jay's plan so perfect.

THIRTY-EIGHT

"I'D BEEN THROUGH *seventeen of those fuckers and I wasn't going to go through another one."*

Having decided that he would make his exit before graduation ("There was a little bit of amorality there, I guess, but I also found it amusing"), Jay worked backward from Sunday, May 23, in putting together the finishing touches to his plan.

On Saturday, May 15, while Nancy went off to the Simpson

wedding and waited for Jay to come to the reception, he was busy.

He wrote his letter of resignation from the college.

In a letter to Dave Lee, the technical director of NOS, he resigned his consultancy position.

He wrote to Dom Monetta, secure in the knowledge that Dom would do as he asked, even though his request—to take care of Nancy "for a while"—was ambiguous.

As he scribbled his message to John Sine on the back of the Ronald and Nancy Reagan postcard, he smiled at the thought of being twenty-six again and playing in *The Rainmaker*, of all the hours they had spent playing tennis and working together, of how much fun it had been "to make rain on Southern Maryland" and how they had laughed and laughed the first time they heard Judge Dudley Digges deliver his speech about A Crossroads at the Top of the Mountain—the point at which Jay had now arrived.

He wrote to his parents. "My biggest guilt in the whole bag," he said, "was my mother. She psychologically had me on a pedestal—God's best gift and all that bullshit—and, as a consequence, I knew it would be very tough on her. That was the reason I mentioned Ernest. I didn't really know him, but I knew he was an adventurer, so I did it as a sop to her, to give her something in her own family to identify with. It was really very diabolical of me, but there you have it."

And he wrote to Nancy. "When I said that I didn't want to drag her down with me, I meant that we had been on an Up escalator for so long that there was no way she could ever have gone in reverse." As for the line about *I'm leaving because I know you can't*, he said he couldn't recall writing that but wouldn't swear that he hadn't. If he had, he said, it would also have been referring to his feeling that she would be incapable of giving up Green's Inheritance, incapable of divesting of any of her possessions, incapable of living any other way—and not to any discussions they might have had about ending their marriage. "The subject of divorce per se had *never* come up," he said. "The subject of whether the marriage might be worth saving may have come up, but I don't recall it. As I've said, verbal communication between us—other than planning our next party or trip—was basically zilch the whole time we were married, and I take full responsibility for that. It was almost like role-playing and I might as well have been a college president playing games with a county commissioner."

But if he really believed that the fault was entirely his, if he was convinced that "the guillotine approach: Go! No warning, no nothing" was the only way he could leave the life he had, why didn't he at least have the note leaving Nancy all the assets and liabilities of the estate either notarized or witnessed? Didn't he feel that was part of his "responsibility"? Or did the anxiety of the last few days before he left result in an honest oversight?

He thought the note was a legally valid piece of paper. He didn't know that it had to be notarized, he claimed, and he was certainly not going to consult a lawyer and risk exposing his intentions. Over and over he insisted there was *no* other reason.

His explanation sounded tinny and unconvincing—especially from a man who would later say that he "developed an enormous respect for the subconscious" as a result of what he did. Pressed again on the subject months afterward, he finally told the truth.

"I didn't want to make it easy for her, so, to a certain extent, there's a punishment mechanism there. Punishing myself and her for a marriage that never should have been, that we both went into for the wrong reasons. I'll admit that the fact I left her with a messy financial situation hardly brings tears to my eyes. After all, you're not talking about leaving someone in a sackcloth. I figured she could hock the jewelry alone and live for two years."

Before leaving the house that Saturday to join Nancy at the wedding reception, he made the tape recording that outlined their financial life and put it in his desk, the tape whose bankerlike tone startled everyone five days later.

On Sunday Jay was in charge of setting up the chairs for the Garden Club party over at Ken Dixon's and he performed his duties perfectly. Having written the letters and feeling one day closer to leaving, he even found it possible to relax, chatting with Louis Jenkins and slyly asking Gordon Barnes about the weather forecast for graduation the following Sunday.

He hadn't decided at that point where he was going to depart from—whether he would fly from National or Dulles, or whether he might make his way to Richmond or Charlottesville, Virginia, and fly from there.

Nor had he definitely settled on a destination. But the more he thought about it that morning as he shaved the more he felt he would be less likely to encounter someone he knew on a flight to Houston than on a plane to Chicago. "Besides," he said, "I knew Houston, I knew the Galleria. I knew that if I stayed near there I would be able to buy the things I needed."

All he was going to take from Green's Inheritance, he decided, was his briefcase and his toiletry kit—and the hope that whatever he found, wherever he found it, would be better than the life he was turning his back on, the life he had enjoyed but no longer wanted.

For someone who said he firmly believed in cycles, he would be coming full circle—leaving the area in the same simple fashion in which he had arrived as a hitchhiker without an overcoat nearly a quarter of a century before. He had gotten what he'd come for and it was time to move on, to begin again.

On Monday, May 17, he and Nancy had lunch at an Italian restaurant in Waldorf and then went to pick up her Triumph, which she had taken to the Simpson wedding and left there. As he drove back to the college, he kept wondering whether he had done anything, anything at all, to make Katharyn Jones suspicious that morning, and he tried to reassure himself that he hadn't. Whenever he traveled by plane, Katharyn always arranged his transportation, but this was one trip he was going to have to arrange himself. He had initially thought he might leave on Tuesday, but then suddenly changed his mind as he closed the door to his office and quietly phoned Pan Am, booking a first-class ticket to Houston from National Airport on Wednesday.

"Will you be needing a return flight, Mr. Carsey?" asked the reservations clerk.

No, he said, he wouldn't.

ON TUESDAY MORNING, just as he was walking out the door to begin his last full day as president, Nancy had a list of things she needed him to do: pick up some of her clothes at the dry cleaners, drop off Courtney Wilson's purse at her house, and go to the grocery store.

Responsible to the end, he of course did all that, even though he had to slip out of an Accokeek meeting to get to the cleaners before it closed. He waited for Loretta Nimmerichter, the county commissioner he thought had a vendetta against him, but she never showed up. If Katharyn Jones had any idea that Jay was going to leave the next day, she of course would have understood why he not only seemed relieved that the meeting didn't take place, but hardly seemed to care.

"Have a good evening, Katharyn," Jay said as he prepared to leave his office for the last time. "I expect to be in for a couple of hours in the morning before my dental appointment."

INSTEAD OF GOING out that night, the Carseys spent a quiet evening at home. Nancy made dinner while Jay spoke on the phone with Spencer Matthews and even went so far as to make plans for lunch the following week.

Once they finally sat down to eat, Jay picked at his food like a child and said that he simply wasn't hungry. As he walked outside afterward, he took in the fragrant spring air and marveled at how lush everything was becoming. The grass was too high, but he knew that it would be mowed in the morning, and even found himself looking forward to the fresh-cut smell.

About two weeks earlier, he had stood outside with John Budzinski, one of his friends from NOS, almost becoming sentimental as he remarked how beautiful everything was. Though John would later think back on that moment and wonder why Jay had said that, the truth is that in all the years he had lived at Green's Inheritance, the only thing Jay had never tired of was the land surrounding it.

But as he came inside and got ready for bed, he put his mask of deception back on. Before switching off the light, he turned to Nancy and suggested they go to Washington later in the week.

THIRTY-NINE

SLEEP, AS HAD BEEN the case for months, was not easy to come by. Jay got up a few times during the night and stood by the window, looking up at the sky. There were so many stars that he felt sure it would be a good day for traveling.

"My most intense feeling the morning I left was continuing to make sure that I didn't tip my hand. I think once you reach that point in a scenario you get—at least I did—terribly tied up in the process of implementation, and that becomes an obsession.

"When I look back on it, it's kind of funny. Here I was, getting ready to hop on a plane and disappear forever, and I actually stopped the car, got out and told the yard men that they weren't doing what they were supposed to be doing. I mean, what the hell did I care? I wasn't planning to ever walk back on the grounds again. But it was an obsession with the process that went on, an obsession with making it as casual as possible."

He was traveling light, as planned. In addition to his briefcase, toiletry kit, and the gray suit he was wearing, the only other things he had with him were his passport and his wallet. The "psychology," he said, of having everything inside a briefcase was pleasing to him.

He didn't kiss Nancy before he left, but there was nothing premeditated about that. "We said our usual, 'See you later, I'm going to the dentist,' and all this, and then I left." As for coming home to lunch, he couldn't recall saying that—especially since he couldn't recall them ever sitting down to lunch on a weekday. "I might come back to the house and grab something out of the icebox, but that's a fantasy on Nancy's part, that I would often come home for lunch."

After talking to the yard men, he parked the car near the entrance and walked around the woods for a few minutes, recalling how it seemed like only yesterday that he had formed the Camelot partnership, and checking to make sure that he had picked up every last vodka bottle. Though he was drinking as heavily as ever, he was adamant that even if he died of cirrhosis, it wouldn't be in Charles County.

During the previous two weeks or so, whenever Jay had gone somewhere, he'd spent even more time than usual talking to people. And though they didn't realize it, of course, he was trying to tell each of them goodbye. That was his hidden reason for driving to the post office in Pomfret that morning. Evelyn Coombs, the postmistress, and he were fond of each other, and he always made her laugh when he threw away nearly all the mail he and Nancy received each day—the majority of which were catalogs. No sooner would he show Evelyn a catalog advertising fur coats than he would say, "I know what I'm going to do with this," and flip it into the trash. "If I took this home, Nancy would see something she wanted."

But on that particular day, May 19, there was none of that banter. He got his mail, they remarked on the weather, and he left. As much as he liked Evelyn Coombs, he wasn't about to give her a forwarding address, even if he had one.

. . .

ONCE HE ARRIVED in Washington and got the twenty-eight thousand dollars converted into traveler's checks, he phoned Katharyn Jones, asking her to cancel his dental appointment. He also "fabricated the story about my sister to give me some excuse to blow the rest of the day away." It was "a smoke mission," he said, "a fog day. I figured that Nancy would not understand it, but wouldn't not accept it. It was clever on my part because there was no way she would try to contact my sister for a day or two."

As he made the phone call to Katharyn from the Army & Navy Club, he could hardly contain himself. Just five minutes earlier he had bought a copy of the *New Yorker* to take on the plane with him. But once he started to flip through it, he changed his mind.

There, on page twenty-nine in the middle of "The Talk of the Town," was a cartoon he would never forget, a cartoon that appealed to his "strange, bizarre sense of humor." In it, a woman in her early fifties was sitting at the breakfast table, drinking coffee. She had set a cup out for her husband, but when he came into the kitchen he didn't sit down. Holding a briefcase in his left hand, he was wearing a hat, dark suit, and glasses and looked painfully meek and timid. His appearance was deceptive though. Standing firmly between the two pieces of luggage at his feet, he began to speak—a speech that left his frowning wife with her hand frozen in mid-air.

> *"Well, goodbye, Emily. It's May 19th. You may remember*
> *my having mentioned some time ago that I was going to*
> *leave you on May 19th."*

When Jay arrived at National Airport after that, he left the magazine in the car. That was hardly surprising. If he had already internalized that the way he was leaving was the *only* way he could, if he was prepared to allow the letters he had written to do his work for him, why not add the cartoon to the mix?

As he walked toward North Terminal he clutched the five letters and the postcard in his left hand. Until he put them into the mailbox, he still had time to alter his plan. But he had no second thoughts. One by one, he dropped them in the box outside the terminal and the release of each one lifted his spirits higher and higher.

"Once those letters were dropped in the mailbox," he said, "that was it. That was the guillotine. It was over with and I had destroyed the way back. That was the point of no return—the single moment of truth."

Since he wore no disguise, he kept looking around to see if he recognized anybody as he stood in line at the Pan Am ticket counter. And even though it was cool inside the terminal, he was perspiring.

"May I help you, sir?" the woman behind the counter asked.

"Yes," Jay said, "my name is Carsey, first initial J. I have a reservation to Houston, Flight 991."

The computer began buzzing and within seconds his one-way ticket appeared.

"And how will you be paying for your ticket, Mr. Carsey?"

"American Express."

"Are you checking any bags?"

"Just this one," Jay said, even though it was really two.

He had had this same dialogue at more ticket counters at more places around the world than he could possibly remember, but it had never had any import until that moment.

As HE SAT in the Clipper Club waiting for his flight, downing one drink after another, he wrote the letter to Ed Loeliger that revealed where he had parked the car, the letter asking him to help Nancy in any way that he could. He made the call to Bob Straus's office saying he was off to Philadelphia and, moments later, settled into the wide, plush first-class seat that would take him to Houston.

He recalled nothing of the long flight, he said, because he kept plying himself with liquor. But as he hoped, there was no one on the plane he knew.

Once in Houston, he went directly to the Houston Oaks, checked in, and collapsed on the bed. When he woke it was Thursday—his first full day of freedom.

HE HAD SOME breakfast sent up to his room and then went on a shopping spree at the Galleria. Using his credit cards, he bought blue jeans, sneakers, T-shirts, underwear, shoes, shirts, ties, and the Pierre Cardin suit that puzzled Nancy and infuriated Evelyn Hungerford.

He also made another decision—to go to San Diego.

"The only reason I decided to go there was that I thought I might either like to be on the West Coast or go to Australia or Mexico. There was an airline ticket agent in the hotel and I paid for the ticket with the cash I had. I wanted to turn the traveler's checks into cash, but I didn't want to do it in Houston because I figured tracing me to Houston was easy. See, you get into this paranoid thing of being traced. I said to myself, 'Well, if they get into a panic and move quickly, they can find out that I've got a ticket to Houston, but they won't find out I've got a ticket to San Diego right away.' "

Even though he felt confident that he had until Monday before anything would happen back in Maryland, his fear of being apprehended was so deep that he was taking no chances. As far as he was concerned, he lived with the constant threat, however irrational, of being "caught," not merely found. As far as he was concerned, his face was bound to turn up, sooner or later, on the sides of milk cartons, or he would be walking down the street, free at last, and someone would say, imitating W. C. Fields, "Hey, I know you. You're that college president who just picked up and ran off. You better come with me, son, I'm gonna turn you in." In his mind he was more than just a missing person—he was a criminal; not because he was, but because he thought he was, because, in his own rebellious way, he *wanted* to be. If you're not a good boy anymore, if you're not kindly Uncle Jay, then you're bad, something, from childhood on, he had never fully *allowed* himself to be.

So he checked out of the hotel and flew on to San Diego later that day. He briefly considered staying at the Hotel del Coronado, but since he and Nancy had stayed there so often he thought it might be one of the places she would check. So he canceled the reservation he had made and opted instead for the Westgate Hotel, which was close to the airport.

He decided not to stay in San Diego past Saturday, but he ran into difficulties. None of the banks he went to that day were open. He would have to wait until Monday before he could convert his traveler's checks into cash.

But things were not so bad. He ate well and bought more clothes, continuing to charge everything. He went to the San Diego Zoo and went trolling for women. And then he sat down on a park bench and carried out the next step in his plan. He pulled out a pair of scissors and proceeded with glee to cut up his credit cards —twenty-eight in all. Like the dropping of the letters in the box four days earlier, it was another moment of truth.

He arrived at more decisions. As much as he loved Australia, he didn't want to "play the passport game." If he wasn't stopped before he left the country, he felt sure that the authorities would have no trouble in tracking him down. So having ruled that out, he thought about going to Tijuana—only to discover that without a credit card it was virtually impossible to rent a car.

By Monday morning his next destination was still uncertain. He went to a bank near the hotel and immediately encountered a problem. Converting twenty-eight thousand dollars of traveler's checks into cash was not so simple as he had thought. He would have to explain to an officer *why* he needed the money right away.

Jay thought fast. He identified himself as a broker from Washington, D.C., in San Diego for one reason only: to buy a yacht for somebody that afternoon. As far as Jay was aware, "*Everybody* buys yachts with cash because it's all underground money. It's offshore money, and people hijack boats from Central America, break them up, sell them for cash."

His request was granted.

WITHIN AN HOUR of leaving the bank, he was back out on the same park bench where he had cut up his credit cards the day before. His bags were packed, but he had nowhere to go. He had the local paper with him and began looking through it. Ten minutes later, having seen something in it that made sense, having thrown away "all responsibility for anything except my tick-tock, day-to-day existence," he went back to the hotel to collect his belongings.

FORTY

AT ABOUT SEVEN O'CLOCK on that Monday evening, the twenty-fourth of May, Jay Martin Adams flew in to one of the few places on the globe where the first world stares directly into the eyes of the third—the border hotbed of El Paso, Texas.

Jay had decided on his alias before he left San Diego. He thought that it made sense to keep his first name because it would be too hard to answer readily to anything else, and he didn't want to arouse suspicion. "Martin" was his paternal grandmother's maiden name. Jimmy Martin was Jay's great-uncle, a famous Dallas trial lawyer who had managed to keep Raymond Hamilton (one of Bonnie and Clyde's confederates) out of the electric chair. "Adams" was chosen arbitrarily, a good, solid name shared by hundreds, including the couple Jay and Nancy played golf with every other Wednesday.

As for El Paso, that jumped out of the paper Jay was reading in the park. A full-page ad said FLY SOUTHWEST TO EL PASO, ONLY $60. "El Paso was totally random," he explained. "I could have gone to Portland, Oregon. I could have gone to Des Moines, Iowa. I could have gone to a million places, but I knew I didn't want to stay on the East Coast. I wanted to stay where it was warm. I didn't want to go to Harlingen or Brownsville [Texas] because it was too close to our condominium on South Padre Island."

As it happens, El Paso wasn't so random a choice; it was actually perfect for what Jay wanted to do. He had been there only one time in his life, on his way to California while he was still in college, and he didn't know anything about it except for one thing—the only thing that now mattered to him. Since it was on the border, he could walk across the bridge into Juárez, Mexico, without having to show his passport. The notion of possibly spending a year or so in a country he had visited many times and loved was even more irresistible to Jay than the price of his ticket.

Having no idea where to stay in El Paso, he wound up checking into the TraveLodge, and soon drifted into a place called Moriarity's—the first step of his journey into a world that was as far removed from the one he had left five days before as he could ever have imagined, a world he wanted to be a part of.

ON TUESDAY MORNING, the first thing Jay did was go searching for a bank. Needing to find someplace to protect the huge amount of cash he was carrying, but with no way of proving that he was who he said he was, he quickly discovered that he couldn't open an account. After a few anxious hours of trying to charm every teller in El Paso, he eventually found a woman at Continental who was willing to give him a safe-deposit box (where he also put his passport and driver's license). He couldn't gain any interest on his money, but he didn't care. Survival and freedom were all that mattered.

Not far from the bank was a YMCA on Montana Avenue. Jay had an affinity for Y's that was nostalgic and genuine. He had stayed at one in New York when he went there with Marilyn Southwell, and when he played in the bridge tournament with Jean

McDonald. But even more important than those memories was that the Y was in keeping with the kind of simple, spartan life that he had lived at one time and now wanted to return to.

And so less than a week after he had left Green's Inheritance he found himself in a second-floor room that, for $160 a month, provided him with a narrow single bed, a thin mattress, a reading light, a desk, two chairs, two threadbare towels, and one minute bar of Ivory soap. The bathroom and shower were down the hall. If he closed his eyes he could have been back in his trailer behind Dick Fuchs's service station. But he was in El Paso and, despite what he had said about never wanting to return to Texas, relieved to be there.

After nearly twenty-five years of getting up in the morning, putting on a coat and tie, and going off to work, he stopped shaving altogether and lived in jeans and tennis shoes. His fear of being caught aside, knowing that he could do whatever he wanted (essentially nothing) filled him with a feeling of luxury that belied his surroundings. Among everyone from down-at-heel transients and teenage runaways to European students exploring America, from widows without money and free spirits working odd jobs to men whose wives had thrown them out of the house, Jay found himself in a situation that was as unfamiliar to him as it was exciting.

As he quickly discovered, El Paso was perfect for more than just a good and easy way into Mexico. It was perfect because Jay had landed in a place where he could be whatever—and whoever—he wanted to be, where he could begin, once again, to seek and search.

El Paso is a place that defies easy labeling, a place that is wild and wide open and always in flux, a place where, someone said, "a person is still admired for figuratively standing in the middle of Main Street at high noon and drawing his gun." Unlike much of Texas, it is not dependent on oil or cattle, and is as different and isolated from a city like Houston as it is from Stuttgart. Being a border town (the world's largest), El Paso has a rootlessness about it, a feeling of anything goes (and literally everything does) that was ideal for a man in Jay's position. Because most people either seem to come to El Paso from somewhere else, or, once they get there (to smuggle drugs, among other commodities), don't seem to stay very long, Jay had arrived in a place made up of so many cultures that he could reinvent himself without ever being too closely questioned by anybody.

And even though he had something to hide, by landing in a city where lithium in the water supply serves as a natural relaxant and no doubt contributes to the general philosophy of mañana, where the very existence of roughly one out of every five households (in El Paso–Juárez) was dependent on some form of illegal activity, Jay would come to feel that he had plenty of time to figure out what he was looking for, among people who accepted him on whatever terms he chose, who themselves perhaps had a past—or a present—they preferred not to talk about.

BOB HARNED WAS one of the first people Jay got to know in El Paso. Four months older than Jay, he worked as a night auditor at the Y and spent a lot of time at Moriarity's, a bar-restaurant whose patrons, Harned said, could have been a stand-in for the crowd at the Dixie Hotel in the stories of Damon Runyon, a curious mix of "dropouts, has-beens, judges, and lawyers."

Harned fell into the first category. He had been an executive with Goodwill Industries in Ohio when he decided to leave his sixty-thousand-dollar-a-year job and marriage (his third) and move to El Paso. He also abandoned his part-time practice as a psychometric psychologist because, after twenty-four years, he couldn't "tell the difference between the nuts and me." He didn't disappear, but he had clearly turned his back on the life he had known, on a life that he no longer felt in control of.

For that reason as much as any, Jay and Bob became friends. Yet Bob knew very little about Jay Martin Adams and he didn't care. All he knew was that "Jay was the type of person you could sit down and talk to. He was a little different from anybody else. You enjoyed him. I never met anybody that didn't think that. He was conversant on just about any subject, and if he wasn't, he could bullshit his way through it.

"He knew way more about me than I ever knew about him, but that didn't matter to me. He said that he was from Chicago, and had gotten a Ph.D. there, and had a child there. I didn't know whether it was a smokescreen or an attempt for acceptance. He so much wanted to be accepted for himself that it seemed he would go out of his way to 'come down.' I remember that he wore the same sort of outfit every day—Levi jacket, workshirt . . . must have had seven or eight of them . . . Nikes, and blue jeans—and he felt himself to be a derelict. In fact, he wanted to be the best derelict, president of the ADA, the American Derelict Association. He would say, 'We're not only derelicts, we're *American* derelicts, we're dropouts, burnouts.' That started the ADA. In order to join, you had to have made it—gotten a master's degree or made a lot of money—and then dropped out."

Even though Jay had moved geographically, his pattern of behavior was unchanged, only underscoring that a person takes himself with him wherever he goes. In his need for acceptance, Jay not only put himself once more in the position of being someone people found they could easily talk to and confide in, someone who could solve their problems, but the rainmaker in him began doing other things to create an aura about himself that people found titillating.

In one of my previous lives soon became the opening line that Jay would use in Moriarity's and the Back Door (a more bohemian bar nearby) in his desire both to blend in and to remain apart. He would hint that he had worked for the Central Intelligence Agency, that he had lived in many different places, that he had a variety of aliases and at least four passports. "As long as people could fantasize about Jay," Harned said, "as long as he had that mystique, they were fascinated. It's like having a big bubble. You don't want to burst it. They didn't want anything to take away from Jay."

In going to El Paso, Jay was not only still playing a role, but ironically he had managed to become what he had willingly allowed Nancy to be for so long—the center of attention.

"THERE IS NO question that I was promoting an underground image," Jay said with a devilish smile. "When you start talking about travel, you don't have to say what you've done. People start assuming things. I'd weave some pretty interesting stories. And by not denying anything, before long it becomes an incredible fantasy. In order to destroy the image, you have only to talk specifically about who you are or what you did.

"In Southern Maryland, the first thing everybody asks is what you do. It's almost like they next want to ask how much money you make, how many cars you have in the backyard. But in El Paso, and this was the great thing about it, people accept you without having to know the kind of Scotch you drink, and the hypocrisy goes out the door.

"Frankly, I was amused at how easily I could build up my image, and your temptation is to leave the string going."

Fun aside, though, was there any truth to the rumor that his disappearance might have had either something to do with the audit going on at NOS at the time he left—or something to do with work he was doing for the CIA?

The answer to the first part was an emphatic no. He reiterated that he would never have done anything to knowingly break the law and jeopardize the way out that he took. The reason he was so paranoid about being caught, about his name's popping up on a computer list of Missing Persons or on a flier at the post office, was that he thought "they could pin desertion" on him.

As for the second part, he just flashed another puckish smile.

. . .

WHEN JAY WASN'T at Moriarity's or the Back Door being a man of mystery, lending people money, discussing everything from sex and nuclear energy to the Soviet Union, and continuing to drink heavily, he was exploring Mexico in a way that he had never done with Nancy. Stopping in whorehouses in Chihuahua and speculating in gold and pesos, he was, as he put it, "experimenting in some other lifestyles." As much as he had come to like El Paso, he did not think of it as a place he wanted to stay for very long and began considering other options—teaching English to Mexicans in Chihuahua or becoming fluent enough in Spanish that he could live in Central or South America without sticking out too much. Beyond that, Australia continued to remain an alluring possibility.

When he talked about promoting an "underground image," he was talking about more than just the aura surrounding him. Rightly or wrongly, Jay came to feel that as long as he was Jay Martin Adams he could only live in one of three different ways—all of which were "underground," all of which intrigued him.

"When I cut up those credit cards in San Diego," he said, "I threw away a biggie. I couldn't rent a car—unless I put down a thousand-dollar deposit—and I couldn't get health insurance. How mundane can I be? On the other hand, I was so healthy I couldn't stand it. But the thought that I might end up in a welfare hospital if something happened was interesting to me psychologically. So one set of underground is the derelict underground. You're homeless and you're broke and you're living off Salvation Armies and you're really in bad shape."

Convinced (at least initially) that he had to "hit bottom" and become a derelict before he could regain his equilibrium, Jay did his best to become a full-fledged member—until something happened at Moriarity's to change his mind. Sitting at the bar one day in an unshaven, sleepless state, he couldn't help but overhear two women say that they were never going to come back in there if "bums" like Jay were allowed to patronize the place as well. Amused yet shamed by their comments, he immediately went back to the Y to clean up and change his clothes, something he hadn't done for a few days. And though he didn't return in his Pierre Cardin suit, the life of the American Derelict Association was a short one indeed.

The only way, Jay realized, to live under an alias and do the things that most people are able to do is to exist in the criminal underground, something he was unwilling to become part of.

"You know," he said, "it's amazing how this country's got you trapped by your Social Security number. I got some identification with Jay Martin Adams, but it wasn't worth a damn. In order to get a passport and a new driver's license you've got to go down in the criminal element." As much as he believed in fate and the degree to which he felt it would deal kindly with him, he wasn't about to tempt it. Flying out of Washington that Wednesday and feeling confident that the plane wouldn't crash was a lot different from becoming a drug smuggler in Mexico. "If I had done that," he said, "with my luck the dogs would have been there that day."

It should be said, however, that Jay did test these particular waters, but not with drugs. Having gotten to Chihuahua by the same route that so many take in Mexico—the route of *mordida*—he was able to persuade a Mexican woman to smuggle some gold back to El Paso for him. But he quickly learned that it was easier to bribe your way in to Mexico than it was to get out. She was stopped at the border and his gold was confiscated.

On another occasion, he found out what dining alfresco really meant.

Bob Harned and he had gone over to Juárez for the evening, hopping from one place to the next, from the Kentucky Club with its mariachi band to the Felliniesque atmosphere of Paraíso. Bob and he had both had a lot to drink (their ability to consume liquor was one more thing they had in common) and they somehow got

JONATHAN COLEMAN

separated. They had driven over in Bob's car, but since Jay couldn't remember exactly where it was parked, he began weaving through the streets of Juárez looking for it.

He never found it, but found his way to jail instead—a jail with no roof on it. Having heard horror stories about Mexican justice, he quickly became acquainted with the police's version of standard operating procedure there: if you either have no identification or not enough *mordida*, they will take all the money you do have (except for one dollar) and throw you in jail. Since Jay had only twenty-six dollars with him at the time (hardly sufficient to interest the officer who stopped him) he was arrested for "loitering."

But as his luck would have it, he was released in the morning, found the car (he had the keys for some reason), and drove back over the bridge to El Paso. Nevertheless, it was too close a call. He hadn't come all that way to be tripped up over something so trivial. When he met up with Harned later that day, he was so angry that he warned Bob never to abandon him like that again.

JAY'S ANGER TOWARD him aside, though, Bob Harned (as much as anyone Jay met in El Paso), represented the underground that Jay discovered he felt most comfortable in, the underground of living minimally, of doing jobs solely for the purpose of having enough money to get by and feel unconstrained, not out of any grand design on power or push for prestige.

It was the world of Cynthia Clifford, the first woman Jay got involved with. She was in her early forties but looked younger, an Irish femme fatale, a poet from New York, a hard drinker, a woman whose tough exterior belied the hurt she had felt since her father abandoned her and her mother when she was fourteen. "Still living in the flower-child age" (according to Jay), she had no steady job, two children who lived elsewhere, a car which didn't run most of the time, and the courage to stand in the lobby of a Juárez whorehouse and deliver a lecture on women's lib.

It was the world of Phyllis Peterson, whom Jay began seeing

after Cynthia, a brilliant woman with a zaftig figure, a free spirit who had never married and who didn't drop out from anything but never really dropped in until she was forty and began teaching on an irregular basis.

It was the world of Connie Day, Phyllis's best friend, who had married young and had decided, in her early forties and long after her divorce, to become a nurse. Like Phyllis, Connie was boisterous and fun-loving, a woman with her heart in the right place. Her first encounter with Jay was at the Back Door, where she worked as a bartender. She had just dropped a chemistry course she was taking and was looking for sympathy from the regulars. All of a sudden Jay piped up, "Well, what's so hard about chemistry?" to which Connie responded, "Hey, who is this guy? He's not one of the group. He's a blowhard." Later, after Connie found a note on her truck that read, "Only People Who Make A's Are Allowed to Park in This Space," she realized that Jay not only had a sense of humor but was "a grain of rice who fit right in with the rest of the bowl."

It was also the world of a Midwesterner named Earl Sloat, known to all as Pancho, a true jack-of-all-trades and a master of most of them, who gave up a management job with IBM to run the Back Door along with his wife Carmen, a famous flamenco dancer whom he had met in Mexico City. And Allan Alexander, a sometime schoolteacher and writer who worked as a night clerk at a small hotel and dreamed of opening an espresso café right there in El Paso. And Mark Regalado, who taught art at the local community college but secretly wanted to rejoin the Merchant Marine and cast off again to sea, whose favorite expression was "Those who dance are thought mad by those who don't hear the music." And Paul Thayer, who had come from Rhode Island at the age of forty-four to take a job as an electronics technician at the White Sands Missile Range but who started his own equipment-rental business instead. And "George" Thayer, the woman Paul married, who was such a famous bullfighter at one time that her picture was a permanent fixture on posters all over Mexico.

And it became, of course, the world of Jay Martin Adams—

"travel writer," "CIA agent," "speculator in gold," all-around "man of the world."

BETWEEN HIS MANY hours at the Back Door and Moriarity's, his frequent trips to Mexico, his beginning to read books again (William Styron's *Sophie's Choice* and Martin Cruz Smith's *Gorky Park* among them) as opposed to "all that silly-assed technical stuff," and his going off to see the El Paso Diablos play baseball, he found that his fear of being caught seemed to diminish each day. In fact, his initial excitement and elation about "cutting loose" had now become excitement and elation about what he might do. "The thing that I found astonishing," Jay said, "after I had gotten out of the game of looking over my shoulder, was that I had absolutely no regret and no sense of depression and anxiety about what I had done."

Perhaps, but he was only speaking about the things he could control. His dreams were another matter.

FORTY-ONE

MY MOST COMMON ONE is *that I've got an airplane I'm supposed to catch. It will be a 3:30 flight, number 783, American Airlines to Chicago, specific time, specific place. I'm trying to get organized, but I can't get packed, I can't find my stuff, the car isn't working right, I get lost on the freeway and go the wrong way. But then it takes on so many flavors that I find myself trying to finish eighteen holes of golf before dark and I can't do it, I'm too slow. . . .*

Another one that I'd have, and continue to have about four or five times a year, is almost totally the same dream and involves either A&M or George Washington University, and I'm trying to get my bachelor's or master's degree, but I haven't been going to class. Suddenly, in the middle of the dream, I will say to myself, You've already done that, you're not in college anymore. But then I find myself going for another master's degree and telling myself, You don't want another master's degree, you don't need it, you've already got a Ph.D.

If his dreams of not making it were the ones that occurred most often, there were others, less frequent but far more threatening, which caused him to wake up in a sweat, flip on the light in his little room at the Y, and write them down.

243

. . .

I WOULD HAVE *what I call go-back dreams, long, involved dreams where I was walking around at the community college, but I wasn't back there as president. I was walking around the Arts Center. Fought like a son of a bitch to get it built—my last big hurrah. Not one of the most popular buildings in Southern Maryland to build by any means. Anyway, I was going to look at it and I was walking to the campus. I didn't want to be seen, recognized, or talk to anybody. But it didn't work. Some of the characters I would run into would really chastise me, say things like, You sorry son of a bitch, I always knew . . .*

Now of course that's the old guilt, nothing but pure-assed guilt, and it would really upset me, but the funny thing is I would have one exactly the opposite and they'd say, Come back. . . .

Another one had to do with a play we were going to put on at the college and involved a cast of thousands. Now whether I was acting one of the parts or not, I don't know, but the play was going to be performed on a kind of mound that sloped up and was half the size of a football field. The only other key actor in the dream was a woman, not a specific person, who was directing the play. It was the middle of the afternoon and we were supposed to put the play on the next night, so we're running around trying to organize a dress rehearsal and we're eating crabs and oysters and all the sort of junk that you eat in Maryland, and then after a while I'm just there by myself, and all of a sudden I see a bunch of ants trying to get into the sack with the leftover fish. And I say, Well, I've got to get this stuff out of here, and so I get a sack in my hands, but no sooner do I start crawling around than the sack falls apart and all the crap falls on the ground.

Now the gal that's the director had a house, and I go in the back door looking for a trash can but I can't find one so I get a brown plastic bag. I get back to the mound and the whole area is absolutely full of the varmints—not large rodents, but kind of like the big red ants in East Texas. I said, My God, we can't use this thing for a play, I'm going home, this is an infested area. Then I run into the guy who used to be my facilities manager and I say, George, you've got to take your troops up there, you've got to find out what's wrong with that thing.

Later that afternoon I go back and there's about ten bulldozers and they tell me that they're going to put a bunch of chemicals down there and try to get rid of the stuff. The guy says it's experimental, doesn't know if it's going to work or not, but that if it does there's a whole bunch of people at the Army depot that would like to use it. His exact words. So I think to myself, Gee, that's interesting. . . .

Anyway, I start to worry that the director hasn't gotten the message that the play needs to be canceled, so I go back to her house and realize that it is Nelda, the gal I used to know in Bryan, and I tell her what has happened, and she gets raging mad and starts throwing things at me— pieces of carpet, pieces of furniture. Now I knew that I wasn't the focus, that the focus was external, but all that kind of excitement in the dream woke me up.

The violence at the end of that dream, though, upsetting as it must have been, was mild compared with the one that followed.

Every once in a while I would have a scary death dream. I'm being killed by a knife, probably the way I would be most scared of going, somebody getting at me with a knife. And it will be so realistic that I actually will feel it going in me, or think I do. And I feel like I'm fading out. And my thought in the dream is, Shit, this is what it feels like to die. Now, when I come out of that dream, I'm soaking wet.

Drinking is part of the problem, I'm sure, particularly drinking late at night. But I sure am a dreamer and I've learned that dreams have got you. You're back there. You can't say, I don't ever remember those people or that place, because you dream about them.

Nancy was in a lot of the early dreams, quite specifically. I can remember one in which we were doing a party to raise money for something like an art festival or charity or some damn thing, and the gist of the dream got involved in what you served, and the complicated question of whether you were going to serve a meal with all the trappings or if you were going to do what I used to call heavy hors d'oeuvres, which meant that you didn't have to bring in thirty-seven caterers to do the job. And since other people were also going to be preparing food, my role in the thing was to try to find out what they were doing, because you didn't want to have a sit-down meal if everybody else was just having finger food. Anyway, I was out getting groceries and began calling from a car phone, people like Buddy Sprague and others, but when I got home, I was harangued for not asking enough questions and not getting enough information. So then I got mad and I said, Well, I'm not any good . . . I don't like to talk on the telephone, and I'm not the one that should be making those calls anyway. Why don't you go make those calls? I can't get the damn information . . . and then I woke up.

But when he did; it was with the knowledge that the person he was reporting back to was no longer Nancy.

FORTY-TWO

BACK IN MARYLAND that summer, Jay continued to be the topic of discussion. A front-page piece in the *Washington Post* gave the story a prominence that caused many people in the area to shake their heads in amazement. Wherever Nancy went, she was constantly asked if she had heard anything, and her reply was always the same—that San Diego was the last place he had definitely been. (Spencer Matthews's stepdaughter thought she had seen him at an airport there, but couldn't be certain.) "If I could just find him and talk to him," she told the *Post*. "I want to tell him how much he is loved and how much I need him."

In the meantime, she was continuing to deal with the legal and financial quagmire Jay's leaving had put her in. She withdrew as a member of the country club, depended on people to help her with everything from trash removal to cutting the grass, and fell far enough behind in paying various taxes that she suffered the embarrassment of seeing her name appear in the local paper. Despite what Jay had said on the tape to Nancy about his back pay, when Buddy Sprague tried to get the money for her he was told that the college's lawyer was opposed to giving it to Nancy, almost as if he expected to be hearing from Jay at any moment. Enraged by that decision, Nancy came up with another solution. If the college really cared about helping her financially, she told Louis Jenkins, why not make her interim president for four or five months? That suggestion was promptly rejected, and John Sine was formally given the position he had lobbied for seventeen years before.

THE COLLEGE LAWYER, it turned out, wasn't the only one who thought he would either be hearing from Jay or that someone must surely know where he was. Evelyn Coombs, the postmistress at Pomfret, was so certain that Louis Jenkins knew of Jay's whereabouts that she phoned his office, asked what she should do with Jay's mail, and was simply told to give it to Nancy. And around the same time, Joe Browning (who still owned a house in the area as an investment) was in the post office in Indian Head (where Jay also kept a box) and was confronted with the same question.

Jay might have been gone, but hardly anyone, it seemed, was willing to accept it, including Bob Schaumburg.

. . .

WHILE JAY WAS having his go-back dreams in Room 201 of the El Paso YMCA, Bob Schaumburg was having dreams of his own. For him the shock of what Jay had done was outweighed by the anger he felt that Jay hadn't either written him a note or somehow been in touch. Jay had been best man at his wedding, they had been close—at least Bob felt they had—and to hear nothing created a hurt so deep that Bob himself wouldn't fully admit to it (even though his wife and son did, with Bob sitting there). Bob would go to sleep at night, fantasize that Jay had called him, and wake in the morning convinced of it. Then, when his wife assured him that it wasn't true, Bob's feeling of disappointment, of being let down, worsened to such a point that his ten-year-old son was cautioned not even to raise the subject of "why Uncle Jay went away."

WHEN THE PHONE call came, the call she had waited for, Nancy reacted with the same numbness she had the day she received Jay's letter.

It wasn't Jay, but it was Sergeant Boone of the Maryland State Police. Even though he had explained to Nancy in May that there was nothing more that the police could officially do in terms of finding Jay, that didn't mean that if something drastic happened they wouldn't try to determine if it had some connection to him.

"Mrs. Carsey," the officer said, "I don't want to alarm you unnecessarily, but I think you should know that a skeleton has turned up near the Eastern Shore. We are going to check to see if it is your husband."

The wait between that phone call and Boone's next one seemed like an eternity to Nancy, even though it wasn't.

The teeth were not Jay's.

FORTY-THREE

O N THE FIRST SUNDAY of August, August 1 to be precise, Jay went to the Back Door with Connie and Phyllis. A few nights earlier the three of them had been sitting around talking about the "hippie days"—or more accurately, Connie and Phyllis had, and Jay as usual just sat there, firing questions without revealing very much about himself.

"You know," Connie said, turning to Phyllis but motioning toward Jay, "it's all kind of mysterious, don't you think, how this guy talks about Australia, and all his degrees, but is never very specific about anything."

"Yeah," Phyllis said, good-naturedly but serious at the same time, "that's what I've been thinking. Listen, Jay Martin Adams, or whoever you are, I've had enough. Shut up. I'm sick of you. I love to talk about myself, but you *never* talk about yourself. What's the deal?"

"Well," Jay said, thoroughly enjoying all this, "while you two were being hippies and smoking dope, I was a college president."

As with the other tales Jay had spun, Connie and Phyllis didn't know whether to believe him. But since their affection for Jay surpassed any irritation they felt, they didn't press the matter further.

But they did, that Sunday night at the Back Door, have a hand in changing the course of his life yet again.

UNDER THE BRIGHT light over the pool table, a woman in a tight jean skirt and halter top was on a run of good luck at a time when everything else in her life was going bad. Head of the city's Department of Aging and sharp as a tack, she was about to lose her job for political reasons. Her third marriage was on the rocks, and this was the first time she had been down to the Back Door in months. As she moved around and around the table, knocking one ball into a pocket after another, Jay found that he couldn't keep his eyes off her and asked Connie and Phyllis who she was.

She was Dawn Garcia, a good friend of Connie and Phyllis's, and when she finished playing pool she came right over and sat down. Not only was she aware that Jay had been staring at her, but she in turn was curious about who he was, not having seen him before. Since Phyllis had told Jay a little about Dawn before she came over, he began asking her questions about her job, saying that he had a lot of experience with bureaucracies and knew how trying they could be.

"Yeah," Connie added, "he's also worked for the CIA, he's been to Russia, he's done a lot of things. At least that's what he says."

When Dawn finally got up to leave, Jay did too, long enough to say that he'd like to see her again.

"All right," she said, not having let on until that moment that she had any interest in him. "Connie and Phyllis know where to find me."

. . .

THE FOLLOWING MORNING at about eleven-thirty Jay showed up at Dawn's office, but the secretary who greeted him was skeptical that anyone as scruffy as Jay would have any business with Ms. Garcia.

"Oh, she knows me," Jay said, "she'll see me."

"I can't believe she knows you," the woman said, "but I'll check."

As Jay sat there he could overhear the secretary say, in a tone of blatant disapproval, "There's a Jay Martin Adams here. *Claims* he knows you."

Knowing how proper her secretary was, Dawn could barely suppress a laugh. "Well, go ahead and let him in," she said.

"Hey, this is some office," Jay said as soon as he settled into a chair, then immediately stated his purpose for being there. "Would you by any chance be free for dinner tonight?"

"Not tonight," Dawn said, "but how about Wednesday?"

That would be fine, Jay said, but since he didn't have a car he was wondering if they could meet at the Stanton Room at seven.

The Stanton Room, Dawn thought to herself, that's a pretty fancy place for a guy who looks as if the source of his next meal could be in doubt.

"Great," she said, becoming more intrigued. Noticing that it was almost time for lunch, she found herself asking if he wanted to have a bite with her and he said sure, he didn't have to be anywhere in particular. But instead of going to a restaurant, Dawn took him to her apartment, introduced him to her dog, and fixed a simple lunch of tuna salad and avocado. Even though Jay had had two months to become accustomed to the casualness of El Paso, he was still astonished that she had taken him into her home just like that.

On the other hand, he knew very little about her—other than his feeling that she had a "field force" surrounding her that drew him like a magnet.

. . .

By Wednesday evening at seven Jay had on the Pierre Cardin suit he had bought in Houston, but it seemed that he was all dressed up with nowhere to go. Dawn had officially lost her job the day before and didn't show up as promised. By the time the phone call came, Jay had already had three martinis.

"Hi, this is Dawn," Jay heard when he picked up the phone at the bar. "I'm sorry I'm late, but I'll be there in ten minutes." On the other end of the line she could hear a sigh of relief so palpable that she was flattered.

If he had been astonished on Monday that she had taken him to her home, she was equally astonished to find him in a suit when she arrived. They drank champagne, ate salmon steaks, went dancing, and made their way back to her apartment.

But no sooner had they got there than she turned to him and said, "There's something I want to ask you, something I was meaning to ask you on Monday. Are you violent?"

"Why would you ask me something like that?" Jay said, taken aback.

"Why would I *ask* you something like that?" she said, then repeated herself. "Because I don't know who you are and nobody else seems to know who you are. You drink a lot, you don't answer questions, and you could be a criminal. Now I don't mind if you're a criminal as long as you didn't murder anybody. I'm not going to turn you in if you escaped, all I'm interested in is if you're violent. When you're a female living alone, you're always more afraid of the Mr. Goodbar person you might run into, and I've got to look after myself.

"Besides, there are some really peculiar things about you. The way you talk," she pointed out, "doesn't match the way you dress," but then, acknowledging that he was in a suit and cleanly shaven, added, "or the way you usually dress. For all I know, you could either be a bank president or a retired mailman fantasizing a romantic past for yourself."

Jay laughed when she said that, assured her that she had nothing to fear, but offered little else in the way of concrete biography.

"He was promoting this image of mysteriousness," Dawn said later, echoing what others had already noticed, "hinting at foreign intrigue, girls with broken hearts who had killed themselves because of him, women in other parts of the world. I didn't know whether to believe him or not."

And what Jay didn't know was that she didn't care about the truth all that much (at least not at that point), that his very image of mysteriousness was one of the reasons Dawn had already fallen for him. "Actually," she confessed, "I fell for him the moment I saw him. What really intrigued me the most was that when we first saw each other, even before we talked, he would be looking at me at the pool table, and our eyes would lock. That was a real strange feeling, something I'd only ever experienced once before."

That wasn't all Jay didn't know about the woman he couldn't stop staring at.

ALMOST FROM THE moment Dawn Peacock was born in Kentucky in 1944, she displayed a streak of independence and rebelliousness so fierce that her parents learned early on to keep a respectful distance from her. "She'd tell me where the cow ate the cabbage," her mother recalled, "and what I could do about it. You simply *don't* tell Dawn what to do. Never could."

Her mother should know. The headstrong quality that she described had come from her, a Kentucky girl from Frankfort, reared among the bluegrass in a house next door to the one that Robert Penn Warren wrote about in *World Enough and Time*. Her given name was Ann, but she answered more readily to "Anna B." and "Sister." Nineteen at the time she met F. Roscoe Peacock one October day in 1942, she was a nurse and he was in the Army at Fort Knox. Even though he was eleven years older, she was determined to marry the soldier who shared her love of music and nicknames, and, four months later in the little town of Vine Grove, she did.

Not long after that, Roscoe (a.k.a. "Peak" or "Pete") was driving to New Mexico, where he was from, and as he passed through Texas, the first sign he saw welcomed him to Dawn, and that was how his only daughter got her name. The family moved to Honduras for a while (Roscoe worked on banana plantations for the United Fruit Company), back to Kentucky, and then on to Mexico City, El Paso, and Carlsbad, New Mexico, before settling in Las Cruces, where he got a job as a supervisor of housing at New Mexico State University. By that point, the Peacocks had three children to support and their many moves and lack of money had put a strain on their marriage, a marriage that strikingly resembled Homer and Bea Carsey's.

Dawn was a straight-A student in high school, an obsessive reader and a snappy piano player, but no sooner had she begun college at New Mexico State than she became pregnant and married Michael Ritchey, a tall, brainy young man from East Texas who loved jazz, studied physics, and read Einstein for fun. By the time they moved to El Paso, he owned close to ten thousand records and was making a living by advising radio stations about what music they should play and servicing jukeboxes.

When the marriage officially ended in 1968, Dawn had already met and was planning to marry a doctor named Lee Morton, a thirty-nine-year-old bachelor whose hobbies were making banjos and engraving precious stones and who was so reclusive that the windows of his house were painted black. Because he had polio as a child he was very pampered by his parents, and as Dawn soon realized, very set in his ways. Nonetheless, he officially adopted Dawn's son, Cody (who changed his name to Morton), and was, according to Dawn, "a wonderful human being." But the marriage lasted only four years, marked by "constant stress." He fervently supported Richard Nixon, while she worked night and day for George McGovern. He wanted her to be a traditional wife and a respectable member of the community. She wanted to be involved in the community, but not drive the Welcome Wagon.

Besides, it's a little hard to play that sort of role if you believe yourself to be a witch.

It's hard to say exactly when the whole idea that Dawn might be a witch began, but it was not an idea that her mother tried to pooh-pooh. "Look," Anna B. said, "I have a sister and an aunt who think they are witches, too. Maybe I'm a witch and don't know it." But when Dawn and her mother are talking about witches, they are not thinking of evil, malicious figures, but people with the ability and instinct to ferret out your darkest secrets, to guess at what you're thinking, to "emotionally and psychologically seduce you" (in the words of one of her close friends, who said she loved Dawn but was afraid of her too).

By the time Dawn married her third husband, Bob Garcia, in 1978, and moved into his house with Cody and her black cat, she had been single for six years. She had graduated from the University of Texas at El Paso, taught medical sociology in Juárez and ESL (English as a second language) in a government program in El Paso, worked for the state Department of Public Welfare, and had begun to focus her energies on the Department of Aging.

Like Lee Morton, Bob Garcia was older than Dawn (by fourteen years) and wanted to possess her. Married once before, he had two daughters—and a capacity for jealousy that was as great as Dawn's need of independence. What drew her to both men was something she was not fully conscious of at the time, the same something that brought Jay to his sister's rescue and fixed him in the role of father confessor to so many people after that. More than any deep love Dawn felt for Lee Morton and Bob Garcia was the fact that whenever she could hear a cry for help she would respond. But once that need was met and she felt unreasonable demands being made on her, she would begin to feel bored and restless, to lash out like the caged tiger she felt she had become. And the moment it happened she knew it was time for her to move on, to seek and search once again in her own particular way.

"Dawn cannot stand an easy life," her mother said. "Pete and I told Lee and Bob time and again, 'We can't *make* Dawn stay with you.' She would always be happier with the men in her life *before* she married them. Now you take Lee. I like him, he's my doctor, never even charges me. But he was thirty-nine and had never been married. Had some strange, weird habits, like those black windows. And with the polio and all, I guess he fought everything he could not be. I told her, 'Dawn, don't marry that man. Just have him as a friend and lover, but don't marry him.'

"She didn't listen. Then she married Bob. He's a nice, nice person, but he had just gotten a divorce after a terrible, troubled, eighteen-year marriage. Now, she did a lot for Bob, trying to straighten his family life out, one of his daughters was always running around and didn't want to go to school. But all the while Dawn was with him, I told her that he hadn't gotten over what he had went through with his wife."

By the time Jay left Dawn's apartment after their dinner at the Stanton Room and the hours and hours of talking that followed it, she had told him of her marital history in a most cryptic way, but gave no hint as to what her next challenge might be.

FORTY-FOUR

OVER THE NEXT FEW WEEKS Dawn and Jay began to spend more and more time together. He would often stay at her place until four in the morning, but then she would insist that he go home, saying that she didn't want to get a reputation, either for her son or in the neighborhood, as someone who had men move in for short stretches of time. Strength, as Jay was finding out, was something Dawn had; having control ("needing to dominate," her son said) was of interest to her.

She told him that she was going to be honored by the Women's Political Caucus at a big dinner and he asked if he could go. Dawn said that would be fine, provided he wore that same nice suit and behaved himself. She was going to be in her "straight world," she told him, and she couldn't risk having him embarrass her.

Not only did he not do that, but every woman at the table was charmed by him, and some even kidded Dawn that if she ever lost interest in Jay, she should let them know.

The following day Jay and Dawn went off by themselves to Cloudcroft, New Mexico, a peaceful spot in the mountains about an hour and a half from El Paso. The trip was his idea, and it came about for a couple of reasons, his disappearance not having diminished his pragmatic side one bit. He wanted to be alone with Dawn for a few days, to be away from her son (whom he liked, but whose presence in the house created an unfamiliar and uncomfortable situation for Jay), and to see, as Dawn said, "if I was decent in the morning."

But if the trip to the Spruce Cabins in Cloudcroft was a "testing ground" in Jay's mind, a barometer of whether Dawn was someone he wanted to be with for more than a few hours here and there, he also saw it as a challenge.

AROUND THE TIME Dawn met Jay she had made plans to visit some friends in New York at the beginning of September, with the possibility looming that she might decide to find a job there and stay indefinitely. She didn't tell Jay about this until a day before the dinner that honored her, and that was why the trip to Cloudcroft happened when it did. Despite his claim that "the last thing I wanted in August of 1982 was to have a one-on-one monogamous relationship with *anybody*," he seemed to be well on his way to having just that—or trying to.

"I was severed from work, severed from my marriage, and, for the most part, severed from my son," Dawn said. "I had sent him off to college and even though he came back and went to UTEP, he was big and didn't need me to stay home with him anymore. So I was getting ready to do the ultimate, which is say bye-bye to friends and family, and go off to New York to have my own non-monogamous life."

Because Dawn knew so little about Jay at that point, she had no idea that in her own way she was about to do what Jay had done three months earlier, albeit far less dramatically. And even though, as he realized, "Dawn was easier for me to get to know than I was for her because she was being herself," Jay didn't fully appreciate the position she was in—a position not unlike his own.

"He thought something about it," Dawn said. "He thought about losing a job, said, 'Yes, I know what you feel like,' a couple of references like that, but he hadn't really put together that all of my strings were being cut, even though my marriage and my son were voluntary ones."

Deciding that she wanted to keep this particular string with Jay going should she decide to return, she gave him the key to her place and said that if he felt like just going over to listen to records he should. But even though their trip to Cloudcroft was a success and he was pleased by her offer, he didn't feel confident that she would come back. Instead of coming right out and telling her that, though, or even trying to persuade her not to go, all he said was that he wasn't about to go to the East Coast, that it would be a "very difficult" area for him to live in.

And so the mystery of Jay Martin Adams continued, while the newest phase of his life was about to begin.

FOR THE BETTER part of late July and all of August, Jay had been driving around El Paso with the idea of doing what he had told John Sine a year before they ought to do in order to be happy. But John was unavailable to tend bar, so Bob Harned took his place.

Jay and Bob had come up with the plan one night at Moriarity's. Not only did the idea of being a small businessman intrigue Jay, but he realized that he could do it under his assumed name, provided he had someone who could front the paperwork. As it happened, there were a lot of bars for sale in El Paso at the time they were looking, many of them on and around Dyer Street, an area of fast-food chains, by-the-hour motels, pawnshops, tattoo parlors, and topless bars that catered primarily to the military men stationed at nearby Fort Bliss, the largest air defense center in the free world. No military base on the globe, it seems, from Athens, Greece, to Anniston, Alabama, is without its Dyer

Street, and any time spent on one of these avenues of endless neon and women hawking their wares seems virtually interchangeable with time spent on another.

And so it was to such a place—TJ's Bar and Grill at 5810 Dyer, with its red door and misleading sign encouraging you to ENJOY COCA-COLA—that Jay and Bob Harned found themselves on September 1. Jay had put up most of the money (a little over ten thousand dollars), Bob found a lawyer to draw up the papers in the name of Push Incorporated (inspired by a waitress at Moriarity's whose constant refrain was "Don't push me"), and the two of them moved out of the Y and rented a small apartment in the back.

If the world of the Back Door was representative of the underground Jay felt he could live in, the world of TJ's struck Jay as a colony of lost souls.

"How can I put it?" Jay said. " 'Archie Bunker's Place' is not what it is. The Pan Am Clipper Club is not what it is. And it sure as hell is not 'Cheers.' It's like a VFW, with mostly retired military guys or their widows. We didn't get too many of the young GIs looking for gals, because we didn't have topless dancing.

"So these old guys"—guys with names such as Hushpuppy and Curly, who had scrawny, half-starved dogs—"would come in and sit there, sucking on a pitcher of beer for three hours and tell you all their war stories. Since you're around people all the time, there's a certain gregariousness to running a bar. *And* you can play a fantasy world with it, especially when you're under an assumed name."

If his ability to dissemble was one of the things Jay liked about his new profession, there was much that he quickly discovered he didn't. For one thing, the hours were crushingly long. He would work every other day from ten in the morning until two the following one. For another, his mild-mannered, nonconfrontational nature would be severely tested when he had to arbitrate any differences of opinion that might arise. One time, some young officers were playing pool and a fight suddenly erupted. When Jay went over to break it up, he felt the sharp whack of a pool cue across his back. Stunned as he was by the blow, he was still able to keep his sense of humor. "The problem with getting in the middle of a dispute among servicemen," he later told Harned, "is that there's *always* so damn much paperwork involved."

But what troubled him more than those things, what dejected him in a way that he hadn't counted on, was that running a bar was agonizingly similar to the job he had left behind—or, perhaps more accurately, to the role he had tried to escape. "The repetitiveness of the lost-soul colony," he said, "is in itself as depressing as being a college president for seventeen years. Bartenders become psychologists. You listen to everybody's story. You consult. You try and help them with their problems. That was one of my weaknesses. I was too fucking softhearted. I must have loaned money to five or six people, and when some of them died, I went to their funerals."

But wasn't he, in his own way, as much a lost soul at that point as he felt they were?

Yes, he said, he was, but with one major difference: "They are who they are. They come in and say, 'I'm Tom Johnstone, retired from the military,' or they say, 'I'm GI Joe and I'm looking for a lay.' Or they want to know if they can buy drugs."

Slowly, though, Jay began to give hints of who he was. He told Tom Johnstone that he had "walked away from a lifestyle back East which he couldn't handle anymore." He didn't elaborate and Johnstone didn't press him ("I learned in the military to let sleeping dogs lie. Too often, if you wake them up, they bite you"). He made mention of Jean's death to Paul Thayer in the most general terms, but it was enough "to change his expression and tone of conversation completely," Thayer recalled. "He wasn't the grinning, happy-go-lucky Jay for a couple of minutes." He told Bob Harned of "hating the house where he lived, the situation he was in, having to raise money, being scheduled seven days a week.

"I had a hard time, frankly, believing that last part," Harned said, "because I felt he was basically a lazy guy. But I only half-listened. As I said, I preferred his mystique to any details that might burst the bubble."

FORTY-FIVE

"I THINK THERE'S SOMETHING you ought to know," Jay said. "Jay Martin Adams is not my real name."

Dawn had come back to El Paso, only for him, and was standing right next to Jay, trimming his beard, when he confirmed what she had already guessed.

"So what else is new," she countered. "Everyone's figured that out already."

Unsure whether she was kidding him or not, he continued.

"My real name is Julian Nance Carsey."

"Oh, that's a good name to choose," she said, continuing to trim.

"No, it really is," he said, reaching into his back pocket for his wallet. "I've got a driver's license to prove it."

She took the license from him and looked at it carefully.

"Nice. How much did this one cost you?" she asked, recalling that he had mentioned a number of times how easy it was to come by items like this.

Jay was becoming a bit exasperated, but he couldn't really blame her. He had told her (and everyone else, for that matter) a wide range of stories, and she didn't know what to believe.

"I just dismissed it really," Dawn explained. "But he said no, no, and he kept insisting. So I said, 'Okay, if that's what you want your name to be, that's all right.'" But aside from asking if he was violent, if he was in any trouble or danger—she did tell him that she didn't care what he did as long as he didn't sell guns to right-wing governments—she didn't probe in any serious way. All their exchanges, up to the one about his real name, had been light-hearted. When she had brought up the issue of selling arms, he had said, "I've already been that route. I don't have to do that again." When he told her that he had been to Russia, she had asked if he was there for the government. "I might have been," was his reply. Or was he just on vacation? Same answer. Or was he a spy? "I might be," he had said. "Somebody might be after me."

Not only did Jay feel that Dawn was not crowding him in any way, but the more diffident she seemed the more he wanted to tell her. "One of her qualities that I found really remarkable," he said, "is her style that suggests when the time comes for you to say something to me, you're gonna say it to me. Same thing about the foibles of life. Comes time to solve those problems you're gonna solve those problems. There's a sense of faith she has which is incredible."

Nevertheless, he didn't want to tell her everything (for the same reason, mainly, that she didn't want to pry; neither wanted to risk offending or scaring the other), but with each passing day, and without his fully realizing it, he came to rely on her more and more, to look to her for the physical and emotional life he hadn't had in his marriage and hadn't even believed he was capable of having until he met Jean in New York.

But with Jean there were no commitments and, from his point of view, no expectations. They were two people having an affair, living outside the law.

With Dawn, it was different. She had taken the first step, had returned from New York when he was convinced she wouldn't. And now he was making his own way toward yet another moment of truth, toward a woman whose big button eyes stared right through him when she spoke or listened, a woman in whose hands he could feel increasingly comfortable and nurtured, who had the uncanny sense of when to give and when to take. In all the ways El Paso had been a perfect place for him to land, meeting Dawn, it seemed, had been the most ideal of all.

But as much as he enjoyed being with her and talking to her, as giddy as she made him feel, he was still wary, still determined to test her whenever and however he could.

OVER THE NEXT month or so, Dawn began to introduce Jay to some of her closest friends, one of whom was Allan Alexander, the hotel clerk who had dreams of opening an espresso café. Though Jay didn't know it at first, Allan and Dawn had seen each other for a while when both of them were students at UTEP and Dawn was between marriages. Allan had not been in El Paso when Jay first arrived, but no sooner had he gotten back and gone to the Back Door than he heard that Dawn was seeing someone who had swept into town from parts unknown with a background equally uncertain.

Fiercely protective of his friend, Allan decided that he wanted to get to know Jay, especially since Dawn was so enthusiastic about him. So the three of them went over to Juárez one evening, to many of the places that Jay had already been frequenting, and soon after that, Allan suggested that the two of them take a walk. Dawn had told Allan little about Jay, other than her concern about the excessive amount he drank, and Allan, not surprisingly, didn't find out much more from Jay himself. But being with the two of them in Juárez had made Allan realize that Jay might indeed be the person Dawn had been searching for, and he came out and told Jay this.

"My sense," Allan recalled, "was that Jay was a strong, bright, romantic guy. Not necessarily as strong as Dawn, but far more interesting than her second and third husbands. I could see the two of them together in my mind's eye. Dawn likes a person that has a world of experience and is multifaceted, and I told Jay that he kind of fit that."

As GLAD AS Dawn was of Allan's impression, the thing that really struck her was how well Jay seemed to get along with her son, Cody. Since Cody had met a number of his mother's boyfriends and had experienced the breakup of her marriages, he took a dim view of any new liaison. Besides, he was more or less on his own by then, trying to finish his studies at UTEP and yearning to be a professional musician.

Nevertheless, he and Jay seemed to hit it off the first time Jay came over for dinner. "My first recollection of him," Cody said, "is his sense of humor, which was a lot better than most people's I'd met. He told me that he'd been in the Army and had traveled all over. Said something about working for the government, something to do with the projection of missiles. He was very easygoing, and I liked that. But to tell you the truth, I didn't take the relationship very seriously, because of my mother's track record."

Jay had always been good with his friends' children back in Maryland, advising them, playing with them, telling them tales both tall and real, and this was no less true of the relationship he was developing with Cody. They talked for hours, in passionate detail, about the respective merits of the Dallas Cowboys (Cody's favorite team) and the Washington Redskins (Jay's), and they talked about Cody's future plans. As Homer had with him, Jay cautioned Cody about the insecurity of a musician's life, but he said it in such a way that Cody felt it was the advice of a friend, not the dictate of a parent.

If someone who knew about Jay's past had stood outside the window of Dawn's little house on Randolph Street, peered in, and seen Jay and Cody together, playing with a dog named Peanut, he might have thought that Jay seemed so at ease in that setting that he wanted to be a part of it always, that he had found what he was looking for.

But as people back in Maryland had already discovered, appearances can be deceptive, and that someone would, for the most part, have been wrong.

FORTY-SIX

THE PLAN WAS as follows:
Jay and Dawn would go to Puerto Vallarta and stay at the Garza Blanca, a monument to luxury that he and Nancy had been to a number of times.

From the moment Dawn met Jay she had wondered how he was managing to lend money to people, buy rounds of drinks, and speculate in gold when he had no visible means of support. Then, when she learned that he had bought a bar on Dyer Street (a bad decision, she was sure) her curiosity was even more piqued. And now, Puerto Vallarta, the Garza Blanca no less.

Even though his "boodle" was dwindling and it took him only one month to realize that TJ's would be a break-even proposition at best, Jay wanted to deliberately put himself in a "high-rolling environment," one where he could find out if he was at all tempted by the way of life he had left behind.

But their trip there in the second week of November was also designed to be another test for Dawn.

The "vacation" began well enough. They settled into their villa, had a candlelit meal with much to drink, and then went to bed. As Jay turned off the light, he seemed, to Dawn anyway, relaxed and content.

But during the night he became increasingly restless and edgy. As he had for more nights than he could even remember during the last six months at Green's Inheritance, he got up and began pacing around, staring out the window, and pacing some more. Dawn didn't hear him at first, but then she did—heard the question he wanted an answer to.

"If I were to ask you to go away with me and promise that you would *never* have any more contact with your family or Cody, would you do it?"

She said nothing, not because she was hardly awake, but because the request had come out of nowhere, one she felt only a true lunatic would make. She was very close to her family, always had been, and even though she had intended to sever from them and her son geographically, that's all that meant. Why on earth would Jay think she would agree to something so irrational and blatantly selfish? Why would he be "so tacky," she wondered, to ask her such a thing?

But when she finally spoke she didn't ask him either of those questions.

"Fine," she said, turning on the light and gazing right at him. "Where to? When do we leave?"

Now it was his turn to be shocked. He never expected that sort of response. He felt sure that she wouldn't agree to being as rootless as he was, as rootless as he felt. Besides, he thought, she couldn't possibly love him enough to do that. He was certain that she would tell him to get out of her life as soon as possible. He didn't want her to, of course, but he was self-destructive enough at that point that he might have been relieved, at least for a while, and self-destructive enough to keep pushing her further.

"We'd have to go live in a foreign country," he went on, knowing that she'd never been to Europe. "You'd have to change your name, like I did, and live underground."

"Great," she said. "Let's leave in the morning. I don't have a job to go back to. Cody will be fine. And I've always wanted to travel more."

She was calling his bluff but he didn't know it. All he knew was that he was "living irresponsibly." He had "thrown away" his family, wife, house, and possessions. "The only thing I had to worry about from day to day," he said, "was whether I got up in the morning, ate, slept. The *only* thing I had to worry about was myself."

When he had been on the beach in Florida exactly one year before, he had convinced himself he would never again experience what he had with Jean if he stayed in the life and marriage he had. But he hadn't counted on meeting someone like Dawn so soon after his exit, and he didn't know whether to embrace her or push her away. That most of his clothes were hanging in her closet back in El Paso both pleased and terrified him at the same time. Even though he was clearly drawn to strong women, and Dawn had given him no reason to fear her, that was beside the point. He might say that he was living irresponsibly and couch it in negative terms, but he also said that he had few, if any, regrets about what he had done. After all, running from responsibility and commitment was as much a part of what brought him to El Paso as his hope of finding another Jean. As long as he could go on being Jay Martin Adams, he could run from himself.

Since Dawn so obviously posed a threat to his newly acquired independence, and since control was something as crucial to him as it was to her, he had no choice but to try and manipulate her into following his agenda, fuzzy as it was. That, at least, was how he saw it. But what he didn't grasp was that Dawn was not only strong, but far less needy and dependent than Nancy. With Dawn, the old pusher-and-junkie game wouldn't fly. That's why she felt confident enough to call his bluff and say that she would follow him anywhere. She felt fairly sure that he wasn't serious about it (and sure that even if he were, she'd be able to sneak out and make a phone call every now and then). "As far as I was concerned," she said, "he had been drinking heavily and not acting normally."

But it was the very fact that she had said yes which had the greatest impact on him.

"That was a real cross point in the relationship," he said. "If she was willing to make that commitment, then I was willing to accept the responsibility for being a professional, reasonably functional, sober human being again."

But wasn't it more complex than that? Wasn't the biggest reason for asking Dawn what he did somehow connected to his sense that had he asked Nancy something like that, her answer would probably be a resounding no? That her dependence on Jay would not necessarily extend to living on a sheep ranch in Alice Springs, Australia? After all, his note to her said that he didn't want to drag her down with him, and yet he was, to some extent, trying to do that with Dawn.

"If I'd have called Nancy from Alice Springs and asked her to sell Green's Inheritance and come out there," he said forcefully, "she wouldn't have come. Or she would have come for the sole purpose of bringing me back. That would have been a test, but an unfair one. After fourteen years, I knew what she would and wouldn't do. I could have said, 'Nancy, I don't want to do this president stuff. I want to go to Alice Springs and teach Swahili to the Aborigines, and we're going to make twelve thousand dollars a year. Let's sell this damn place, get rid of the jewelry, get rid of the cat and dog [both of which ran away shortly after Jay did], quit the country club.'

"She *might* have done it, but she would have been miserable. And I would have been miserable because she was. She didn't have the capacity to do that. As I've said, there was only one way to go and that was up."

. . .

BENEATH ALL THE rhetoric, though, all the talk of being noncon-frontational, was the distinct sense that something else was at work here, something that perhaps was buried as deep within his soul and psyche as he said his anger toward Nancy was, something he was not fully conscious of, but which had begun moving him toward the decision to leave long before he sat on the beach that day in November of 1981. The sense that his own actions, as much as his response to Nancy's and his growing disenchantment with his role as college president and the overall life he was leading, had put him in a position where he perhaps deluded himself into thinking that the way he left was the *only* way he could.

For someone as smart about money as Jay was, it didn't make sense that he would pay cash for the time-sharing units in Florida and borrow money when interest rates were exorbitant. It didn't make sense that he would allow their cash-flow situation to grow progressively worse and not discuss it with Nancy. It didn't make sense that he wouldn't urge her to begin working again (especially since they were not going to have a child) or make concrete sug-gestions for paring back and divesting.

But if he had done it any differently, or if he had agreed to adopt a child, or had chosen to consult full-time, or had focused harder on the college's problems, or sought counseling, or gone to AA in Washington as Nancy had pleaded with him to, or even if he had looked for and found another Jean—if he had done any of those things, he might have found himself in deeper than he was before, even more trapped and entrenched in a life and a marriage that he desperately wanted to escape.

Didn't it seem that his inability to open up to Nancy and others had as much to do with his total unwillingness to make that effort as any belief that he was emotionally shallow or any fear that she or anybody else would talk him out of what he was planning, as he claimed Joe Miller had that day in 1968? That by doing all the things he did and refusing to do others, he was painting himself into such a corner—the little box perhaps that Nancy said she couldn't enter—that the means he took were designed to justify the end he chose on May 19? After all, he was a chemical engineer, a man who passionately believed that Machiavelli was a great guy. Hadn't Jay on some unconscious level, *especially* on some unconscious level, been planning this all along, as a way of punishing both Nancy and himself, long before and much more severely than the note that deprived her of power of attorney?

If what he did could be seen, depending on one's point of view, as an act of weakness or an act of courage (or a combination of both), as an act of fantasy or an act of change (stemming from a need to survive), as an act of sanity or insanity, wasn't the one indisputable thing about his flight the sense that, like suicide, it was an act of hostility, a statement to which there could be no response?

JAY STOOD UP and began pacing, as he had in Puerto Vallarta. But Puerto Vallarta, or Alice Springs, for that matter, was not what he was thinking about now.

"You know, as I look back on it, I probably should have gotten out of the marriage four years earlier," he said, continuing to try to explain, as much to himself, it seemed, as anyone else. "And probably if it was *only* the marriage, I might have sorted it out in a different way. But to answer your question, I don't know that I wasn't building up to the decision without realizing it—particularly in those last two years after the Camelot days were over. Buying Green's Inheritance, for instance, could have been a psychological wish to reach the point where leaving made more sense than it would have meant otherwise. Or buying all the time-shares for cash and then borrowing money when interest rates were fourteen, sixteen percent. Maybe I *was* working myself into a position where the cash flow would be a problem. We had very few liquid assets. Everything we owned was property. So in order to make cash out of it, you've got to make the decision to divest, and I had come to the conclusion that was an impossible psychological problem for Nancy. But if I had confronted Nancy about the spending a few years earlier, let's say, it might have made it more difficult to exit the marriage.

"Or take the kid thing. I felt guilty about that. But here we go. How much of that was way down deep inside of me already—psychologically knowing I wasn't going to stay in the marriage? If we had had a child, and that child would have been under the age of eighteen, what I call kicking-out-of-the-saddle age, I want to tell you right now that I wouldn't have done it. That's too much guilt. . . .

"And one of my problems, partially, with the decision when I was conceiving it is that Nancy is dependent on a one-on-one relationship. Doesn't like to be alone. But I was absolutely convinced that the guillotine approach, in the long run, was not going to be any more painful than the other, and that is Rationalization 101. To be perfectly honest, I think my greatest guilt is that I don't feel more guilty in terms of Nancy. If you feel it's an act of hostility, I'm not going to argue with you. We already talked about the note, and I admitted that there was a punishment mechanism to it. But despite the complications of the estate—and I know this will come across as cruel and incredibly cold—I wasn't exactly leaving her with nothing.

"So I go back to what I've said. As bizarre and selfish as it may have been, the way I left was the only way *I* could have done it."

No SOONER HAD Dawn said that she would essentially follow Jay anywhere than he delivered some more news.

"Even if you go away with me," he said, "I can't marry you. I'm already married."

"Well, I thought you might be," she said. "But why do you think I would want to marry you anyway?" she asked, once again not knowing whether he was telling the truth, whether it was another one of his stories. (He had told her about Jean before they got to Puerto Vallarta, but she didn't know whether to believe that story either. "He told lots of stories, and the only way I could pick out the truth was to listen real hard. When some things kept repeating themselves, I figured that was the truth. Or when some things contradicted themselves, then I'd dismiss both versions. But my biggest concern was that the more I got to know about him, the more truth I found, the more dull he would seem in comparison to what he built up.")

Jay laughed when she said that, laughed because Dawn's sarcastic response to his presumptuousness was precisely the kind of thing he treasured about her.

But shortly after they returned from Puerto Vallarta, the laughing stopped.

FORTY-SEVEN

A	T FIRST GLANCE, Mike Cascio looks like a mad scientist for whom sunlight is a foreign country. In truth, though, he was another of the regulars at the Back Door and Moriarity's, an almost painfully shy man in his early forties who had come to El Paso from somewhere else, lived with his aging mother, and was pursuing a degree in computer science at UTEP. A friend of Connie Day's, Mike had met Jay a few times, was always impressed by how much he seemed to know about education, but never asked him why that was.

He soon found out.

One day in early November, Mike was at home when his mother returned from the hospital with a recent copy of *People* magazine, the issue of September 27 with Princess Grace on the cover. Mike was not a regular reader of the magazine, nor was his mother, who had picked it up in the waiting room and accidentally brought it home, where Mike started thumbing through it.

"When I first saw it," Mike recalled, "I didn't want to read it. I wanted someone else to look at it and tell me what the tone of it was. I simply didn't want to know something about him that might be derogatory."

The first thing Mike saw was a picture of Jay, dressed in a white turtleneck, his hair slightly windswept, his face shaven, eyes squinting toward the camera. It was one of the photographs that Nancy had made copies of, sent out to friends in different places, and given to the media. Above the photograph was the headline, A QUIET COLLEGE PRESIDENT SOLVES JOB STRESS HIS WAY: ONE DAY HE JUST DISAPPEARS; below it, a picture of the college's administration building. On the following page, there was a picture of Nancy.

When Mike's mother, who had never met Jay, read the two-page article at her son's request and told him that the person in question had not committed a crime, Mike was surprised.

"I just assumed that the only people in *People* magazine were either famous, like some senator or entertainer or the mother of quintuplets, or had done something wrong. Anyway, I remember reading the article and thinking how hilarious it was, the idea of someone kind of giving up everything and just running off. Now, maybe that's just my sense of humor, but that was my first reaction."

As amused as Mike was, he was shocked too, and didn't quite know what to do. He finally decided that he would drive over to see Jay at TJ's, slide the magazine across the bar face down, and leave without comment.

But when he got there, he was told that Jay had gone to Chihuahua and wouldn't be back for a day or two.

The following day Mike went to the university's library. Wanting to see if there were any other articles about "Jay Carsey," he checked the computer for "Missing Persons" and found something else: the front-page piece that had appeared in the *Washington Post* in June.

This was no longer so funny, Mike realized. He was in a quandary. On the one hand, he felt extremely uncomfortable "knowing anything about anybody," felt it was his responsibility to protect Jay's privacy. On the other, though, he felt "like Woodward and Bernstein."

For a week or so he did nothing, paralyzed by indecision. Then, as discreetly as possible, he began asking if anyone knew "anything out of the ordinary" about Jay, but learned nothing that matched what he had read in the articles.

Each night he went to Moriarity's and the Back Door he kept the pieces on the front seat of his car—until one night, his nerve fueled by alcohol, he came to a decision. He was going to turn them over to Ed Foster, another regular who just happened to be a newspaper columnist for the *El Paso Times*. Thinking that it might be "a story Ed could handle *and* keep quiet about," Mike made his way in Ed's direction.

But no sooner had he sat next to Ed at the bar, clutching the information in his hand, than he changed his mind, realizing there was no way Ed could just sit on a story like that.

Before leaving Moriarity's that night, though, the amateur sleuth showed the articles to someone else.

"I'LL NEVER FORGET that," Connie Day said. "When Mike gave that to me, I was really shocked. He said, 'Did you know about this?' and I just immediately downplayed it and lied, 'Yeah, I know some of it, not all of it.' He told me that he wanted to give the stuff to Ed—it wasn't malicious on Mike's part, he was just thinking more in terms of it being funny—but I talked him out of it, told him the man's not going around holding up liquor stores or anything."

Jay and Dawn had already left for Puerto Vallarta when Mike agreed to "loan" the pieces to Connie (whom he had a crush on), and as soon as she had them in her hands, she began to feel the burden of what they contained. "In reading all of that stuff, and especially reading that his parents in East Texas didn't know anything about it, my feeling was when somebody wants to get away that badly, they want to get away. If somebody's your friend, you're obligated to respect their privacy. If he wanted everybody to know what he did, he would have told everyone. He obviously didn't."

But she did decide to show the material to Phyllis Peterson, and together they considered going around to every doctor's and dentist's office in town and removing any copies of that issue of *People* they could find. And night after night they argued what Connie should do when Jay and Dawn got back. Phyllis was adamant that Jay had a right to know, that Connie should seek him out instantly and privately. As far as Phyllis was concerned, it took a lot of courage to do what Jay had done. "He just shot up in my estimation, and I already thought the world of him."

But as Connie listened to her best friend's opinion, her mind was elsewhere, focused on something she hadn't thought about for quite some time, hadn't, in truth, ever wanted to think about again—the stifling marriage she had been in, a life in Louisiana which produced a daughter, born at the wrong time and for the wrong reasons, whom she now only saw irregularly. "It's amazing," she said, "how something like this forces you to re-evaluate your life—your own sense of values, your own beliefs—to ask, 'What *is* my breaking point?' It makes you want to know the secret. There was no way I could verbalize it at the time, no way I could even have *thought* about doing what he did, but *that's* what I was feeling, that I wanted to walk out and never have to deal with any of that again."

JAY AND DAWN got back from Mexico on November 17, and the following night he received a phone call.

"Hi, Jay, it's Connie. How was your trip?"

"Wonderful," he said. "What's up?"

"I need to talk to you."

Since Jay was used to people needing to speak to him, he didn't press her on the phone, but assumed it had something to do with her daughter.

"Why don't you come by TJ's tomorrow morning. I'll be there."

Connie arrived about eleven and suggested they get some coffee. Jay told Hushpuppy to tend bar while he was gone, and then he and Connie drove to the Oasis, a few blocks away. She said nothing on the way there, and neither did he. But as soon as they sat down, he turned to her and asked what he had asked so many people so many times before.

"What's the problem, Connie? How can I help?"

"Well," she said uneasily, "it's a big one, *Julian*."

His face went white, her emphasis on his given name unmistakable.

"I sure hope this isn't going to be another 'Exit the Rainmaker.' I mean, here's all this stuff, Jay," she said, pushing the two articles across the formica table.

"Connie," he said, without even looking at them, "it's important to me that you know that I *never* would have done this had there been children."

"Hey," she said, hurt and offended that he would even think she might not understand, "I'm not your Acme Value Judgment Service. I'm not judging you or condemning you or anything."

A few minutes passed while Jay forced himself to skim the articles. More than the words, more than his utter amazement that

277

what he did had found its way to the front page of the *Washington Post* and into a national magazine, the thing that absorbed him the most was the photograph of Nancy in *People*. He kept staring at it and staring at it. It hardly mattered whose idea it was to have Nancy stand in the dining room of Green's Inheritance wearing the same low-cut gown and holding her hands the same way as she appeared in the portrait behind her. No, what mattered to Jay, far beyond her saying that if he were to contact her, she would join him, wherever he was, was that that picture told the story. That picture was now bluntly informing him that *nothing had changed*.

As soon as he looked up, Connie continued.

"Look, I kind of didn't want to show you this stuff, because I was afraid if you saw it you'd feel like you had to leave town. You're too good a friend. We don't want you to leave town."

"*We?*" he said. "Who else knows?"

"Well, I told Phyllis and Pancho," she said, quickly deciding it would be a mistake to tell him about Mike. "That's all."

"Look," he said, as calmly as he could, "I need to get back."

On the short drive there in Jay's beat-up white Volkswagen (purchased when he got TJ's), he began trying to explain, but Connie held up her hand.

"Look, Jay," she said, realizing now how important her approval was to him but irritated nonetheless, "if you want to talk about it, fine. But don't feel like you owe me some big explanation or that I'm prying or anything. It's just that that stuff about the detectives concerns me."

That afternoon, exactly six months to the day that he disappeared from Maryland and only one week after Dawn told him that she would go with him anywhere, Jay fled El Paso, alone.

FORTY-EIGHT

DAWN WAS AT the laundromat that day, reliving their trip, when the explosion came.

"It was about noon," she said, "and all of a sudden he comes roaring in, wanting to have the key to the house, said he had misplaced his, and needed to get something out. He was very agitated and I said, 'What's the problem, what's the matter?' and he said, 'Later, I'll talk to you later,' and he just rushed out again."

When she got home, Jay's clothes weren't there. He had cleared out all his stuff, except for a little file folder with his Army severance papers and his transcript from college.

She searched for the key to his safe-deposit box.

Gone.

She looked everywhere for a note.

None.

She drove out to TJ's and asked Bob where Jay was.

"I have no idea," Bob said. "Hush was filling in while Jay went to the bank, but he should have been back by now."

Connie was sitting at the bar when Dawn came in, but sa nothing, unsure of what to do, there for the same reason D was: they were troubled.

"Have you been to the back?" Bob asked, referring to t

ment he and Jay shared, even though nearly everything Jay had was at Dawn's—or had been.

No, she said, but when they went to take a look the only thing they found was a secondhand record player Jay had bought.

"Look," Bob said, "maybe he had to make a little trip or something. I'm sure he'll show up."

"I WAS JUST beside myself," Dawn recalled. "I stayed at the bar a long time before I realized it was Friday afternoon and the bank was closed. My first thought was he went to Chihuahua. Something had happened to scare him—whatever it was—and I was thinking of going to Chihuahua and look for him, but I didn't have enough money.

"I was really worried because I couldn't imagine what could be so bad that he couldn't tell me about it, that he couldn't trust me to know it. Or that was so frightening that he had to just take off that way. Here we had just had this perfectly wonderful week in Puerto Vallarta, everything was really beautiful between us, and then he up and disappears like that."

But on Saturday morning, after a night when she couldn't sleep, and her son, not used to seeing her rattled, told her that he had never seen her in such shape, a car arrived.

Jay wasn't in it, but an explanation was.

"When I saw you at the bar yesterday," Connie said, practically hyperventilating, "I felt so guilty, I was so worried, and Phyllis said I had to come tell you the truth."

"About what?"

"Well, I know why Jay left." As she had the day before, Connie produced the articles. "I knew he was upset, but he told me not to worry, that it wasn't important. He *never* said anything about leaving."

"I knew his real name," Dawn confessed, her hands trembling as she sipped black coffee, "and I knew he was married. But I sure didn't know about this."

After Connie left, Dawn continued searching for Jay in El Paso and asking questions. Crying was not something that came naturally to her, but she had begun to do that too. She considered going to visit her parents in Las Cruces, but thought better of it. On the few occasions she had taken Jay there the visits had not gone well, to say the least.

Sister and Roscoe were used to her bringing "stray cats" home, so it wasn't that. And it wasn't that Jay usually came there wearing old jeans and tennis shoes without socks, though that didn't help. No, it was something he did the first time he was there, almost as soon as he walked in the door and was introduced as Jay Adams, owner of a bar in El Paso.

He went right over to the Peacocks' liquor cabinet, pulled out a bottle of whiskey, and poured himself a drink.

"Why, he didn't even say boo to anybody," Sister said, adding that "nobody touches Mama's liquor and gets away with it."

Drink in hand, Jay proceeded to regale the Peacocks with what Sister called "big stories," as she and Roscoe just sat there, seething, feeling as if Jay were trying to take over the place. They didn't say anything at the time, but after Dawn and Jay left, Roscoe told Dawn that he didn't want her to bring Jay back anymore. It wasn't just the audacity with which he helped himself to liquor, he said; they simply didn't like him, and that was that.

But the following Sunday, when the Peacocks opened the door, there were Dawn and Jay—and a new bottle of whiskey that Jay had brought. That appeased Sister somewhat, until Jay took a copy of *Reader's Digest* and disappeared into the bathroom for hours. In Jay's defense, Roscoe had started needling him about how convinced he was that Jay had been a janitor somewhere, but instead of taking the bait, Jay said nothing, just picked up the magazine and vanished.

"He bothered me to death," Sister said. "He wouldn't talk to anybody, and then when he did he rambled so. He reminded me of one of my brothers who was in the Air Force in World War II and came home with battle fatigue. So I just went over and said, 'Jay, you know you're just like my brother and people think he's crazy.'

"Now this thing with the bathroom was something else. We have *one* bathroom, and he just stayed and stayed in there. I got so mad that I just went to the door and started asking him questions. He'd answer me, and then I'd ask him another. Finally, he came out, but then he took the magazine into the backyard with him. We were having a picnic and he just sat there at the table reading and I said, 'Roscoe, how rude can he get?' but Jay just kept on reading. So I kept asking him questions until he put that thing down."

The more Sister and Roscoe told Dawn not to bring Jay back to Las Cruces, the more determined she seemed to get them to like him. "She didn't pay any attention to her daddy or me," Sister said. "Just kept bringing him back up."

THINGS HAD CERTAINLY taken a weird and ironic turn. Not only did Dawn have the truth she partly dreaded, but she had some understanding of how Nancy, at whose face she kept staring, felt.

FORTY-NINE

"THERE'S NO WAY you can get deep enough in my psyche to know exactly what I was feeling," Jay said. "Relief initially, because the most important thing those articles said was that the police had investigated and decided I hadn't committed a crime. Relief that John had gotten the job, and relief that Nancy hadn't killed herself. A little bit of guilt, I guess, some sense from the articles of *How could this guy do this to Charles County and his wife and friends and mother and father?*"

But the main thing he felt was anger—anger that he had been "blasted out," anger that he had lost control of when he would become Julian Nance Carsey again, anger not only at the picture of Nancy, but at her closing quote in *People*, her sentiment that "it would be nice if he could give me power of attorney." Any hope he harbored that his leaving might force her to alter her way of life evaporated the moment he saw that picture and read that comment. He always said he loved strong women, and he was going to continue finding out just how strong Nancy could be.

"I never doubted, in November of 1982, that I was going to use my real name again, because I had already decided that the only way to stay under an assumed one, unless you've got a million dollars in a Swiss bank, is to go into the criminal underground. But it made me mad that the moment of truth had come and I was no longer in control of it. I had had a year [from the time he made his decision in Florida to leave] in which I was totally in control, and then that darn magazine came along. I mean, *People* magazine is a biggie in the sense that everybody in the damn United States picks it up. And when I saw that it said September, hell, I didn't know how many people in El Paso had read it. I figured that somebody had called the Washington area, fantasized that a whole planeload of people would be flying down to pick me up and haul me from El Paso. The thought of that happening absolutely petrified me, and my reaction was to get away."

That decision was significantly helped along, as it was in May, by alcohol. The first thing Jay did after he brought Connie back to her car and told Hushpuppy to hold the fort a little longer was get himself a fifth of vodka and drink it in about five minutes. He then went to the laundromat, got the house key from Dawn, cleared out the little he had, and headed for the bank. He had a little more than eight thousand dollars left in his safe-deposit box and took it all, as well as his passport, and headed west, thinking he might go to Phoenix or Albuquerque, check in at a Y, and "buy more time." It didn't matter that the articles said he hadn't committed a crime; the paranoia that someone from Maryland, or some private detective, might find him and even try to persuade him to return was a kind of pressure he was determined to resist.

"If there was ever a period," he reflected, "when my thought process was totally irrational, when I was close to crazy, it was those two hours between whenever Connie showed me those articles and I got into the car and headed out. The alcohol-crazed obsession was to get out of town and *then* pick up the pieces. I had to be out of town in the next two hours—before the plane landed and carried me back to Maryland."

But what about Dawn? Didn't he want to find out if she meant what she said the week before?

"I didn't want to . . . I wasn't at that time psychologically ready to put her through that. Maybe I was afraid she would say no. I don't know. It's hard to judge those kinds of situations."

ABOUT TEN OR SO miles outside El Paso, Jay stopped to pick up a hitchhiker, a young man in his mid-twenties with a beard and a destination—California. Since Jay had done a lot of hitchhiking himself when he was the same age and the fellow looked pleasant enough, Jay didn't hesitate to help him out.

Needing gas, Jay pulled into a self-service station in Vinton, right on the border of Texas and New Mexico. He filled up the VW, walked about two hundred yards to the window where he needed to pay, and returned to find no passenger in the front seat—and no black satchel in the back, the one that contained the eight thousand and his passport.

For someone who had talked about how important he thought it was to "hit bottom" before he could rise like a phoenix, it certainly seemed he had.

"SO THERE I was, forty-seven years old, drunk, no passport, no credit cards, sitting in the middle of the desert with forty dollars in my pocket and a Volkswagen which, if I took it to Albuquerque and hocked it, I could probably get four hundred bucks. Now you talk about sobering up. Took me about two seconds. I said, Well, this *is* the end of the road. I've got to really think through this."

But he didn't. He drove to Deming, New Mexico, got another quart of vodka, and picked up a woman at whose place he spent the night. By Sunday, he was back in Las Cruces, flat broke and out of options—except one.

. . .

ONE OF CODY'S friends was coming over for supper on Sunday, and by late afternoon Dawn was glad to have that to occupy her. Throughout the weekend, each time the phone rang she was sure it would be Jay, but each time it wasn't. Sometimes she would answer it, and sometimes Cody would, and it was Cody who picked it up a little after five that Sunday.

"Mom," he said, looking as if someone had died, "it's for you. I think it's important."

"Well, who *is* it?" she said, irritated that he hadn't asked.

"It's Jay."

She picked up that phone as if it were a lifeline.

"Where are you?"

"At a Best Western in Las Cruces, in the bar."

"Are you okay?"

"Not really. My car's not running, and I've got no money."

"Look, stay right there and I'll come and get you. *Don't go away.* I'll be there in fifty minutes."

Dawn had lived in Las Cruces and El Paso for enough years to know exactly how long it would take her to get there. She had made the drive along Interstate 10 countless times, but never with the urgency that would mark this trip. Figuring that if Jay had no money he was probably desperate for a drink, she put a bottle of vodka in the car and set off.

When she arrived he was where he said he would be, and she went right over to him and gave him a hug. He didn't say a word, not one, just rested his head on her shoulder and began to cry.

ON THE WAY back to El Paso, they said little. Dawn mentioned that she had seen the articles and said, as softly but firmly as she could, that he should never do that again. If he felt the need to leave in the future, that was one thing, she told him, but don't just leave without saying a word.

She took a risk in saying that, and she knew it. But Dawn was always one to speak her mind, and her not attacking him on the phone but coming there to bring him home instead meant more to Jay than words could ever express.

THE FOLLOWING DAY they drove back to get his car fixed, and they searched the area where he had been robbed, hoping that the young man had taken only the money and left Jay's passport—"my last link to identification that was important."

But they found nothing.

Jay did not return to TJ's right away, nor did he do anything else, except stay inside and, with Dawn's help, try to dry out. She gave him long, hot baths (to stop his delirium tremens) and protected him like a fugitive—the fugitive he thought he was. They decided not to tell anyone he was back (at least for a while), and he told her how afraid he was that somebody was looking for him. And even though she reminded him that the articles said the police felt he had committed no crime, his fear, however irrational, that he might be listed on a computer as a missing person was so great that Dawn actually prevailed upon a detective she knew to find out.

Jay's name was nowhere to be found.

THANKSGIVING WAS THAT Thursday and Dawn had in mind that a nice family dinner at her parents' house in Las Cruces might be a good idea. It was a risk, she knew that, but she felt it was one worth taking. She promised Jay that she wouldn't tell them who he was—at least not then—and he agreed to go. Just before they left she gave him something she had written, something, she hoped, that would continue to reinforce her importance in his life, his confidence in her love.

The Similarity of El Paso to Other Romantic Places
(for J.N.C.)

Caviar and vodka
in the Russian Tea Room;
Eastern Europe, that you loved;
and the ghost of a girl who loved you.

Memories eroding
in this hot border town
like the desert's gypsum sand
slipping away in a duststorm.

Except for her—again—
who listens lovingly
(accepting even truths), and
for your sake would study foreign ways.

And, for your sake, would
gentle your existence
with gifts you thought forsaken;
laughter in loving, song, and poetry.

ALL THROUGHOUT DINNER that Thursday, Sister couldn't help noticing how much attention Dawn paid to Jay. She had seen that quality in her daughter before, that response to other people's needs, but never with the sort of intensity and vigilance that she displayed that Thanksgiving.

"Dawn led him just like a child," Sister said, "told him what to do, and he loved her just like a little baby would his mama. To me, it indicated that he was very sick, because he was so meek and so quiet. He didn't ever object, didn't ever say, 'No, Dawn, I want to sit here,' or anything like that. He just got up and followed her when she said jump."

FIFTY

Dawn had not had a lot of time to think about the articles she had read, but enough, at least, to form some understanding of why Jay had fled from Maryland in the way that he had. As with the few morsels of detail he had given her *before* she read the pieces, Jay was less than forthcoming about this subject as well. Knowing that she didn't want to scare him away, she made a decision not to push him too much.

Just as he felt he had "hit bottom" that Friday in the middle of the desert, Dawn viewed his situation that way too. Not only was he drunk and without any money whatsoever, but "he had lost a little bit of his dignity," she felt, "and more than that, he was suddenly totally dependent on a woman that he loved and had reason to feel he might have totally alienated."

Part of the reason he hadn't was that Dawn felt sympathetic to the predicament he found himself in. "How would you feel," she asked, forgetting that her reaction was much different on the morning Connie came over, "if you picked up that magazine and the first thing you see is that picture, and the main thing you read is that the woman you were married to for fourteen years wants you to give her power of attorney more than anything else?

289

Now you tell me what the hell else there is in that article? If I had been his wife all that length of time and cared about him, there are just some things you make sure get printed and some things you make sure don't get printed. Now, I ask you, how would you feel?"

For one thing, the articles said a lot more than Dawn's comments would indicate, and she knew that. But her reaction did not stem just from her, but from the way Jay recoiled from the pieces as well, leading her to believe that the things that prompted him to leave were only barely touched on in the articles, were much deeper and darker and far more complex.

"You have to remember that we started in the same place," she said. "We were severed from work, severed from marriage, and had little money. What I got from reading those pieces and, slowly, from him, was the sense that he didn't feel loved for who he was, only for what he could provide. Now that may seem a bit harsh, but that was the feeling I had. I, on the other hand, was someone he could be himself with, and our life was this side of reality more than it was any other kind of pretending.

"I wasn't looking to him for support. Whatever money he had he put into the bar, and I was supporting us with money from unemployment, and borrowing it from my parents and my ex-husband. The hardest thing Jay had to face after he ran off from El Paso was that he had nothing. He had to face that before he could deal with anything else. Otherwise, how could any of it be honest, how could he deal with where he was, how and why he had gotten there, or what he intended to do, if he was unable to say that he couldn't afford a new pair of pants to go interview for a job?"

But forgetting Jay for a second, how was *she* able to reconcile his disappearing from Maryland in her own mind?

In the *only* way she could, she said. "I had to view him as a temporarily insane normal person. If not, then I had gotten myself tangled up with Bluebeard."

In a larger sense, though, she had to do more than just say she was someone he could be himself with; she had to believe, from that point forward, that she was an exception, that what had happened to Nancy could not possibly happen to her, even though he had given her enough of a scare that she couldn't erase the possibility from her mind with any degree of comfort. And even though Dawn was smart enough to know that no one is ever safe, not entirely, that at certain points in time we are all up for grabs, she was also sure that the more she could understand Jay, the more he could feel that she was not someone to fear, the more remote would become the chance that he would run off again.

THE NEXT STEP she took toward achieving that was having Jay officially move in with her, even though he had essentially been living at her place for months.

As of December 1 he gave up the apartment behind the bar. He went back to work at TJ's, but with the hope that at some time in the near future he would resume some sort of professional life as Julian Nance Carsey, having more of an idea of what it *wouldn't* be than any clear sense of what it would.

As of December 1 Dawn had shown Cody and her parents the articles, and she planned to do the same when her brother Frank arrived from California later that month.

That wasn't all.

Once Jay was told that his name was not on any computer listing of Missing Persons and his fear that someone was actively looking for him had lessened, he reluctantly agreed to Dawn's suggestion that he see Malcolm McGregor.

McGregor was one of the most prominent attorneys in El Paso, and since Jay did not want to be declared dead under any circumstances, he sought out his advice.

Dawn had spoken with McGregor ahead of time, and assured Jay that anything he told the attorney would be held in strict confidence. The main thing Jay wanted to know, he said almost as soon as he got to the lawyer's office, was whether he could arrange to get a divorce without leaving Texas.

"If I were you," McGregor said, leaning his poker face toward Jay, "I'd get the first plane back to Maryland, drive straight to your house, knock on the door, and when your wife answers I'd say, 'Hi, honey, I'm home. All is forgiven.'"

Jay cracked up. McGregor wanted to inject some levity into the situation and it worked. But once Jay regained his composure, he was all business. He told McGregor there was no way on earth that he would ever go back to Maryland, and McGregor told him that if that was the case, he was better off dealing with someone back East who could represent his interests while his whereabouts remained unknown.

As Jay thanked him for his time and left, he knew exactly who that someone would be.

FIFTY-ONE

WENDY BRUCK WAS the head of the Shelter for Battered Women in El Paso, a no-nonsense type who was one of Dawn's good friends. Dawn had told her a little about Jay Adams in the fall, but for one reason or another, she had not managed to meet him. On the weekend Jay left town Dawn had phoned Wendy, but aside from telling her that he had taken off and she didn't know why, gave no other details. But now that he had returned, Dawn was especially eager for Wendy to meet him.

When Dawn called and invited her over, she told Wendy of the change of circumstances (that she would be meeting someone whose last name was Carsey, not Adams), let her read the articles, and said that her only request was that she not ask Jay anything directly related to what he had done.

So by the time Wendy appeared for dinner in early December, she came not only as a friend whose curiosity was piqued, but a friend with deep reservations and concern about the situation Dawn had apparently gotten herself into.

When Dawn called her in distress just a few weeks before, Wendy had wasted no time in letting Dawn know what she felt ("Screw him and get on with your life" was her advice; better for him to vanish now rather than later) and she fully expected to meet "some wild-haired, off-the-wall kind of borderline crazy person." She knew Dawn well enough to know that what Jay had done would hold a special fascination for her, that Dawn would find "that kind of radical step" close to her own rebellious personality, and she worried that perhaps it was the drama of it all more than Jay himself that Dawn was attracted to.

Much to her surprise, she took to Jay instantly. "I just knew the minute I went over there that they were soulmates. That's not to say that I wasn't concerned that if he took off once, he might take off again, and I told Dawn that, but he just seemed to be so comfortable, so happy, so relaxed. You can't be an intimate stranger with Dawn. You're either going to be one or the other, and I just sensed that whatever he was escaping from, he wouldn't be able to escape from that with her."

Given her background in counseling and psychology, Wendy would have loved to ask Jay questions, but she had to be satisfied with just observing and listening, and from that she began to glean some things. When the discussion that evening turned to "the system" and bureaucracy and politics, specifically to Dawn's losing her job, she was startled by the anger he displayed, anger that she felt was "inappropriate," all the more so because Jay struck her as quiet and fairly reserved.

But his anger served a purpose: it made her wonder about the toll his previous life must have taken on him. "The more public a figure you are," Wendy felt, "the more power that you wield, the more you wonder if people like you for you, or if they like you because when they're around you *they* are in the spotlight."

Nevertheless, Wendy's initial feeling about what Jay had done, quite apart from how it might affect Dawn, was that it was a crazy, stupid thing to do, an act of desperation. "I kept thinking, Why would he leave all of that, come to El Paso, live in almost poverty, and work in a bar? If I had that money and that power and that prestige, I'd have figured out another way to do it."

As it happened, her saying that turned out not to be true, a mask for her own desire (most of the time) to leave her job, "pop out of sight," and reemerge as a nameless, faceless, blackjack dealer in Las Vegas. "As a director of an agency like the Shelter for Battered Women," she explained, "where the responsibility and stress is phenomenal and where people are depending on you—my staff depends on me to fund the shelter so they get a salary; the women depend on me to provide protection; the community, in a sense, depends on me to provide information to continue the shelter—you begin to think about what people would think if you left the job. What will happen? I don't want to see what will happen. One of the things I've said is, 'If I leave, I'm out of here.' I don't want to be in El Paso and see the shelter fold after everything I've put into it.

"Now, I go to Las Vegas a lot. I love to gamble. And so I sit and think, Wouldn't it be wonderful to go there, not know or care about any other people that are there, and just deal blackjack and have fun?"

So what was stopping her from doing that?

"My personal relationship with my mate is such that I wouldn't want to drop out of his life. But if that compelling reason was not there, I could easily understand just dropping out of sight."

She could easily understand it because she had already done it once. Not nearly so dramatically as Jay had, or even as her fantasy would have it, but it had changed the course of her life. She had been living in Las Cruces and was separated from her husband, sharing a house with a group of people whom she felt close to. But not close enough, it seemed, to prevent her from moving to El Paso without telling anyone—not at first anyway. Even though she "wanted to escape from a life," she eventually did tell the people she had lived with where she was, but asked them not to tell anyone else or to give out her unlisted number. The problem she had with Jay's doing what he did in the way that he did it, she kept insisting, was that he didn't notify anybody. The "hostility" of that, she said, was what would continue to bother her as long as he and Dawn remained together.

But that concern would be greater, she said, were it not for the fact that Dawn had qualities which set her apart. If Jay was testing Dawn when he ran off from El Paso, Wendy said, he had some surprises in store. "Dawn's the sort of person who wants to see how far she can go, how much you can take. It's something she needs. She needs someone that she can't predict what he's going to say or do. She needs something to push at. If she can't do that, she's bored. From what I saw [on that evening and others] she's not going to be able to budge him that easily. And that's good. But I promise you, she will go on testing him until the day he passes over to a new life, and she may follow him to test him there, too."

FIFTY-TWO

WHEN JAY TOLD DAWN what Malcolm McGregor had said, she had the same reaction he had had—a mixture of humor and dread. And even though they had both satisfied themselves that it was unlikely that anyone had phoned Maryland and said that Jay could be found for a price, Dawn and Jay both knew that McGregor was right. Hard as Jay found it to admit to himself, and as potentially threatening as it was to both of them, if Jay was intent on surfacing again under his real name, he needed to do some things.

But that didn't mean the call would be any easier to make.

When he first dialed the number there was no answer, and he was relieved. When he tried it again a few days later, late one Wednesday night, the eighth of December, the bouncy voice that answered "Hello" on the other end of the line was a familiar one.

"How ya doing?" Jay said, struggling to conceal his nervousness.

"Fine," the other person said slowly, unsure of who it was.

After nine in the evening, Dom Monetta usually unplugged his phone and didn't take calls, but since the phone was ringing as he came in the door he had picked it up without thinking about the time.

"What you been up to, Hoss?"

There was only one person who called Dom that, and he came from Texas.

"Jay, you sonofabitch, you have the audacity to ask me what I've been up to when you've been gone since the nineteenth of May?"

"Well, you know how it is."

"What do you mean, *how it is*?" At least Jay hadn't lost his sense of humor, Dom thought. "What's happening?" He was dying to ask Jay where he was, but was smart enough not to.

"Well, I'm just thinking a whole lot of things through."

"What do you need?"

There it was, the question Jay was hoping for, the reason he had decided to call Dom in the first place. Not only was Dom a good friend, Jay told Dawn when they were discussing this, but as a Sicilian he was someone Jay knew he could count on completely, someone who felt he owed Jay a lot, someone who could be the intermediary Jay needed. Jay and Dom dealt in a world of chits, and now Jay was calling his in.

"I'm going to ask you to do something that might be very difficult, and I want you to think about it before you answer."

"What do you need?"

"I don't want to be declared dead. I've seen a couple of articles. I want you to make a few calls to let people know I'm alive and well. You're probably going to have the media knocking at your door, and I'm concerned about the disruption that will cause."

"Well, I've been talking to a guy from CBS News named Coleman. He was down in Maryland a few weeks ago. But you know me, Jay. I'm careful. I won't tell anyone anything unless you and I agree on it."

Jay said he appreciated that, then asked Dom to phone the following people: Nancy, John Sine, Joe Browning, and Bob Straus.

"Just tell them I'm okay, recovering, and working things out," he said, then paused. "And that I'm not coming back."

That was not what Dom wanted to hear, but it didn't surprise him. Despite Nancy's telling him over and over that even if Jay had done this to punish her he would come back when he decided he had had enough, Dom was not confident about that. He wished it wasn't the case, but whenever Jay had embarked on something in the past, he never changed course.

"By the way," Jay said, as if he were asking about the weather, "how's Nancy?"

"Fine," Dom said, not wanting to go into detail, sensing that Jay wanted to get off. "But before you go, I'd like to ask you something."

"What?"

"When you said 'take care of Nancy for a while,' how long does that mean?"

The reason he wrote that, Jay said, was that he thought she might do something silly, like kill herself, after he left. By no means did it suggest that he planned to come back.

"Well," Dom said, "I feel I've done all I can do." What he didn't say was that he had faithfully phoned Nancy nearly every day since Jay had left, and visited her every other weekend. Not only did he feel drained by the energy he had devoted to her, he had become resentful. He felt that in doing what Jay asked he was giving Nancy a gift, but that for the past few months especially, she had begun defining the nature of it. Even though he preferred going to see her in Maryland (always taking a female friend along, so he could control the length of the visit *and* make sure people didn't draw the wrong conclusions), Nancy would often come into Washington and stay at his apartment. As he had always known, it was virtually impossible to say no to Nancy; and even when he tried to alert her to how he felt, it didn't matter. As skilled in the art of maneuvering as Dom was, Nancy's sense of entitlement was too formidable even for him.

On the other end of the line, Jay released him from those duties.

"So what happens next?" Dom asked.

"I'll call you in a few days, around the same time."

DOM HAD WAITED for this call ever since he returned from New Mexico seven months earlier and read Jay's farewell letter. He had worried and he had probed (himself as well as Nancy) and, most of all, he had mourned, mourned the absence of a friend whom he saw frequently and spoke to on the phone nearly every day. Once he knew it was Jay who was calling that night, what he felt, more than the relief that Jay was all right, was a determination to stay free of his own expectations, of any hope that Jay would come back. In telling Nancy that he thought she was wrong in thinking Jay would return, in urging her, almost from the start, to forget Jay and get on with her life, he was trying to protect himself as much as he was trying to protect her.

And it was Nancy he needed to call now, a call that he dreaded making even more than Jay had dreaded calling him. In order to make sure that he wouldn't be on the phone endlessly, he decided to try her from a pay phone at, of all places, the YMCA (where, as a member of the board of directors, he had to attend a meeting on Thursday afternoon).

Nancy had landed a temporary consulting job in education, and Dom was fairly certain that she would be at her Washington office that day.

She was, and he wasted no time.

It was not only May 20 all over again for Nancy, it was worse. Just at the moment when she had begun to find her feet again, however unsteadily, she was getting a phone call that not only reinforced what Jay had said in his letter to her, but was now being conveyed, in all its deadly finality, through someone else.

"Goddamnit, Dom," she said, barely able to hold the phone, "if you don't know where he is, at least tell him to call me when you next hear from him."

"Look," he said, sympathetically but firmly, "I will not lobby

Jay on your behalf. I've given you nearly seven months of unconditional support and now I want to give him that."

First Jay abandoned me, now Dom is about to. That's the way she looked at it—the only way she *could* look at it. She tried, of course, to squeeze as much information out of Dom as she could—she was sure that Dom knew where Jay was, even though Dom said over and over that he didn't—but Dom said that he couldn't stay on the phone because people were waiting for it.

He hung up, then she did. And without a word to anybody, she fled the building at One Dupont Circle and began walking the streets of Washington, streets that she and Jay had walked together, past stores that were open late and filled with Christmas shoppers. She stopped briefly and looked at a window. But instead of finding distraction she saw only a reflection of herself, nearly forty-six, still beautiful, and achingly alone.

"I JUST FELL apart again when Jay didn't contact me," she said. "I mean, this was a call I had waited months for, and it was from Dom, not Jay. I had been a yo-yo emotionally, and had just gotten myself 'up' again to do some consulting when this knocked me down. It was such a relief, of course, to know that he was alive, but when Dom said that he didn't want any more to do with me, that was such a shock. And I just kept saying to Dom, 'Why can't he call me? Why can't he call me? Why can't *he* say to me that he doesn't want anything more to do with our past life?' "

FIFTY-THREE

"As a female," Dawn said, "I think that was the unkindest cut of all. I felt he definitely ought to deal with Nancy directly and told him that. It troubled me that after such a lengthy marriage someone couldn't even deal on a personal basis."

And since it also troubled Dawn that Jay might never be hers until he was able to do that, even by letter, they clashed about the matter, one-way arguments that only heightened her determination to understand more about the man who was living under her roof, who would only say, "I got my message across. I *got* my message across. I didn't want to leave any doubt in Nancy's mind that I wasn't going back."

Much as he might have been trying to adhere to his hard-line, tough-guy, guillotine approach, there was more to it than that, as Dawn would find out.

If Dawn's first real lessons in understanding Jay Carsey had begun with the articles—articles that said he had always been all things to all people—and especially with the photograph of Nancy, she felt that even as "Jay Adams" he had given her some very

301

important clues, clues that had nothing to do with her difficulty in knowing when he was lying and when he was not.

"I somehow sensed," she said, "that he had never allowed himself to be emotionally close to anyone. He can flippantly say that he is 'emotionally shallow,' but then he can't discuss why he feels that is. The things he says are not always an accurate reflection of what he really thinks. He keeps so much deep down inside himself that it's hard for him to be gut-honest about anything. He says that he's emotionally shallow, I think, because he's always worked to keep things on the level where he wouldn't get too close to anyone. He might complain about all the social circles he and Nancy had, but it served his purpose: it enabled him to keep moving, to never get too close."

And yet she began to realize before he made that first phone call to Dom precisely how important other people's approval was to him.

"Jay is the most perfect other-directed person I've ever seen," she said, drawing on the term that David Riesman put forth in *The Lonely Crowd*. "It made me see that if he had told *anybody* what he had in mind, his desire to leave would have crumbled under the pressure of his desire to please. The thought of all those people unhappy with him disturbed him greatly."

While her previous worry was that he might turn out to be dull and commonplace were she to find out who he really was, she now realized that his concern had been that she would reject him if the unvarnished truth ever surfaced. And once she understood that, it made her feel even more protective of him, made her want, literally, to be his courage.

But if Nancy's needing his attention and his needing her approval had formed the chemistry that kept them together, wasn't it unsettling to Dawn—as unsettling as his refusal to contact Nancy directly—that her own apparent need, as much as her desire, to save him might be the only new variable in the equation? That she was living with someone whose only change had been one of geography?

The short answer was no. Even though she had read the articles and read Nancy's comments, comments that were hauntingly similar to her own, her confidence that she stood "totally apart from the rest of the world in my relationship with him" stemmed from her belief that if she could continue to nurture him, continue to make him feel that he could trust her and that she wanted him for himself, she could eventually get him to open up and communicate in a way that he had never done before—a way that might even include persuading him to contact Nancy.

But as she would soon discover, the rest of the world she claimed to feel apart from—specifically, Jay's previous life—would enter that relationship more quickly than she expected, and would affect her in ways she hadn't even imagined.

BY THE TIME Dom received Jay's next phone call, two nights after the first one, he had done what his friend had asked. In addition to speaking with Nancy, who promptly let the local newspaper know that Jay had contacted him, Dom sent Jay's regards to John Sine, Bob Straus, and Joe Browning. He told Jay that not only did everyone want to know where he was, how he was, and what he was doing, but that the college was holding some money for him.

Jay's reaction to all that was an odd blend of surprise, pleasure, anger, and guilt. He figured that the college would be so furious about his abrupt departure that even if they didn't give the money to Nancy they never would save it for him. He figured that people would be so threatened by what he had done they couldn't care less about the things Dom claimed they did. What they didn't understand was that Jay wanted them to be angry with him. He *needed* them to perceive him and what he did as villainous. After all, one of the things he had run away from was his role as "good old Uncle Jay." How else could his flight be successful if people's opinions about him hadn't changed?

On the other hand, it occurred to him that Dom could just be saying that; giving him the impression that people were not upset with him could just be a ploy to lure him back. Dom was as clever as Jay was, and Jay knew that. While it was true the overall tone of the articles was one of concern, they had appeared in June and September. It was now December, he thought to himself, and surely whatever concern people had had about his well-being had turned into anger, not to mention mounting sympathy for Nancy.

But there were things Jay didn't know.

He didn't know that his reaction of disgust toward the photograph of Nancy in *People* was shared by many people in Maryland, so much so that loyal friends like Evelyn Hungerford and Jackie Matthews felt that even if Jay had the slightest wish to return, seeing that picture would change his mind in a hurry.

He didn't know that many people felt Nancy had just about used up their reservoir of sympathy for her, that like Dom, they too felt she had been defining the nature of their gifts—everything from running errands for her and taking her to the country club to helping her get a permanent job—and that it had to stop. And though it didn't mean they were any less hurt by Jay's not being in contact with them, they began to have an even clearer understanding of what role Nancy may have played in his decision to flee—especially since he had chosen to contact Dom, not her.

But on the phone that Friday night, regardless of his internal reaction and what he didn't know, Jay made a decision to tell Dom where he was—more or less. He said that he was going back and forth across the border a great deal, but could be reached through "a friend" of his in El Paso. He also said that a message could be left for him at a bar where he occasionally worked, a bar that was near Fort Bliss. (Jay mentioned the base because he recalled that Dom had been there on business once.)

"I don't want anyone else to know where I am," Jay said.

"What about Joe?" Dom asked.

Jay had to think about that. One of the reasons he hadn't written Joe a note in May was because he knew Joe would never approve of what he had done. Sheer guilt over displeasing his mentor simply prevented him from doing that. But to not have any contact with him now, Jay felt, would be pointless and unnecessarily hurtful. Like Dom, Joe could be trusted; he was friendly with Nancy, but his loyalty, Jay hoped, was to him.

"I've never lied to Joe," Jay said. "You can tell him anything you want. But no one else."

Finally, Jay got around to telling Dom what he needed: a copy of his résumé, and his contact lens prescription from Sterling Optical. On the surface, it didn't seem like much, but it was a start, helped, of course, by the back pay (more than four thousand dollars), which he said would be particularly useful since he had been robbed and had no money.

Dom didn't press him for any details about that, but was bold enough to ask if there was any chance they might meet at some point in the future. Hearing Jay say he was okay was one thing; making that determination for himself quite another. For all Dom knew these phone calls could be a last-gasp attempt for help before he did something more drastic. He didn't believe that to be the case, but he was also well aware, *now*, of all the signals he had missed—some of which he had wanted to miss—in the time leading up to Jay's leaving.

"Let me think it over," Jay said.

AT THE SAME time those first two conversations with Dom were taking place, Homer and Bea received a letter from Jay. In the months since he had been gone, they had done what they said they were going to do—not discussed his disappearance with anyone except family.

But all that changed when a friend of Bea's brought over a copy of *People* when she arrived to play bridge one late September afternoon. Not long after that, Bea suffered a heart attack.

So Jay's letter, which essentially told them what he had told

Dom, obviously came as a great relief. But there was something it didn't tell them: it didn't tell them about El Paso. In fact, it left the impression that he was living in California.

THE LETTER HAD been mailed from San Rafael, courtesy of Frank Peacock.

Before Frank came home that December, before he had any idea that Jay was involved with his sister, Dawn had contacted him and asked him for a favor. All she said was that she had a friend who needed something mailed—from someplace other than El Paso.

Frank, as it happened, had a fascination with "covert activities," but it stopped short of *his* doing anything illegal. Over and over again he asked Dawn for assurances that he wouldn't get into any trouble if he did this, and over and over again, she promised him that he wouldn't.

Of all the people in his family, Frank was closest to Dawn, probably understood her better than anyone else. In his thirties, Frank was a painter, an artist with eyes that assured you of his unending belief and determination that no matter how long it took he would eventually make a living through his art—and with a personality so genial and lacking in pretense that it instantly won you over and made you permanently root for him to achieve his dream. Like Wendy Bruck, he was convinced of his sister's uniqueness; and like Wendy, he had reasons to be concerned when Dawn pulled him aside one day in Las Cruces and showed him the articles about the man he had just met—the same man, he now realized, whose letter he had mailed just one week before.

"Frankly, I was worried that my sister was attracted to him for the wrong reasons," he said, "that the mystique of what he had done might be influencing her to help his cause. It occurred to me that he might be using her as a safe haven, that he was just passing through. Now I'll admit that my sister was far from an ingenue, not at all like the girl in *The Rainmaker*, yet I didn't want to have someone come in and disrupt her life or bring external consequences to her. After all, not too many people in their lives get to harbor a felon—and if you do, you're guilty of a felony."

But if Frank was willing to concede that Dawn was not like the unmarried Lizzie of the play, in every other respect he viewed Jay as a haunting reminder of how life often imitated art. As far as Frank was concerned, Jay was a man repainting the canvas of his life.

And as he stared at Jay standing across the room with a drink in his hand, he couldn't stop thinking about *The Rainmaker*, about "the tremendous insight into the psychology of people and what motivated them" that both the lead character and the Jay of the articles seemed to share—the ability to be charismatic and genuinely charming and, at the same time, have the power to ultimately hurt people.

Nevertheless, Frank was not unsympathetic to the things that might have caused Jay to walk away from the life he had. On two separate occasions, he had given up a steady paycheck in order to paint full-time. He had read a number of articles about "executive burnout," about upper-level managers in the San Francisco area who had walked away from big, stressful jobs and become custodians in junior highs. He understood how a person could get to a point where he might feel so "starved for oxygen" that in order to purchase his freedom he might have to cause other people pain. So as he sat there, watching Jay with Dawn, reminding himself that he was, at heart, a sensitive, live-and-let-live person, he realized that it would be hypocritical of him not to counter his deep skepticism with an honest attempt to give Jay the benefit of the doubt.

By ACTING AS an accomplice in Jay's scheme, Dawn was not only trying to protect Jay; she was, whether she realized it fully or not, serving to reinforce his own continuing need for drama. That, at least, was the way it seemed. For the longest time, Nancy had provided enough of a light show for both of them, but his departure had certainly matched any performance she had ever put on, and he certainly didn't stop once he got to El Paso, spinning stories and holding everyone he met in thrall.

And even though he had started to tire of trying to be someone he wasn't, had realized that running a bar was not going to be an adequate antidote to what he'd been doing, it was crucial to him that he regain the control he felt those articles had taken away.

By calling in his chits with Dom and falsely leading everyone else but Joe Browning to believe he was living in California, he was only doing what he had done for so long and been so good at.

His note to his parents had told them not to worry, but as Homer wrote to Nancy a few days after he received it, "I worry that at middle age he has made a complete shambles of his marriage, his life's work to date. His future credibility is suspect and the pain he caused his loved ones will remain with him the rest of his life. I know, normally, he is more sensitive."

Since Jay's note also told them he was not going to return to Maryland (and Nancy had previously made them aware of her financial difficulties), Homer sent along a Christmas present of twenty-five dollars a few days later.

FIFTY-FOUR

As 1982 GAVE WAY to a new year, Jay had more reason than ever to brush gold dust off his shoulders.

It had nothing to do with TJ's, which continued to be, as Jay had predicted, a hard dollar to make.

Nor did it involve any firm plans to do something else. There weren't any.

No, it had to do with a level of acceptance among the people he had met since he descended on El Paso more than seven months before. Even though he had sensed, early on, that El Paso was a perfect place for him to land, it wasn't until after "the *People* magazine incident," as it came to be called, that he fully realized the degree of that perfection.

Once he felt pulled enough together to circulate again, though still nervous as to how people might react, he discovered that *no one* had seen the article at the time it appeared. When he mentioned to Dawn how incredulous he was about that, she calmly reminded him that *People* magazine was "mainstream America," and El Paso was not.

And he discovered that he was wrong to think he had to create a persona all those months before in order to make himself more exciting or appealing than his low self-esteem had led him to believe. To the Back Door crowd, it didn't matter whether he was Jay Martin Adams or Jay Carsey, he was still the same person. If Dawn was trying in their private life to show him that she loved him for nothing but himself, these individuals were doing it in their own way, with their own brand of humor.

Connie and Phyllis would kid him that here he was, trying to start over, and *People* had the audacity to come along and ruin everything. Or they would threaten blackmail, saying that if he didn't do this or that (like get them both fur coats), they were going to pick up the phone that instant and tell Nancy exactly where he was. And they would warn Dawn that if he ever had to go to the dentist, she should make sure to go with him.

Paul and George Thayer would tease him that they had it on good authority that a news crew from the local television station was about to burst into TJ's at any minute for an "exclusive interview."

And even Cody got into the act. One evening, after the three of them finished dinner at home, he got up from the table and headed for the door. But instead of just saying good night and walking through it, he turned to Jay and said, "Well, exit the rainmaker."

Jay smiled; they all smiled. All around El Paso, it seemed, humor—not unlike the kind that surfaced the night at Hawthorne Country Club when Mike Sprague said to a group of men how inconsiderate it was of Jay not to charter a plane so they all could have gone—greeted Jay wherever he turned.

But just as with everyone back in Maryland, Jay had no idea what these people were really thinking. And since he didn't, on a certain level, completely trust the terms on which they seemed to take him, he kept trying, in his own peculiarly circuitous, less-than-totally-forthcoming way, to explain himself, to ensure they didn't turn their backs on him.

Yet if he had come right out and asked Paul Thayer his reaction, Paul would have told him that "I think any man fifty years old and up can identify with it. He might not do it, but I don't think there's a man who went through his forties who didn't have the desire to do it—or hardly any that I know. And a lot of them did do it, not as drastically because they had underaged kids they felt they couldn't just leave out in the cold, but they changed careers." He would also have told Jay that he didn't think Jay had any idea what he was trying to do when he left, would have likened it to being in jail when all of a sudden a bulldozer breaks through the wall of your cell. "You'd run through it, but you wouldn't have any idea where you were running."

What Allan Alexander would have told him coincided with one of Nancy's greatest fears—that some people might perceive Jay as a hero of sorts. When Dawn told Allan what Jay had done, Allan immediately thought of Gauguin, of how "history views the romance of what Gauguin did more than the tragedy of it—the tragic aspects of Gauguin's life and what his wife went through." He would have told him that a good friend of his, a college English professor, "walked out the door, never said he was quitting, and became a Greyhound bus driver." And he would have told him things about himself that Jay didn't know—things that were completely opposite from the life Jay had had, but which made him sympathetic to what Jay had done. He would have told him that commitments and responsibilities of any kind were things he had always traveled great lengths to avoid. The reason he was living minimally and working as a night clerk at a hotel was not so much that he needed the time to write, but because he had convinced himself that he had no facility for making money (having made more than five thousand dollars a year only twice in his life). He had grown up wanting to be a cowboy or a trapper, and even though he hadn't become either, the romantic vision of that sort of life had always stayed with him, a vision helped, he strongly believed, by living in an unregimented place like El Paso, steeped in the lore of such figures as Big Foot Wallace and John Wesley Hardin, Pancho Villa and Ambrose Bierce.

And Polly Harris, a feisty politician in her sixties who met Jay at the dinner honoring Dawn in late August and was one of Dawn's closest friends, would have told him that she viewed what he did as "a healthy thing. As a feminist, I should not condone this at all, but he was only leaving people in a quandary, not a real bind. Is it any more wrong for him to have done that as a matter of survival than it was for him to do what other men have done—destroyed themselves and everything around them? I don't see that disappearing is any more cruel than the kind of mental cruelty men are capable of inflicting when they decide they're going to leave, or worse, when they stay and are abusive.

"The fact is, he didn't leave his wife in dire straits. I read the articles about 'the brave little woman bearing up to all this who doesn't know what could have come over him,' but something's wrong with her story. How much is real and how much is pretense? *'Why didn't he confide in me? I could have helped him.'* Baloney. A lot of it has to be ego and a lot of it has to be role-playing. Obviously, he couldn't confide in her because he felt she couldn't help him. I'm sorry, but women can be the bitches of the world. If it was a shell of a relationship, you haven't really broken anything that's that fragile. I think his leaving was part of his own emotional salvation—either go or go under."

BUT POLLY HARRIS wasn't living with Jay, Dawn was, and as she continued to observe and listen to him, the portrait that was forming in her mind took on new shape and complexity. If part of that portrait was her belief that Jay was "a very warm, generous, sensitive, caring human being who had never really learned to say 'I'm a warm, sensitive, caring human being,'" another part revealed that a good deal of his "likability" was learned behavior, not always intuitive.

"I never *learned* to be 'Aunt Dawn.' He's a real actor sometimes, shows a lot more warmth toward people than he's feeling at all. As far as I can tell, he has a basic personality, three or four well-developed masks, and a couple of roles he can put on very comfortably. Now you take those notes he wrote to Dom Monetta and John Sine. As far as I'm concerned, they were 'grand gestures' inspired by alcohol, and I think a lot of grand gestures are masks. I don't think a lot of those people understood some of his insecurities or some of his shyness. If you talk to him, he'll have you believe that he doesn't get hurt. I don't think you could ever get him to deal directly with whether Nancy or even Marilyn [Southwell] really hurt him, but if you watch closely you can tell by the way he reacts. That's why I say he has an inability to be gut-honest with himself, an unwillingness to dig inside."

Not only had Nancy voiced many of the same things after Jay left, about how difficult it was for him ever to express emotion, to come right out and say that he loved her, to hold her when she needed holding, but she had also begun to wonder if all the things Jay bought for her—whether it was the Iron Duke, the now infamous portrait, or even the tank of kissing fish—were, on some level, just a substitute for this inability on his part, an offering of more material goods and more trips around the world in exchange, perhaps, for feeling less guilt. (Or, looked at another way, that her incessant acquiring, and even her verbal and physical outbursts, were a reaction of deep frustration to the lack of physical and emotional contact.)

"I really do think she loved him a lot," Dawn said, "and I think the real fault of unloving was more on his side. But I also think she didn't know how to come around that. It was really a question of not talking to each other much in the beginning. Had she been very nurturing, he might have been more comfortable with her in the marriage.

"A lot of couples don't really love each other very much, but they're so comfortable that they don't leave each other. I think Jay loved Nancy in a way he was capable of when he married her, and I think it was an exciting love. But he had no idea what it meant to 'go to the head of the class,' to 'make it.' And since he wasn't that comfortable to begin with—since he saw himself as being there to provide, since his mother had impressed upon him the importance of the social veneer, of 'what's expected'—he realized, once he gained a little maturity, that he didn't have anything particularly to keep him. There was no more love. . . .

"But he didn't know how to turn Dr. Jekyll into Mr. Hyde—and he couldn't face the idea of all those people being unhappy with him—so it was best, *for him*, just to escape."

When Jay and Nancy came back from that sensitivity-training session in Maine and Nancy told the Schaumburgs that, more than anything, they needed to be with people who loved them, she couldn't have known all that her statement meant.

FIFTY-FIVE

DEAR JOHN,

Hear good things about you from Dom. Good training watching me make mistakes.

Still floating—went through my money so my lifestyle is now modeled after a young Oliver Twist—good for character building. Dom tells me you have some checks for me in escrow. If that's still true, give them to Dom please. We're going to rendezvous in a neutral corner.

Also: Go see Ed Digges. Ask him if he is willing to take my

side of the divorce proceedings I assume are in process. If he says "yes" tell him I'll call him in late January. If "no" ask him who he would recommend. Tell Dom what you find out.

Have a hell of a great '83!

Jay

P.S. I've become a fair to middling bartender.

Once again, Frank Peacock mailed Jay's letter from California. The "rendezvous" with Dom was arranged for Friday, January 21. He would be returning home to Washington from New Mexico, and would fly into El Paso that evening. Joe Browning had wanted to come to El Paso too, but Jay said no: he wanted to see Dom first.

Not surprisingly, Jay anticipated that the meeting would be the next moment of truth. What he didn't anticipate was that that moment would arrive a few days ahead of time.

EARLY ON THE morning of January 18 at Fort Bliss, Sergeant Bill Johnson was, like most people who watch television at that hour, trying to watch and do something else at the same time; in his case, polishing his shoes and brass to such a degree that he could, if he wanted to, use them as a mirror.

At about eight minutes past eight, it just so happened, the television had his full attention. Diane Sawyer, co-anchor of the "CBS Morning News," was introducing a story about a missing person, a college president who had run away from Maryland for mysterious reasons, when suddenly a photograph of Jay (the one Nancy had sent everywhere) appeared on the screen and seemed to stay there interminably. Bill stared, dropped his head, then looked again, inching closer to the screen.

"Hey," he said to his wife, sitting right beside him, "that's no missing person. *That's* my bartender."

Within two hours, shortly after TJ's opened up, Bill was sitting on his favorite stool, sipping a beer and staring some more.

"Hey," he finally said, "didn't I see—"

"Yeah, yeah," Jay said quickly, making no attempt to deny it, "that was me."

Indeed it was, and he knew it was coming. As soon as Dom heard from CBS when the piece was scheduled, he let Jay know, and there had even been a promotional spot for it the night before.

It was unsettling to discover himself on national television; to see Nancy in the living room of Green's Inheritance and hear her remark that she had often said to some of her closest friends how Jay could be Thoreau and live on Walden Pond, but that she didn't really think he would ever do it. He was startled to hear that the state police put his disappearance in the same category with John Wilkes Booth's fleeing to Charles County after shooting Lincoln as one of the biggest things to ever happen in those parts. He laughed when Nancy said she had prepared lunch for them that day, and solemnly nodded when she said that had he confronted her she would have talked him out of it—and that he probably knew that.

It was eerie for him to see a shot of his empty office, and the long approach to Green's Inheritance, and students on the campus. And it was eerie to see John Sine holding the postcard that Jay had sent him and reading the message out loud; to see Buddy Sprague shake his head in frustration as he said that Jay would always be so interested in *your* problems but you could never get anything out of *him*.

But the thing that had the greatest impact of all had to do with the one person in the piece Jay had never met—a clinical psychologist named Herbert J. Freudenberger. When he appeared on camera, Jay heard the doctor say that even though what Jay had done was uncommon, the "fantasy of wanting out" was *very* common. Based on what he had been told, he said he viewed people like Jay as "the mules of society," people who felt they had a certain image to maintain, an image of being "dedicated, committed, helping individuals," but who in turn also felt they never needed any help. To admit needing help, he said, would be an unbearable admission of weakness and personal failure, would entail the risk that people would no longer seek them out.

What Jay had done, he said, was an act of desperation—"a *need* to do this, and almost a sense, which I sometimes feel, that if that isn't done, when things are that bad, there's really one other solution: either to give in and give up, or to become an alcoholic, or to become involved in drugs, or to commit suicide."

As for Jay's not leaving Nancy clear-cut power of attorney, Freudenberger said it was no oversight, not when the departure was that clearly planned, not when it was carried out by a chemical engineer. "No," he said, "this was a final, you know, 'We're evening the score, kid. Now you're going to struggle with a bunch of years for what I probably struggled with with you for years—except you weren't listening to me, or you didn't hear me.' It's conjecture, but it's a possibility."

At the end of the piece, the same picture of Jay that appeared at the beginning returned—with a final bit of information:

Last month, late one night, Jay Carsey phoned a close friend. Carsey would not say where he was. He did say he was recovering . . . but had no plans to come back.

No PLANS TO *come back*. Those words had a nice ring for Jay, made him feel that he was back in control. The interviews for the piece had taken place in November, and there was much that couldn't be included, much that would have interested him.

Had he been able to hear more of Freudenberger's comments, he would have heard that he imagined Jay was probably doing something quite different (this was before Dom had found out he was working in a bar), that Jay's story reminded him of a man who had come up to him after a speech once, and said that he was a nuclear physicist who had run away a few years before and was now doing what he had always dreamed of doing, from the moment he had had his first ride on a merry-go-round: he was running an amusement park. He would have heard him say that flight was basically a lower- or lower-middle-class phenomenon, usually done for economic reasons, but that the number of men *and* women who had come to him as patients in the past few years—people in high-pressured jobs, people of accomplishment who had received the accolades of their colleagues, their family, and their community and yet who felt something was missing, who wanted to buy a boat and get away, most temporarily, some permanently—had risen dramatically. From about 1975 on, he said, given everything from changes brought on by the women's movement (the enormous increase in dual-career couples especially) to increased violence in society to a feeling among younger people that they might not succeed to the degree their parents had, he had treated more patients who had come to the conclusion that they couldn't cope with all the demands and pressures being put on them (real or imagined, by others and themselves) than in his previous twenty years of practice.

So often, he said, a husband and wife would come in to see him and not only seem like strangers to each other, but the only reason they were there was because of something catastrophic that had happened to their child, something that had forced them to seek help. The more successful either or both of them were in their professional lives could often be an indicator of how poorly they fared, of how little they communicated, in their personal ones.

In Jay and Nancy's case, of course, the lack of communication was a serious problem, and the lack of a child—the "familial glue," as Evelyn Hungerford saw it—made it easier for him to flee. But there was still the question of the image Jay had built up, his role as everyone's Uncle Jay. That, more than anything, was what made him a prisoner—a prisoner in a jail he had constructed for himself. He didn't know that even "helping individuals" become depleted. He didn't know that even people who were "giants in their own mind" eventually fall, too. And, frankly, if he was so averse to seeking help (which of course he couldn't do, given his belief in this image), how could he know?

Fear of the unknown, he would have heard Freudenberger say, was what prevented more people from doing what Jay did, and that was precisely the opposite of what Jay had felt when he took that plane the previous May.

THE DAY AFTER the piece appeared, Jay spoke with Dom on the phone and pointed out, among other things, that the reporter had curly hair. But before Dom had a chance to wonder why he said that, Jay quickly followed with "So do I now," almost as if he worried that Dom might not recognize him when Jay came to the airport on Friday night.

Since Jay had received his money from the college by then, he sat down to write a letter to Louis Jenkins.

Louis et al.

. . . I had no idea that my leaving would create such a "stir" outside the Southern Maryland press and for that I apologize. What I am writing to say is that in *no* way did my departure have anything to do with the "super seven." I have nothing but fond and pleasant memories of our years together. . . .

I particularly appreciate your releasing the check. It represents a salute to me more meaningful than 10,000 gold watches.

I was especially pleased that you picked John. After all, he was the only one who knew how to run a graduation!

Jay

Eight months after Jay had left, his ability to play a role showed no signs of weakening.

FIFTY-SIX

Dom was as nervous about seeing Jay again as Jay was about seeing him. They had talked a number of times on the phone since December 8, and the CBS News piece had only heightened Dom's apprehension about the visit.

His plane arrived at nine that Friday evening and the first thing he noticed was that his friend was standing up straight, a good sign, an indication that Jay's back wasn't bothering him. As he moved closer to Jay he saw that he was tan, that in fact he looked quite well.

"You look great," Dom said as he shook Jay's hand. "Better than I've seen you look in ten years."

"Why, thank you," Jay said. He had come alone to meet Dom, and as they walked toward the baggage claim area it seemed as if they had never been apart—to Dom anyway.

Before going to the house, Jay drove Dom around a bit, showing him the sights (including TJ's), and kidding him that if he had never left Maryland he'd be freezing his ass off at this time of year. He was glad to see Dom, but wary. For all he knew, Dom was going to make a strong pitch for him to come back and try to work things out.

Dom didn't do that—not really, and not at first. Since Jay had already told him by that point that Dawn was "more than a friend," he tried to size up the situation as best he could, a situation that was unsettling to him. After all, here he was, more than two thousand miles from home, sitting with the one person whom he thought he knew better than any other, who had done something which shattered that notion, whom he had worried about for months; here he was, suddenly being introduced to somebody who, he was led to believe, was an important part of Jay's new life, a life that might not hold a place for him. And even though he had no clear sense whether Jay realized, or truly cared about, the agony he had put his friends through, Dom was determined to try and accept what his friend had chosen, at least verbally, even if he didn't fully understand it.

The three of them had dinner. They talked, they drank wine, they said nothing, then they talked some more. Dawn went to bed, and Jay and Dom continued talking through the night, talking like they used to. By morning, though, out of all the hours and hours of conversation, only two things were clear: Jay had no intention of ever going back to Maryland, and no idea of what he wanted to do next.

Jay's letter to John Sine had said that he and Dom were going to rendezvous in a neutral corner, and Dom still wanted to do that. Before boarding the plane for Washington only fourteen hours after he had arrived, Dom proposed that they meet the following month at Joe Browning's house in Miami. At the very least, Dom said, he and Joe could brainstorm in the meantime and come up with some things Jay might be interested in.

ON THE FLIGHT back, Dom felt like the odd man out. As good as it was to see Jay, to see him looking well and full of humor, Dom couldn't help feeling he'd lost him, that what they'd had they might never have again. It wasn't that he didn't like Dawn; he did. In fact, she not only impressed him with her intelligence and the fierceness of her liberal politics (he couldn't ever remember spending that much time with "such a committed, dyed-in-the-wool liberal"), but with how supportive of Jay she seemed, with how "right they looked together."

Nevertheless, Miami would enable him and Joe to probe, to find out whether the situation Jay gave every sign of being happy in was one he genuinely wanted—as they had thought for the longest time about his life with Nancy—or whether Jay was acting out his greatest role yet.

DAWN SOON BEGAN to worry as the trip to Miami approached. Jay had given her enough background about Dom and Joe that she was sure (as Jay was) they would never really understand why he had done what he did, even if they tried to make Jay think otherwise. And knowing how susceptible Jay was to pleasing people, she worried that the trip to Miami would turn out to be an under-a-bare-light-bulb assault on their part to convince Jay that he had done something stupid, an assault he might not be strong enough to withstand.

"How would you expect them to feel?" Dawn wondered. "The longer Jay stays away, the more they have to examine themselves. Take Dom. He admired Jay. I told Jay that he probably left Dom feeling out on a limb in the sense that Jay showed him a certain way to live, then helped him create it for himself. If he accepts what Jay did as permanent and good for Jay, then he has to scrutinize himself. He has to deal with the fact that he admired Jay, all that he had done, but that Jay turned away from all that. Doesn't Dom have to wonder if he should say goodbye too—or wonder if there's something the matter with him if he doesn't?"

But Dawn also knew that Dom or Joe might not do that at all, that it would be human nature for them to have already decided that Jay was "crazy" or "not normal" (just as she had, for different reasons) in order to simply block it out and live with themselves. The reason they might do that, she explained, was that "people can't stand the thought that *they*, not Jay, might be failures.

"From all that Jay told me, I got the sense that Dom and Joe were two people who will *never* feel they have enough money, enough sense of security about what they already have."

As MUCH AS she wanted to protect Jay, she was also perceptive enough to know that this was a trip he had to make alone.

FIFTY-SEVEN

ON FRIDAY, FEBRUARY 11, Jay went to the Circle K and came back with more than just a few groceries. He returned with a copy of *USA Today*, which had his picture and a story about him on the front page, a story with the headline 'DROP OUT' TURNS UP IN CALIF.

Pleased by the success of his ruse yet puzzled by the continuing publicity, Jay arrived in Miami two days later with a Valentine's Day present in his suitcase—a T-shirt from Dawn that said SOME BODY IN EL PASO LOVES YOU. Since Dom's plane had come in from Washington a few hours earlier, both Dom and Joe were there to meet him. (And since it was a Sunday and the financial markets were closed, Joe actually went as far as the gate.)

Joe, as it happened, had seen Jay in El Paso not long after Dom had (he was passing through in his DeLorean on the way to California), and they had talked on the phone once or twice. Having learned of Jay's ordeal with the hitchhiker, Joe had given him a thousand dollars (making the check payable to Jay Martin Adams just in case the Maryland National Bank, where Nancy had an account, got curious), and, along with Dom, had chipped in for his plane ticket to Florida. Like Dom, Joe thought Jay looked very well ("like someone who had had a great burden lifted from his shoulders") and hadn't lost his sense of humor ("You'll never hear me criticize the small businessman again," he said about his struggles with the bar), but Joe was convinced that Jay's situation, and his alliance with Dawn, were temporary. He might not go back to Maryland or to Nancy, Joe felt, but there was no way he could go on living minimally and ever be happy about it. *If I can only get him down to Florida*, Joe's thinking went, *I can talk some sense into him, especially since my approval has always been so important to him.*

He tried and Dom tried. They tried to kid him, telling him that in all the months they had been looking for him they fully expected to discover he had become the most successful doorman in New York. And they joked, as Malcolm McGregor had, that he should go back to Green's Inheritance and inform Nancy that all was forgiven.

When Nancy's name came up, Jay became visibly angry, something Dom and Joe had never seen before, wanting to know why she hadn't tried to sell (or at least rent out) the house or get rid of some of the possessions, why she wasn't working full-time. "I am pissed by the implication that she is destitute," he said. "You don't have a twenty-three-room house on thirty-three acres and a condominium and seven time-sharing units and all that sort of junk and a Ph.D. and say you're destitute."

They told him that he had to get beyond his anger and get practical again—that he had left "too much on the table" and it was important that the three of them figure out how he could "optimize" his situation. Joe had even arranged for them to go up to Orlando and look at a company he was thinking of taking public. "I mean, here was a guy who is worth x amount of dollars," Joe said later, "and it's tough to start over from zero. I was trying to figure out how he could 'come out' and reinstate himself someplace with some decent standard of living. I wanted Jay to see the kinds of things that could be done, the kinds of things we were encouraging him to do before he disappeared. *'Come on out, let's get with it, there are opportunities!'* I told him, but he was so damn indecisive."

Actually, Jay told them, he was thinking about doing some teaching.

"Look," Joe said, one eye on Jay, the other fixed to the Financial News Network, "you're bare-assed broke and you've got to get established somehow. There's a real question whether the academic community would be willing to accept you. How do they know if you're going to be with them three weeks, three months, six months, and do it again? The best thing to do is just sell your soul and put yourself in the best financial position you can be."

Dom pulled out a piece from the *Washington Post* that he had brought down with him (FROM SELF-IMPOSED SECLUSION, THE RAINMAKER DROPS A LINE), a piece that had appeared the day after the one in *USA Today*. If the media was so hot for his story, they told him, why not see if they would pay for it?

No, Jay shot back, he had no interest in selling his story to anyone.

They were becoming frustrated, and so was he. But he didn't blame them. "The Joes and the Doms—and I could name thirty-five hundred other people—" he explained, "just can't conceive of leaving the life I had, it clogs them up. All I was trying to do was get across the message that I only wanted to make enough money to live on—that I needed a job in order to get health insurance and didn't want to end up on Skid Row."

In saying they didn't understand, he was only partly right, but that didn't matter. All that mattered was that he felt that way about it.

DURING THE THREE days he was there, Jay began drinking heavily again, but secretly.

At least he was trying to. But whenever Joe got up in the morning, he noticed his vodka and whiskey bottles were lighter than the night before. Joe didn't confront Jay about it, but did say something to Dom—another uncomfortable reminder to him of all the signs he had missed leading up to Jay's departure. Nonetheless, Dom had to admit to himself that even though Jay seemed different to him, those differences, now that Dom was finally forcing himself to face some things about his friend's life, were positive ones. Even if the booze was making Jay appear more relaxed than he really was, Dom thought he seemed more "at peace with himself." And however threatening that might have been to Dom personally (in Dawn's view of things), the fact remained that Dom wanted the best for his friend, and always would.

But beyond the secret drinking and the anger toward Nancy, the one thing that came out in Florida that startled Dom and crystallized his missing of signs was Jay's mention of Jean.

Jay didn't announce it to both of them, but chose to tell only Dom about her, casually and briefly. At the time, his reaction was one of total surprise—surprise that Jay could have been in New York that many Wednesdays without his knowing about it. And even though Jay told him that her death had a large impact on him, Dom didn't know whether to believe him or not. Perhaps Dom didn't want to believe him—didn't want to believe that this could have been going on. Or perhaps Dom simply didn't buy it, felt that it was some sort of fantasy, built up by liquor—another bone Jay was throwing him in an effort to help him understand.

Perhaps it was.

. . .

FOR WHATEVER REASON, Dom didn't tell Joe about Jean after the rendezvous in Miami was over. But then again, there was something Jay didn't tell Dawn.

Nobody from the New York City Ballet—or from any other ballet for that matter—was murdered in Central Park during 1981. In fact, the only people who were murdered in the park that year were male.

Nobody named Jean—nobody even matching her description or occupation—lived in the St. Moritz on a permanent basis.

Nancy didn't recall Jay's being away in New York on Wednesdays, even on an irregular basis, and neither did Katharyn Jones.

So why would Jay come up with such an elaborate, emotion-filled story that was so easy to disprove? Was this the ultimate example of his clogging things up so much that the truth would never be known—the one thing, more than any other, that he was determined to take to the grave with him?

He didn't blanch when these questions were put to him, months after he had first related the story. And far from being in the least bit offended, he looked genuinely, disarmingly pleased that the person he had decided, for reasons far from clear, to recount his story to had confronted him about it.

"You're a tough person, aren't you?" he said, smiling.

"Not really, but I'd like you to tell me the truth."

"The *essential* story is true," he said, all business now. "I had an affair with a woman, it had a tragic ending, and it opened my eyes to the two things I mentioned. Number one, that I had the ability to open up emotionally in a way that I really hadn't been prepared to feel, and two, that it opened up an awareness of a sexuality that I thought I had totally suppressed to the point that it made no difference. Hell, I didn't even have a platonic love affair in Southern Maryland at that time. Those are the facts.

"I knew you'd check out the story. In fact, I would have been pretty disappointed if you hadn't. It was a test in a sense. But I wasn't going to tell you the exact story so you could bring somebody that's innocent into it. I don't want that. I told you, *There's some parts of me I'm going to keep private.* The story is true. It was significant to me. It might have been in Washington, could have been in Baltimore, could have been in Philadelphia, but it *wasn't* in Southern Maryland."

IT WAS IN Washington. It slipped out when he said that she lived in a high-rise apartment near "that bridge with the two lions"— the one on Connecticut Avenue that connects the Kalorama section to the south with Calvert Street to the north.

Washington made sense. Since Jay was there at least twice a week on legitimate business, there was no reason for suspicion—from Nancy, from Katharyn, from anybody. He often would have lunch alone. In fact, he liked to have lunch alone, especially once his drinking began to escalate. And it was over such a lunch one day that he met Jean.

It was in 1979—a year earlier than his original version of the story; they were both sitting at banquettes, facing each other. She was tall, in her late thirties, and expensively dressed. Her hair was jet black (not blond, as he had previously claimed). He struck up a conversation with her, did she eat there often, that sort of thing. Yes, she said, she did. Without being specific, she mentioned that she worked in a government office, and that this particular restaurant (which Jay declined to name) was convenient.

Jay didn't believe her. In his opinion, she just didn't look like the sort of person who worked in an office, even though he couldn't articulate precisely what he thought that kind of person looked like. In his opinion, she had an air of mystery about her, which prompted him to ask if she would be willing to meet him for lunch the following week, same time, same place.

She would, she said, but Jay didn't believe that either.

But the following Wednesday, there she was, as promised. They talked about the ballet and the theater, and how often each of them went to the Kennedy Center and the Arena Stage. From her reedlike build, Jay guessed that she must have been a dancer at one time, but since he didn't ask, he didn't know for sure. All he knew was that he wanted to see her again.

And so they did, the next week. But at the end of that lunch, just as Jay was preparing to say that he would be back in town the following Wednesday, she invited him to lunch at her apartment. From the moment they met, Jay felt sure there was a mutual "electric stroke across the way," and this invitation, he hoped, only confirmed that.

IF SHE WORKED in an office, Jay thought as he sat in her tastefully decorated apartment that Wednesday and sipped a glass of wine, she must have a fairly high-level job, because he had been there for three hours, and she had given no indication of needing to be anywhere other than where she was. In fact, even before he arrived for lunch, he had begun to wonder, as people would later wonder of him, whether she was a drug runner who commanded top dollar, or a spy who had more than proven her mettle.

As it happened, he didn't have to wait that long to find out.

Back during his seek-and-search days, Jay had developed a theory, a theory based on the notion that if you came right out and asked ten women to go to bed with you, nine would almost certainly turn you down flat, but one would probably say yes. The Random Sample Approach to Life, he called it at the time. Since it had worked for him then, he thought, perhaps it would work for him now.

To say it did would be an understatement. For someone who had "barely got past the missionary position," the time Jay would spend with Jean was a revelation to him, time that was all the sweeter because it was free of gamesmanship, because he wasn't, to the best of his knowledge, "stealing her from someone else," the guilt of his courtship of Jessica Ross and Nancy Brumfield clearly still with him.

He didn't see her every week (either he would be out of town or she would) and he never saw her at night. Quite apart from his dread of rush-hour traffic (he always headed for home before three-thirty), he knew that it would be impossible for him to keep the affair going if he got careless, if he tried pushing the boundaries back more than he had already.

He needn't have worried. He couldn't have seen Jean at night even if he had wanted to. He could only have seen her at night if he could have afforded her.

Not long after they began spending time together, going out to lunch at the Iron Gate Inn on N Street or to the Normandy Farms Inn slightly north of town or having food brought in to Jean's apartment, time in which they would listen to music, talk, and, almost always, eagerly find their way to bed, Jay asked and she answered: she worked for an escort service; her evenings could be engaged for a thousand dollars.

Instead of being put off, Jay was (as ever) fascinated. Since he was uneasy with the word prostitute, no matter the price, he came to prefer thinking of Jean's nocturnal adventures as her "concubine world." As to why she never charged him for her time, he wasn't sure, his only thought being that she wanted "an emotional connection" that she was unable to have—that she couldn't allow herself to have—in the name of business. (But in the name of business, she implied that some of her clients were influential congressmen—influential enough, it appeared, that Jay was able to gain valuable information about certain bills long before they were ever introduced.)

He made no demands, she made no demands. They would kid about what they would do if they bumped into each other at the Kennedy Center, whether they were good enough actors to keep their secret secret, but they never talked about a future together. Jay might have been enchanted by Jean, he might have found a kind of happiness with her that he hadn't known before, but he was not going to leave Nancy for her. He knew enough about roles to know that he couldn't marry Jean, continue both as president of the college and traveling in the wide circles he did, and run the risk that someone might recognize her. Depending on one's point of view, he wasn't courageous enough, or stupid enough, to do that.

Nevertheless, when the end came, he was devastated.

He was supposed to see her one Tuesday, but couldn't get away. Nor was he able to phone. By the time he finally did, though, he got a recording: the phone was disconnected. So he drove up on Thursday and was told by the doorman, who knew him, that Jean had been killed. He provided no other details, and, of course, Jay didn't ask. He immediately got back into his car and took a cir-cuitous route to the Market Inn, a famous watering hole near the Capitol whose dim atmosphere would enable him to cry, and drink, as inconspicuously as possible.

He couldn't remember now exactly how many martinis he had that afternoon, but forty dollars' worth somehow still stuck out in his mind. And also in his mind, as he sat there, was the headline PRESIDENT QUESTIONED IN DEATH OF PROSTITUTE, the headline he feared would be in all the papers just as soon as the D.C. police got around to talking to him. Even though he was pretty sure the doorman didn't know his name, he worried that the doorman could not only describe him, but add much more. Doormen know things, things you often wish they didn't.

On the other hand, Jay thought to himself, what if she wasn't murdered by a client or a pimp? What if she wasn't killed by a burglar whom she might have surprised? What if she died in a car accident or was hit by a bus? Then he wouldn't have to worry about being questioned at all. At least that's the hopeful way he looked at it.

Over the next few weeks, he didn't listen to the radio and he didn't look at the papers. When he was at work, he occasionally found himself looking out the window of his office for either a police car or plainclothes detectives. But instead of feeling relieved when no one came, he cynically took it as confirmation of how incompetent he always felt the D.C. police were.

But in the end, it didn't matter. As he had said before, all that mattered was that Jean was gone, and a part of him had gone with her.

FOR THE PERSON hearing the story a second time, seeing him relive the experience with the same emotion he displayed the first time around, it was nearly impossible to doubt the "essential truth" of what he was saying without seeming callous and insensitive.

Perhaps it didn't matter that the only prostitute killed in Washington around the time Jay spoke of (*and* whose death was reported in the press) did not fit Jean's description—or more accurately, Jay's description of her—did not have her name (either professionally or privately), and did not live in the area Jay claimed to have visited.

Perhaps it didn't matter that Jay wouldn't reveal her last name, or that Jean might not be her first one; that he wouldn't be specific about the building she lived in, or that he might be protecting someone, someone who might have killed herself—the one form of dying he didn't consider that afternoon at the Market Inn. Perhaps, as he said over and over, all that finally did matter was that he had this experience, and that positive things had come from it.

But what if it *never* happened, if it was some elaborate fantasy so deeply woven into his subconscious that he had thoroughly convinced himself it had? And that the shaking and crying over her death, over his not being there when he said he would, was really just his way, his need, of expressing guilt for leaving Nancy in the manner that he did?

FIFTY-EIGHT

WHEN JAY RETURNED to El Paso from Miami, his frustration with Joe and Dom had turned to a gnawing agitation. As Dawn patiently listened to Jay describe the conversations he had with them, she became fearful that Joe or Dom might cause Jay "some psychological harm" by spreading stories about him and his current situation that weren't true.

Though her fear was unfounded, it was easy to understand from where it had sprung: the same him-us, bad-good theory she had already expressed, except that it now became more personal—it now included her role in all this. If Joe felt that Jay's situation was temporary, that it was some bizarre aberration which would eventually pass, then Dawn knew that they could only view her as part of the aberration, as "the whore waiting in the alley" who could satisfy his needs until he got his mind right and became respectable again.

But to Jay, becoming respectable again not only meant finding the sort of work that would enable him to support Dawn and himself (though forced to depend on Dawn financially after the loss of his boodle in November, he had never accepted it), it meant creating even more distance between himself and his life in Maryland than he already had.

Jay couldn't have cared less that Nancy's reasons for filing for a "limited divorce" were, far from malicious, the only response she could make to the legal haze he had created with his unnotarized note. He couldn't have cared less that she wanted a reconciliation. All he could think about was that she had moved, and moved quickly; that she had posed in that dress; that nothing had changed. She hadn't found a full-time job; she hadn't sold her jewelry; and, as best he could tell from speaking with Dom and Joe, she was still operating as she always had, the only difference being her switch from dependency on Jay to everyone else. These were the things—more than his feeling unable to make Joe and Dom understand, more than his inability either to make a small profit from TJ's or to find satisfaction in that line of work, more than the loss of control over his life that the discovery of *People* represented—that utterly frustrated him. He had expressed this to Dawn, he had expressed this to Joe and Dom, and now he was about to do something about it. He wasn't just going to obtain a divorce; he was going to "swing the pendulum" by making an effort to gain some part of the very estate he had so adamantly said he no longer wanted.

On the surface, Jay's decision made no sense. If one looked at it rationally, given everything he had done and said, one could justifiably wonder why he would want to engage in that pursuit, in all that it might entail; why he wouldn't just want to get his divorce and be done with it, a conventional ending to his unconventional act.

On the surface, one could think, given Jay's need of other people's approval, that the decision to do this was more Dawn's than his, that she had more or less told him he had to do it in order to prove he had regained his "sanity," and to demonstrate the strength—and permanence—of his commitment to her.

But it wasn't. She didn't care if they married or not, and she certainly didn't care about any of the trappings he had left behind. Even if he had impulsively purchased a diamond ring for her, she would have reminded him how many people could have been fed for what it had cost him. As she kept saying, they had started in the same place—started with essentially nothing, other than their love—and she was not about to begin making the kinds of demands that had eventually driven him away from Nancy.

That's not to say that she was some odd combination of saint and doormat. She certainly wasn't. That's not to say she wanted to continue being the one who, time and again, would dictate the level at which they lived. She emphatically didn't. But she was not going to quit on him. She would see to it that they found a way for him to cut down on his drinking, to become more and more honest with himself, and to get back on his feet. Dawn had watched him like the all-knowing witch she claimed to be, and she had listened, looking for signs and answers. And she could tell, as he prepared to get in touch with the lawyer Ed Digges had recommended, that he wanted to "create the circumstances where he could talk about something more solid between us." And even though it didn't matter to her either way, she was still touched by that, touched by the fact that, despite what he had done, he was someone who still clung to a traditional view of what his role should be.

But she didn't confuse being touched by that with her determination that he not slip back into viewing himself a failure if he couldn't provide for them in the way that he, not she, felt to be his responsibility. It's not that she didn't understand why Jay felt like that, and understood even better once she learned more about his upbringing and his care of Susie. It's just that she was convinced it could only lead to misery.

But none of that prevented her from challenging him when

he later tried to explain why he wanted to swing the pendulum.

AT FIRST HE said it was more out of "intrigue" with the legal process than any real hope of getting anything—an explanation that was as laughable and insulting as it was unconvincing. After all, how could he expect anyone to accept his recurring claim of endless fascination with the world as a plausible reason to put himself through what was bound to be torturous, even if from a distance? After all, this was the same person who had talked at length about the joys of the guillotine, how you cut and run and never go back. More than a slight contradiction, this seemed a supreme act of both masochism and hypocrisy.

But perhaps that's too simple and rational a way of approaching something that defied logic. Perhaps "frustration" was too mild a noun for the considerable anger Jay was feeling—anger that the punishment his leaving was meant to have inflicted had not cut as deeply as he had hoped. Not only was he upset that Nancy was living, more or less, as before, but he hadn't even been able to make everyone else turn against him. He picked up and walked away without a word, essentially thumbing his nose at everybody, and some of them *still* had good feelings about him, still wished him well? What, short of committing murder, would he have to have done before he could cease being good and heroic in their minds?

Could these have been the sorts of things, driven by a mixture of guilt and stubborn willfulness, that were swirling around in his head?

Or was he in fact so malleable (and, as ever, so pragmatic) that he could be influenced by Dom's advising him to get what he could—as well as by a chiding letter from his father? (When Jay got back from Florida he decided to tell his parents he was in El Paso. Not long afterward, he received the following note.

Dear Julian:

Glad to hear from you and be assured that you are in better emotional, physical and mental state than ever. As to you having your drinking under control, I never thought you had a drinking problem.

Your behavioral aberration caused your mother and me considerable anxiety. We worried about your mental state, what kind of trouble you might encounter, and where we went wrong in your upbringing.

Your mother has been seriously ill since October of '82, three weeks in the hospital and is having a slow recovery. She is finally getting to the place where she can manage to get about alone. I've learned that keeping house, cooking and grocery shopping is time consuming and frustrating. Frankly I had fears I might be losing her. I am much of a recluse, so the prospect of living alone devastated me . . . no close friends to lighten the loneliness.

Unemployment, crime, Reaganomics . . . what a time to abandon all you had worked 20 years to accumulate and achieve!

Well, I must run; will write again when I have time to think over a suitable summation of your great adventure in nonconventional behavior.

> Love you,
> Dad

What his father didn't tell Jay until later was that his "great adventure" had cost Homer two hundred dollars: one hundred to take Jay out of his will, another hundred to put him back in.)

JAY WAS SLOW to respond at first, but then launched forth.
"Look, assuming that Nancy had taken what, to give the devil its due, was a courageous position—to stand there and deal with it—I decided on two tactics: talk to Dom and Joe, deal with John and others, but *never* speak or deal with her. So people start saying, 'Jesus, that son of a bitch was a bastard, wouldn't talk to his wife,

won't speak to her now, and won't write her.' Second thing is, you go for the gusto."

"Spare me," Dawn broke in.

"You go for the money," Jay continued. "Go for part of the estate. What a son of a bitch. He left her a note leaving her everything, now he wants some of it back. If she's going to stay there and I'm *never* going to go back there, then the image has to be reversed. You've got to say, 'God, I thought Jay was a really good guy. Son of a bitch, he's a bastard.' "

"Spare me," Dawn said again. "Spare me the idea that you have so much influence over Southern Maryland you can still conduct the direction of their prejudices, that by going for part of the estate *you* can direct all of their sympathy to Nancy. Goddamn, Jay, I said it before and I'll say it again: they're going to reject you and eventually come to that anyway, without your help."

But Dawn's pleas notwithstanding, didn't that attitude on Jay's part, however irrational and almost egomaniacal it might have been, finally align with his own thinking of himself as a rainmaker? Someone for whom control remained a boundless desire?

"Well," he said, "look at it this way. There are certain things in life that you don't have any control over, like having your damn plane hijacked, or even getting electrocuted in the bathtub. But I think if you're in a position to control things, you should try to control them—"

"Like falling in love with me?" Dawn said sarcastically, having heard him say a thousand times that that was the last thing he was looking to do in August of 1982.

"Well, now, that's different," he said, flashing a smile. "Falling in love with you was the biggest delight of my life. I didn't have any control over that."

FIFTY-NINE

NEARLY A YEAR after he left Maryland, Jay wandered back onto a college campus. Dawn had known Bob Shepack, the president of El Paso Community College, for quite a while (they had worked on a project for the city together and she had taught sociology at the college part-time), had always admired him, and thought that he might be willing to meet with Jay. Not wanting to scare Shepack off, however, all she told him was that Jay was a former educator, nothing more.

When Dawn and Jay arrived at his office, Jay was as nervous as a child on his first day of school. But instead of bringing a bookbag, Jay had the articles from *People* and the *Washington Post* in his sportcoat. If he was trying to surface as Julian Nance Carsey, full disclosure, he figured, was the only way to do it.

He needn't have bothered. Shepack knew who he was. Not from the articles Jay had with him, but from two pieces that had appeared in the *Chronicle of Higher Education*, one as recently as late February, which had placed him in California. Yes, Shepack knew who he was all right, but much to Jay's amazement, didn't seem to care. Far from being troubled by what Jay had done, he felt he understood it, an understanding he had come to long before, one that had nothing to do with the person sitting across from him.

"You know," he said later, "jobs like these are like practicing for dying. You can't do it. What do you do after the faculty takes its first annual vote of no-confidence after you've given them a whopping raise? Basically you have no personal friends on the staff. People don't even think they can be your friend. Anytime someone sues the college your name is first on the papers. You're always at risk in some way. The job is pure masochism, Chinese water torture. It drives one toward fantasizing about doing other things. I don't blame anyone for getting out."

Even in the way Jay chose?

"I, personally, wouldn't do what he did. I would never consider it, because I've got some very strong and healthy relationships with my family. An awful lot of this job is putting on a good public face, and I have no personal life outside of the locked doors of my house. You're under a microscope all the time. Now if what Jay was feeling was suffocation—all he said to me was that it was something he *had* to do—I've been in that position before. In the two instances I am thinking of, I was able to leave those jobs in a way that everybody saw it as 'Bob is moving up the ladder logically' and that sort of thing. But the truth is, I felt the suffocation so strongly that I would have started all over again, and my family would have supported my decision.

"My wife and I have an understanding. I could go home from here this afternoon and say, 'Joan, I really have had it. I really can't and don't want to put up with so and so and so and so anymore. I think we'd better leave,' and she'd start packing. That's my security blanket. Maybe he didn't have that. You only want ivy to grow so far across the walk before you take a hatchet and chop it at the edge and say this far and no further. I've tried to reserve a chunk of Joan's and my life separate from the job. After all, we're entitled to something of our own."

It was precisely that kind of thinking that made Shepack feel that Jay was entitled to a fair hearing, to not be judged—especially since Jay did not try to use him in any way. He didn't ask him for a job, and he didn't act desperate. He simply said he was running a bar and had begun to miss being around an educational setting and that if there was anything, anything at all, that Shepack felt he might do that could be useful, he hoped the president would call on him.

Fearing that Shepack might reject the idea out of hand, Jay was relieved when he didn't, when he said that he would give it some thought and get back to him.

As he left Shepack's office and for days afterward, Jay fluctuated—fluctuated between being totally confounded by Shepack's apparent acceptance of him and feeling that perhaps fate, once again, was shining down and playing its role.

IT WOULDN'T HAVE been easy for anyone to go to Shepack's office that day, hat in hand, but it was particularly difficult for someone as proud as Jay, partly because he was still convinced that no one, despite evidence to the contrary, would ever understand why he had fled, and partly because if anybody truly did, it would only undercut his actions. Catch-22, it seemed, was not only becoming a permanent state of mind for Jay, but a sad commentary on his underestimation and lack of faith in other people. Just as people in Maryland had wondered, after he left, whether he ever knew how much they loved and cared about him, had worried that it had been their fault if he didn't, Jay was now the one who, two months after meeting Bob Shepack, found himself wondering why he was being offered work.

Had he asked Shepack to pinpoint all the reasons for his job offer (which, of course, he didn't), he might have been moved to hear of the empathy Shepack felt, to hear him say that "sometimes some of the most important things that we do in life require very little effort and are things we're unconscious of. In friendships, for instance, I think there are some rules and some boundaries that parties agree to even in an unspoken way. When those rules and boundaries are respected, I believe those relationships are likely to persist. There's an unfortunate tendency in this country, I think, to have to explain and rationalize everything in order to accept or reject it. It's like being a nurseryman and pulling all the trees up to see how the roots are doing. You can only do that so many times before you kill the tree.

"Human qualities, I feel, defy all that. I tend to trust my gut. What he did was a very private act, and I felt that as long as he was living the life he wanted and wasn't hurting anybody else, what he had done before, what he was doing now, really wasn't anybody's business. My assumption was that at least for a time he was living a life that didn't feel natural to him, and so he decided to end it. But for me to have probed into all that with him [other than making a discreet check that Jay hadn't embezzled any money from the college in Maryland] would have been injudicious.

"He understood what I could do for him. I understood what he needed. My instinct was to accept him."

IF JAY HAD become, as Nancy feared, a hero to those who could only dream about what he had done, he had now found a hero of his own.

On July 18, Jay began teaching math part-time at El Paso Community College. And though, on the surface, this was more like coming full circle than advancing to a new stage of development, it was a significant step toward the kind of work he thought he wanted, and toward helping him regain a crucial sense of self-esteem.

But, Jay being Jay, it wouldn't be long before more would be asked of him.

SIXTY

J AMES KENKEL WAS his name, the
point man entrusted with try-
ing to swing the pendulum for Jay in Maryland. When Ed Digges
contacted him about representing Jay, Kenkel listened carefully.
He had handled a thousand divorces, but none with elements like
this one. If he was interested, Digges said, Jay would phone him
from somewhere in California. In the meantime, he should just
stay posted.

All Kenkel knew about Jay was what he had read in the papers.
Since he practiced in Prince George's County and didn't know
Nancy (it took Digges only a minute to figure that no Charles
County attorney could handle the case without incurring her
wrath), he would have more room to maneuver.

That, at least, was the way Kenkel initially viewed it—before
he actually got entangled and began stitching his own pattern into
the emotional tapestry.

ONCE WORD GOT out and around of Jay's intentions to get his
share of the estate, he seemed well on his way, in absentia, to
regaining control.

Even though Joe Browning wasn't caught completely off guard by the news (it had come up in Florida, but Joe thought it was more Dom's prodding than something Jay would or wanted to do), he was extremely disappointed in his Fair-Haired Boy. As unhappy as he was about Jay's refusal to contact Nancy, this was worse—this was hypocrisy of the most venal kind. As much as he loved Jay, Joe's position was blunt and simple: *Once you've cut your deal, you don't go back and slop in the trough.*

And when word reached John Sine, his feelings were not markedly different, but had a more literary flavor. "Pure Sartre" was the way he viewed it, reinforcing what his colleague Josephine Williams felt that commencement day. "He was not behaving according to the Hemingway code of conduct," Sine said, explaining why he had lost some respect for Jay. "After you kill the bull, you don't carve it up for steaks."

There were many who reacted in the way that Browning and Sine did. Spencer Matthews deplored it as "a deliberate second shot," and his wife, Jackie, who had discovered the cartoon in the *New Yorker* and showed it to Nancy, felt that Jay was "a rat. He didn't keep his marriage vows and now he didn't even keep to his note"—the note that gave everything to Nancy.

Yet there were others who (regardless of Jay's longing to be a villain) not only felt they understood why he was doing it, but were sympathetic as well. People like Buddy Sprague and Ellie Straus (Bob's wife) and Hilda Herbert (John Sine's secretary and a friend of Nancy's), who felt that Jay was "in very bad shape, in a state of irrationality," when he wrote that note, and that he was now "entitled" to his share of an estate he had worked long and hard to build up.

But despite the differences in opinion, there was one thing that everyone in Maryland—including Nancy—could agree on in hindsight: that the anger which had fueled his decision to leave, an anger whose depth none of them had accurately gauged, was clearly motivating him still.

Even though they, too, continued to feel angry and sad and

abandoned (something they wouldn't express to Nancy for the longest time for fear she would accuse them of being more concerned with *their* loss than hers); and even though many of them would, as Dawn predicted, choose to see what Jay did as insane and irrational because they were too afraid to view it otherwise and too responsible to start anew . . . the pendulum Jay was hoping to swing would, in the end, advance only so far. The affection so many of them still had for him would outlast his desire to destroy his image and his need to lessen his guilt.

But Jay, master manipulator that he was, wanted it both ways.

He might have wanted everyone to think he was a son of a bitch for trying to get his share of the estate (a metaphor, some felt, for trying to destroy Nancy by attempting to force her into selling Green's Inheritance), he might have been convinced that they would never understand why he had left without a word, but he didn't, despite what he *said*, want them to hate him.

In an effort to ensure that, he sent flowers to Hilda Herbert, he called Vince Hungerford (to commiserate with him about not getting a position Vince had coveted with the Air National Guard), and he sent John Sine a photograph of Dawn and himself (bearing only the message "Re-Entry").

Yet by the beginning of September, there was still no one in Charles County who could say with any certainty where Jay was, and Joe Browning and Dom Monetta weren't about to tell anyone.

SIXTY-ONE

WHILE THE PEOPLE of Jay's former life were dealing with the fallout of his latest actions, the people of his present one were forming opinions of their own.

As Bob Harned and Jay prepared to sell TJ's, Bob was worried about his friend. When Bob first found out what Jay had done, his admiration and affection for him only increased. Bob had dropped out, it was true, but not in the way Jay had. He never even considered it because he knew he couldn't have done it, even without obligations or ties. But when *People* appeared, Bob felt he saw a change in Jay, felt he became more tense, less easygoing. So when Jay put on a coat and tie and went back to a more conventional job, Bob worried that he had "compromised himself," and now he was worried about the emotional toll (not to mention the financial one) that pursuing the estate was bound to take on him. But when he tried to talk with Jay about it, he got nowhere.

Wendy Bruck was, not surprisingly, opposed to his effort as well ("If I were Nancy, I'd feel the same way: *You didn't want it, that's it. You wanted to disappear, you disappeared. You want another estate, build it*"), but had no trouble in understanding it. She not only felt he was doing it because of his new life with Dawn, but sensed (as Harned and others did) the element of punishment attached to it—the fact that Nancy seemed to be going on with her life without him "perhaps told him she hadn't noticed he was gone."

At the college, the only person Bob Shepack told anything about Jay's past to was Bill Williams, the vice-president to whom Jay was ultimately responsible. But it wasn't long before word slipped out (Jay told a few people himself) and a dog-eared copy of *People* began to slowly circulate.

Aside from the fact that he wasn't president, the most crucial difference between Jay's being at the college in El Paso and the one in Maryland was that he had no intention of staying for very long, and, more important, no intention of getting locked into the type of role-playing, administrative position that had worn him down before.

So when he was asked to be the director of the Worker Training Institute just two months after coming to the college, he said he would only do it temporarily. "When you advertise the position," he told Shepack and Williams, "I *won't* apply for it." He was sure they didn't believe him, but when the job was posted, he was true to his word.

The quick offer of more money and more power was, of course, a tribute to Jay's considerable experience, but to him it represented something even more significant—another form of reassurance about his worth to other people, another boost to an ego in need of them.

Jay didn't get close to many people at the college, didn't really allow himself to, but it should be no surprise that he won over virtually everyone he came into contact with, won them over with his charm and irreverence, his sense of play, his talent for dealing with people. It didn't matter where Jay was, whether he was in Charles County or El Paso, in Alabama or in Bryan, people were drawn to him. As much as he might have come to hate his role of leader and father confessor, he would never be able to stop this human stream unless he became a total recluse, and he was too much a rainmaker for that to ever happen. People came to him in hordes well before he drew attention to himself in May of 1982, and that would never have changed even if he had left and gone elsewhere by more conventional means.

Instead of feeling anxious because he didn't have tenure, it was his very lack of desire for such security that enabled him to operate as a free spirit and breathe fresh air into the halls of academe. He wore a multicolored clown wig to teach math on one occasion, and on another, began breakdancing in his office. Often seen in a white sportcoat with red pinstripes (his "Baskin Robbins jacket") or an electric-blue shirt and white slacks (his " 'Miami Vice' outfit"), he would take a group of secretaries out for piña coladas and spin their heads with tales of—what else?—his adventures with the CIA. When his VW (with no backseat and windows that wouldn't roll down) finally quit, he began driving Polly Harris's turquoise Oldsmobile, and could often be spotted roaring past the college and blaring the horn.

As had been true from the moment he came to El Paso, Jay's ability both to entertain and to energize was undiminished. But had he not also been talented, he might just have been dismissed as a merry prankster or a nut. He was good and everybody knew it, from Bob Shepack on down.

To Raul Ramirez, Jay was someone "who knows human behavior better than anybody. It was apparent in ten minutes that he knew what he was talking about."

To Earl York, a Hispanic who, like Ramirez, reported to Jay, he was the Big Enchilada. "I loved his nontraditional style. He made us *think* before we reacted. In fact, he is the only white dude I know that's got charisma, and the best storyteller I've ever encountered." As for what Jay had done, York was in awe. "The guy had it made. He had the money; he had the position; he had the house. So it must have torn him up at first to give all that up—and to go against his own grain, the paradox of influencing so many people about social values and morals as an educator and then disappearing." Hearing him say that, one sensed that York's awe of Jay was combined with feeling it was a crazy thing to do. On the contrary. Some day, York told Jay, he would do the same thing.

BY MARCH OF 1984, another position became available at the college, a much bigger job than the one Jay had. Once again the powers that be turned to him, and once again he said no. He would serve as the *acting* dean of occupational education, but had no interest in anything more permanent. That his decision puzzled everyone (except Shepack) was more of a delight to Jay than the offer itself.

Since the college was large and spread over a number of campuses, Mark Regalado, who taught there and was one of the Back Door regulars, had no idea that "TJ" was even associated with the school until the day he was introduced to his new dean at a large faculty meeting. In no time at all, Mark said, "TJ got things moving and rolling."

To say the least. Only a few months into the job, Jay sent out a memo that almost destroyed the academic Richter scale, a memo that essentially argued for abolishing tenure. If Jay had wanted to maintain a low profile, this wasn't exactly the way to do it.

The hue and cry, in fact, was so loud that Jay sought to explain himself, not to mention prevent bodily harm.

"Before I find myself floating face down in the Rio Grande," he wrote in a follow-up note, "let me clarify my DAM [Dean's Action Memorandum] on tenure. First, I am *not* busily preparing a document through channels recommending the abolition of tenure for occupational faculty. However, tenure should be periodically deliberated, ironically, to strengthen the commitment of an institution toward the concept.

"There is a tendency for faculty to believe that tenure is inviolate.

There have been numerous examples in the past decade in which Boards of Trustees summarily removed tenure and replaced it with multi-year contracts. In every case, the Courts have upheld their right to do so.

"There also is an increasing volume of research data that indicate an alarming trend for occupational faculty to have a reduced motivation to keep abreast of the fast-paced changes in technology once they are tenured. . . .

"I perceive no proclivities on the part of the current President and Board to 'toy' with tenure. However, Boards, Presidents, and yes, Deans, often 'turn-over' rapidly. I felt obliged to write this when the *nicest* thing I heard through the rumor-mill was that I was being called 'the Grinch who stole Christmas.' "

THAT WAS WHAT he was saying publicly. In private, though, he was more graphic, telling Mark Regalado that "what this college needs is more street fighters, gunfighters, and prizefighters," and Mark agreed. "Everybody was playing by the book," Mark said. "It took an outsider like TJ to come here and remind us of that."

SIXTY-TWO

JOHN SINE WAS the first one in Charles County to find out where Jay was living because Jay wrote in the autumn of 1983 and told him. After briefly sketching his movements from the day he left Maryland, he focused on the woman in the photograph John had seen ("Dawn is bright, sensual, and, importantly, non-materialistic") and that her influence on him was such that he now mowed lawns, did laundry, read books, and didn't "go to thirteen parties each weekend!"

Perhaps feeling guilty that he had made John go through Dom as an intermediary, he said he had done that because "I had total faith in a Sicilian," but then quickly added that "Now that I've cleaned up pertinent items with my lawyer I could care less who knows where I am or why, but I have total faith in your discretion vis-à-vis my current situation." And by the way, he wrote, "The local theater group had auditions for *The Rainmaker* and the father role"—the part Jay had played—"was up for grabs. I decided that was too much, especially since my previous director never taught me how to say 'dawg.' "

. . .

JAY WAS RIGHT in thinking John might be irritated that he had had to communicate through Monetta for as long as he had. For one thing, Monetta was far too smooth for John's taste; for another, he simply felt that Jay owed him more than that. But John, like Dom, was a loyal person. Even if Jay hadn't asked him to be discreet about El Paso, John was not the sort of person to gossip or put out a special press release. But that didn't mean he could prevent someone else from doing so.

Dave Lee was the technical director of the Naval Ordnance Station at the time Jay left Maryland, the recipient of one of his farewell letters (resigning his consultant's job). As it happened, Lee had a son in El Paso, and Jay knew that. Since one of the options Jay had considered (if all else failed) was a return to government work, he needed to find out if his billet was still open. So he went to see Randy Lee not long before he wrote to John and asked him to find out.

In no time at all, it seemed, Dave Lee appeared in El Paso. Much to Jay's amazement, Lee had kept a slot for him, and Jay was grateful. They talked, Lee met Dawn, saw his son, and then went home, apparently satisfied that his friend was okay.

But when Lee arrived back in Maryland he told one and all that Jay's life was in shambles, his great escape a crashing failure; he was living with a whore, drinking so heavily that Lee had to have him admitted to a dry-out center, and needed to be saved.

When Joe Browning heard of Lee's comments, he was livid. But when Jay learned of them, he just laughed. There was a plausible reason, he explained, why Lee would invent such a story. "More than any person I knew," Jay said, "Dave Lee would have liked to do what I had done. And nothing would have pleased him more if I had had to come back, tail between my legs."

. . .

As IT TURNED out, Jay did have to come back, but not for the reasons Dave Lee had said. He had to come back to give a deposition, and it had to be done in Maryland.

The deposition was scheduled for Monday, June 11, slightly more than two years from the day he had left. In truth, no time would have been a good one for Jay to do this, but this was particularly bad. His mother had died the previous month (fortunately, Jay and Dawn had finally gone to Bryan shortly before that, the best visit he ever recalled having with his parents), and he was just settling into his job as dean. His drinking had tailed off somewhat by then, but the prospect of flying back to the same airport from which he had departed filled him with dread.

He arrived on Sunday and stayed at Embassy Square, the same place Dom had an apartment. Jay and Kenkel had dinner that night, but it wasn't until the following morning, the day of the deposition, that Jay almost turned back. Kenkel had told him to take the Metro out to Silver Spring, and he would pick him up there. But as soon as Jay got into the car, Kenkel said they were going to Nancy's lawyer's office, and that Nancy would be there.

Nancy will be there, Jay began saying over and over to himself, almost wondering if he was somehow being set up. "I was in a state of total shock," Jay recalled. "I almost said, 'Please stop the car and let me out, that's the end of this case.' Jim thought I knew things about law and knew that was going to happen. And I want to tell you, right now, that if I had known that, I *never* would have pursued the damn thing. But there I was, and I was trapped."

When they arrived at Tom Yewell's office in Greenbelt (like Jay, Nancy had chosen a lawyer from outside Charles County), the first person Jay saw was a man whom he had known from Hawthorne Country Club but whose name escaped him. Jay nodded, and the man nodded, his face turning ashen. "You would have thought that

I was the Ghost of Christmas Past," Jay said. "I would have given ten million dollars for a picture of his face. He stammered away at hello and I said, 'It's good to see you.' "

But when he saw Nancy a moment later, the woman he had been married to for fourteen years, he said nothing of the kind. In fact, he barely acknowledged her at all, quickly taking his seat, about to experience some of the most grueling hours of his life.

Nancy was deposed first, and Jay heard her say that she had made numerous efforts to find full-time employment but had been unsuccessful so far; that she had been unable to obtain proper health insurance since her husband's "dramatic exit"; that she had sold two of the time-sharing units in Florida and the condominium on South Padre Island in Texas, had liquidated her life insurance policy and a Keogh account, and had sold the Mercedes and was now driving a Honda. When she was asked about Green's Inheritance, she made it very clear that none of its possessions were anywhere near as valuable as Jay seemed to think they were, but that even though things were tight, she had no plans to move from there.

When Jay's turn finally came, he followed his lawyer's game plan. In order for Jay to have any chance of gaining his share of the estate, Kenkel had decided to suggest that Jay was not in his right mind when he wrote the note that essentially gave Nancy everything; that if he had been truly serious about it, he would have had it notarized. Unfortunately, the other note—the one that would help this argument of temporary insanity, the one in which he told Nancy that he was a physical and emotional disaster and didn't want to drag her down with him—had somehow disappeared. "In the confusion of being so emotionally distraught when this occurred," Nancy said in her testimony, "I have no idea what happened to it."

. . .

FROM THE MOMENT the depositions began until the time they concluded four hours later, Nancy never took her eyes off Jay. "I wanted him to look at me," she said. "I wanted to see his eyes. After all"—she paused—"he *must* have been feeling guilt. He *must* have been feeling ashamed."

Instead of going home afterward, she got onto the Beltway and drove for hours, smoking one cigarette after another. Joe Browning had told her that Jay was living with someone, but it didn't seem real to her until she heard *him* say it. As for herself, there was no shortage of men who wanted either to be seen in her company or to marry her, but she was not about to tie herself down with anyone, no matter how much she enjoyed his company. Even after all that had gone on, she still loved Jay. In fact, when she got dressed that morning, she had fantasized that perhaps they might "click again" when they saw each other, that there would be some spark.

Having always known how difficult it was for Jay to look at people directly, she certainly got a harsh reminder of that.

"There were so many things I wanted answers to," she said, "so much I needed to know, and wanted to know." Whatever *she* had done to contribute to his departure was far outweighed, she felt, by the fact that it was *his* problem, that he should have been able to sit down and talk to her about it, and that she didn't deserve all the pain and humiliation he had caused her. It would be a long, long time before she could ever put her trust in any man again. If she was unsure of everything else, she was certain of that.

The answers she said she wanted, though, would apparently have to come from the various things she had heard Jay say under questioning and from the one thing she had observed him do—the thing she had seen him do to others, but which she still couldn't accept had been done to her. When Jay was asked if he felt "the only way you could manage to do what you wanted to do was to break it off and leave," he had slowly put his hand in the air, then swiftly brought it down like a meat cleaver.

He may have had to come back to do it, but he had certainly gotten his message across.

As NANCY CONTINUED chainsmoking and driving around in circles, James Kenkel had someone for Jay to see in Bethesda before he flew back to El Paso—a Belgian-born psychiatrist named Jean Feys, who, Kenkel hoped, would be able to support the defense he was planning.

In his late fifties, Feys looked years younger, and considered himself an anomaly. Not only was he "a psychiatrist who happened to be a Republican," but the credo of his practice was "mental health is abnormal," the notion that no more than 15 percent of the population ever had their lives in balance at any one time.

Jay spent about an hour and a half with Feys, recounting his version of things. Not long after that, the doctor read the transcripts of Jay's deposition and the tape he left Nancy; read the note that left her everything, as well as the articles that appeared in the *Washington Post, People*, the *Chronicle of Higher Education*, and *USA Today*; and he watched a videotape of a piece on CBS's "Nightwatch," a longer version of the one that had been broadcast on the "CBS Morning News."

In the letter he eventually wrote to Kenkel, Feys stressed that his professional opinion was arrived at solely from talking with Jay, and that the additional information he received only confirmed that opinion in his mind.

"My perception of Dr. Carsey," the psychiatrist wrote, "is that of a man who suffered from, in technical language, a tyrannical superego, that is an extraordinarily demanding sense of conscience, in which this inner force in him was always and constantly demanding a maximum level of achievement, in the direction of pleasing and satisfying others, under the penalty of severe and disorganizing guilt.

"He was able, for a number of years, to keep this demanding

entity in him assuaged, and everybody around him was happy with him. Then various factors around him which were beyond his control caused him to fail at his mission, and many people became unhappy with him. He started using alcohol as an anesthetic, and by April 1982 he was clearly an uncontrolled alcoholic; but his internal failure was only further progressing: he was not living up to what he was supposed to be.

"[I believe] that this internal conflict had reached a point, by April/May 1982, where Dr. Carsey could not handle the stress of his internal guilt anymore, his failure to make everyone happy. I am in full agreement with Dr. Freudenberger's conjectural analysis that at that time Dr. Carsey was getting in a mental state where there were, *for him internally* (everyone's reality in the final analysis is how we perceive [it] internally), very few options available—there was so much guilt, someone had to be punished by being destroyed. He could not confide his troubles to his wife or close friends: that would be burdening them, instead of making them happy. He could not seek professional help, as he was advised to: he was supposed to give, give, give. . . . So rather than continuing to commit suicide slowly (which he was doing through alcoholism), or killing himself all at once, he jumped into a desperate act of killing the whole life of Dr. Julian Nance Carsey, College President, and guiltily scooting out the back door, saving his own neck and expecting to be arrested any time.

"This, however, would only aggravate the sense of guilt at not doing the Right Thing. I imagine that he went through the torture of the damned, psyching himself up to that decision, and was eventually able to do it only by throwing everything away, in an act which I will call a paranoid fugue—projecting away from himself the terrible guilt he felt, divesting himself of being Dr. Carsey and all he was and had, leaving it all behind; take Dr. Julian N. Carsey, College President, you can have all of him, I no longer am him—I am the child running away. And with the rational compartmentalization typical of paranoid processes he could make sure the little boy in him would have something to subsist on."

In essence, Feys said, he would be prepared to say much the same thing in court—that in the days prior to his leaving, Jay "no longer had a healthy, rational control of his mental processes, or was capable of making sound and proper judgments or decisions."

WHILE IT'S HARD to say exactly how much of Feys's assessment Jay truly agreed with, it didn't matter: admitting weakness at that point was far less important to him than continuing to swing that anger-filled pendulum.

SIXTY-THREE

JAY'S DRINKING PICKED UP considerably after his return to El
Paso. For the most part, he was enjoying his job as dean (as well
as a course on management he was teaching at Fort Bliss), but the
few days in Maryland had been brutal. He became even more flip
and sarcastic than he usually was, and though Dawn continued to
be supportive, she also continued to worry how the ongoing situation and ultimate outcome would affect him, and them.

With Dawn's help, Jay had mentally walked through Green's
Inheritance and made a list of everything he could think of. There
were certain personal possessions he was determined to have back,
regardless of whether he received a share of the estate, and he
stressed the importance of some of these things to Kenkel: the
Harvard Classics his father had bought for him, his college ring,
his golf clubs, some brass cartridge cases that Dom had given him,
and two Washington Redskins season tickets, tickets even sane
people would kill for, tickets he had held long before he ever met
Nancy.

But when Kenkel tried on a couple of occasions to retrieve
these things, Nancy would either not be at the house or say that
she hadn't had a chance to sort through it all. That, naturally,

only fueled Jay's anger; how difficult the depositions must have been for Nancy was not something that especially concerned him.

Along with Feys's opinion, one of the things Kenkel was hoping to do was bring some witnesses from El Paso who could buttress it, who could say that they had met Jay Adams when he first came to town, that he was drinking heavily and didn't seem particularly stable. But Jay was adamantly opposed to involving anyone from his new life, and that was that.

The court date was set for the first of November, and, this time, Jay had no doubt where he would be going.

THE COURTHOUSE IN La Plata, Maryland, was a familiar place to him, as was the Howard Johnson's just down the road, the restaurant where he and Dom met Kenkel and Feys to talk things over before the proceedings began.

As he had in June, Jay flew into Washington early and stayed at Embassy Square. He had arranged for Tommy Sexton from the college to meet him in D.C. for lunch the day before (Kenkel was not only hoping to use him as a witness, but to see if the college could supply a VCR; Nancy's comments on CBS News were the only record now of Jay's note to Nancy about what a physical and emotional disaster he was, and the lawyer wanted to admit the piece as evidence). But when Sexton arrived at the Gangplank, he brought someone with him, Hilda Herbert, John Sine's secretary.

Instead of feeling irked by that, Jay wasn't. He had already prepared himself for seeing a good number of Charles County people in court, many of whom would no doubt be testifying for Nancy. Besides, he liked Hilda (had, after all, sent her flowers), and the three of them had the kind of lunch that made it hard for Tommy and Hilda to accept that Jay had ever left in the first place.

But later that night, as Jay was dining alone in a Washington restaurant, he wasn't the only one to get a Halloween surprise.

Reading a magazine and finishing his dessert and coffee, he suddenly became aware that someone was standing by his table.

"JesusChristJayfancymeetingyouhere."

Jay didn't even have to look up. He would have recognized Billy Zantzinger's rapid-fire voice anywhere.

"Well, howdy," Jay said when he raised his eyes, seeing that Billy's wife, Jane, was with him. Jay was fond of both of them, and he had spent hours with their children. In fact, he had been to their house the Sunday night before he disappeared. But he hadn't had any contact with them since.

The five awkward minutes or so they spent talking together seemed like five hours to Jay. They seemed that way because he could see the hurt in Jane Zantzinger's eyes.

As HE SAT in the Howard Johnson's the following morning over another cup of coffee, he wondered if that unexpected meeting would be a harbinger of the day ahead.

Nancy's lawyer had subpoenaed a flock of witnesses—everyone from Spencer Matthews to Bobbie Baldus—and Jay couldn't exactly hide from them once he got to the courthouse. Even though they were there (many of them quite reluctantly) to testify that Jay didn't seem any different two days before he left than he had ever been, that didn't prevent some of them from coming right up to Jay and telling him how glad they were to see him and that he would be welcome back in Southern Maryland anytime. This kind of sentiment only made Jay more uncomfortable, made him wonder if he had been wrong, if his pendulum was perhaps not as forceful as he'd hoped it would be.

On the other hand, he felt they were probably just being polite. Since he was a master at that, he thought, why shouldn't they be? After all, he observed, others kept their distance, and some people didn't even show up at all—a statement of disapproval, Jay was sure.

As it turned out, Jay never got into court that day. The judge suggested both sides come to a settlement, implying that Jay's note wasn't binding. When Jay heard this, he was stunned, as stunned as he had been when people came up to him. And even though he didn't look at Nancy, not once, he didn't have to. He had witnessed her fury before.

After an hour of huddling, the two lawyers (who had become co-trustees of the estate two months earlier) emerged. Nancy's offer to Jay was eighty-nine thousand dollars, take it or leave it.

More time passed, and then he left it. Both Dom and Kenkel (who was working on a modest retainer and would receive 15 percent of whatever settlement Jay got) advised Jay that he should hold out for more. When the judge was informed of this, he requested separate appraisals of the house and all its contents.

Returning to El Paso late that night, the only thing Jay could think of was how surreal the whole trip had been. When Dawn picked him up at the airport, he hugged her as if he had been away for months instead of days. And then he suddenly stepped back and said, "Well, you're now dealing with an insane person."

Perhaps Jay's instincts were right. Perhaps humor was the best way to downplay such extraordinary willfulness.

SIXTY-FOUR

O NCE AGAIN, Jay was making plans to leave El Paso. But this time, he was going to take Dawn with him.

He had applied for teaching jobs in South Carolina and Washington State, but hadn't gotten them. Perhaps that was just as well, because he became aware of something else that, were he to land it, would be perfect for the kind of life he wanted to lead. Through Troy State University in Alabama, there was a program that hired teachers to go to Air Force bases overseas so that enlisted men could attain graduate degrees. You spent ten weeks at one particular base (the Air Force would provide free accommodations nearby), had two to three weeks off in between, and then moved on to the next base. Four different spots a year, at a salary of two thousand dollars a month.

Dawn was as excited by the possibility of Jay's getting such a job as he was. After all, he was the only reason she was still in El Paso, and she had never been to Europe. This would be a way to do that, without having to abide by any of the ball-and-chain conditions Jay had raised when they were in Puerto Vallarta.

So off he went to Alabama for an interview. He gave John Sine as one of his references and told them he wanted to teach public administration. They asked him if he was married, and he said no, he was living with somebody. Well, they said, if they were to offer him a job he would need to be married by May. Military rules, no exceptions.

Not long after that, Troy got in touch with John Sine. When John learned all that the job entailed, he just laughed for about two minutes over the phone. Once he regained his composure, he told the man from Troy that the job he was describing couldn't be more ideal for his former colleague than if Jay had sat down and designed the job for himself. "That's like throwing Br'er Rabbit into the Brier Patch," John said, still having trouble containing himself. "Jay Carsey is the most traveled person I've ever known. This is a guy who could live out of a suitcase for the rest of his life."

IN LATE FEBRUARY of 1985 Jay went back to Maryland and, with Dom as a witness, quietly obtained the divorce he wanted. Even though the estate question was still to be settled, Nancy did not stand in his way, nor did she see him on that cold winter afternoon. She was in Florida, trying to go on with her life.

Two weeks later, on the Ides of March, Jay and Dawn returned to Bryan, Texas, their first trip there since the death of Jay's mother. They went back to Bryan because Jay needed a best man, and wanted his father to be that person. Homer not only approved of the match, he couldn't imagine how his son could be so lucky, to find someone like Dawn after the damn fool thing that he did; and he couldn't get over how different Jay acted with her, engaging in the kind of playful cuddling that Homer had never seen with Nancy, and that was foreign to his own marriage.

Before Dawn had said yes to Jay's proposal, though, she wanted him to promise, once more, that no matter how desperate things might become in their financial future, he would *never* sell arms to right-wing governments. He not only agreed to that, but more: that he would try to "go left-wing intelligently" (his liberal side, inspired by JFK, having died when the president did), learn Spanish, stay in good health, and handle small children better.

Once the three of them finished their nuptial business at the courthouse, they went back to the house for a little reception that Bea's old bridge partners had organized. Jay had seen them the previous May at the funeral but didn't remember all of their names.

They didn't care. What mattered to them was that by doing something for the son Bea had never stopped idolizing, they were doing something for her.

In the same way that Jay always had.

As WORD SOON spread that Jay would be leaving El Paso Community College at the end of the school year, no one seemed sadder about that than Mark Regalado. In a memo to Jay, he wrote: "You truly are the best administrator I have worked for in my 16 years of public education. Since you began your work here at the college I have been reminded of the old Roman legion tradition when the conquering general would parade in review before the emperor, he had a slave in his chariot to whisper in his ear that glory and the sense of accomplishment was fleeting. I never wanted to believe in the slave in my chariot but it came to pass. You are leaving.

"All seriousness aside, we are going to miss you. I mean, the cast from *Star Wars* at the Back Door lounge will not be up to full performance capacity. . . . I hear you & Dawn tied the knot. You're both very lucky—especially you, TJ. Congratulations!

"I know you're going to knock 'em dead at Troy U. After that, come on back to El Paso, your tab will probably still be running at the Back Door and we can once again relive all the Woody Allen movies we play in here at the college. . . .

"There are countless people who will miss you. There are countless people that missed you with snowballs at the faculty retreat. But if you keep moving no one can draw a bead on you, right? . . .

"May the gods smile upon your wildest dreams!"

JAY WAS TOUCHED by Mark's note, and oddly gratified that at least one of his colleagues understood: *If you keep moving no one can draw a bead on you*—his sentiments exactly. But if Mark was unequivocally admiring of Jay—of his ability and courage to take only interim appointments and then pick up and move on—most of his colleagues, as Jay suspected, were not. While they were sad he was leaving, their overall feelings were marked by a belief, partly rooted no doubt in envy, that Jay's desire to "keep moving" was just another form of fleeing responsibility.

Before Jay did any fleeing anywhere, though, he had to fly back to Maryland in June, his fourth trip (and third to Charles County) in a year.

SIXTY-FIVE

T HE SAME CAST of characters (except one) assembled on June 17 as had gathered seven and a half months earlier, and, this time, testimony was given.

Nancy unfolded her story, then told the court that "Jay has not spoken one word to me, not one syllable . . . he doesn't even look at me." Another witness said that Jay certainly seemed the "same old Jay" to her a few days before he left and, when asked about his drinking, remarked that observing how much someone drank was not something you do, "not in Southern Maryland, anyway." Dom Monetta said he was aware of all the pressure and stress Jay was under, but admitted that even though he considered himself Jay's best friend, "I could never get beyond a certain very carefully guarded level." Jean Feys, the psychiatrist, said that Jay was an "extremely suppressed person" who did not have "internal permission" to burden Nancy or others with his problems, that he "had to be the rainmaker, the source of good things." When he could no longer be that, Feys said, he "split himself in two" (this was how Feys interpreted Jay's talk of the guillotine) and irrationally ran away—"like Huck Finn or Tom Sawyer," he would later say.

JONATHAN COLEMAN

After Jay gave his version of things, Nancy's lawyer claimed that Jay got a lot more than the twenty-eight thousand dollars he took. "He got what practically everybody who leads a fairly high-pressure-type existence would really like to have," Tom Yewell said. "There is not a single one of us who has not thought at some given time, you know, 'I would really like to leave it all behind and walk down the road.' . . . He did it. He got freedom. . . . He really got the American dream. He got independent from obligations, responsibilities, the burden imposed by having someone get on you." But, Yewell said, to come back now, having realized "he made a bad bargain for himself," and try to "get back those things he had given up" was unacceptable. While in human terms it might be "about as normal a reaction as you could possibly expect," Yewell said, Jay couldn't do it in legal ones. "You can't be an Indian giver in the law. *He* chose out the deal."

As it happened, the judge that Yewell was addressing was not the same one as before. Through some sharp legal maneuvering, Yewell had been able to arrange a change. Though the first judge hadn't explicitly said that the note Jay wrote was invalid, the new judge left no one in doubt as to where he stood.

As far as the Honorable Perry G. Bowen, Jr., was concerned, the note was a "model of brevity and clarity and exactitude. It says *Take the property, take all my debts, it is yours to keep.* . . . Absolute proof that he was sane and competent and knew what he was doing and how it would relate to him."

Not only would Jay get nothing, Bowen said, but he wanted everyone to know how lucky Jay was. "If I had done to my wife what he did to Mrs. Carsey," the judge boomed, looking straight at Jay, "there would have been nothing left when I resurfaced but to have a funeral—providing they found enough of me to pick up with a blotter."

JAY'S DAY IN court was over, and he was free to go. On the surface, of course, he had lost. He had lost some money (the cost of his trips, a modest retainer to Kenkel, and the eighty-nine thousand previously offered) and he had lost in terms of all the emotion that had gone into coming back.

But beneath the surface, on the level that most interested him, he had apparently won. Better than anyone, the Honorable Perry G. Bowen had said, on the record, what Jay wanted everyone to hear—that he was dishonorable, that he wasn't who everybody thought he was. For the person who had always held the lantern while everybody else chopped wood, perhaps it was only fitting that someone else take that final swing of the pendulum for him.

But as Nancy soon learned, the punishment would continue.

Not only did she feel like she was the last one to know that Jay had gotten married three months earlier, but a week after the court proceedings, still shaking from what she *thought* was "final closure," she received a new blow: Jay was going to appeal.

When Kenkel asked Jay if he wanted to do that (citing the fact that Bowen's decisions were often overturned), Jay didn't say yes right away. After all, he had gotten back most of his personal belongings (and some golf clubs that weren't), and had roared with laughter when he threw out his green Charles County Community College blazer and wound up seeing a homeless man wearing it the next day (a haunting glimpse, no doubt, of what might have happened to him had he really "hit bottom"). He had a job to go to in Europe, a woman he loved, and who, he was finally convinced, loved him, loved him for who he was, human and imperfect, not for some idea of who he ought to be.

Nevertheless, once Jay asked Kenkel if he would have to return in order to appeal and Kenkel said he wouldn't, he immediately said, "What the hell, I've gone this far with it. I've got nothing to lose, except a little money."

SIXTY-SIX

"You know," Nancy said months later, still grappling with all that had happened, "I keep coming back to the same thing: I don't think Jay knew what he wanted."

It was a cold Saturday in March and she had just gotten back from Florida. Though the immediate effect of Jay's appeal was that she couldn't gain control of the estate and still had to be accountable to the lawyers until it was acted on, it hadn't stopped Nancy from traveling far and wide, continuing what Evelyn Hungerford sadly called her "long, frantic search."

When she was invited somewhere, which was often, she went, and it was almost always paid for. She hadn't found the full-time job she was apparently looking for, but whether it was because she was "overqualified" or had "just missed out," the truth was, a friend said, that she was "not just seeking any kind of job. She is seeking a very *special* position—one in which she can work when *she* wants to, and take off when she wants to. Let's face it," Dick Steffens went on, his face breaking into a smile, "those kinds of jobs are a little hard to find." (And until she found such a position, she was working as an unpaid member of the Maryland Arts Council.)

She was nine months short of her fiftieth birthday as she sat in the den of Green's Inheritance that day, in the room off the kitchen where she and Jay had their last supper together the night before he disappeared, the room where in winter she would often sleep in order to save on heat in the rest of the house. Nine months short of her fiftieth birthday and still striking, still the first person you would see when you entered a room.

As it had been from the beginning, it was painful for her to talk about all this. She was exceedingly wary as to how she would be perceived. She felt misunderstood by nearly everyone who knew her. For that reason, perhaps, more than any other, she hoped that it would somehow be cathartic for her to continue trying to explain herself.

"I promise you he got the life he wanted—or thought he wanted. He loved having me out front, and I enjoyed what I was doing. And I *thought* he did. And it's going to be very hard for him to sit over there in Europe with a new wife and tell you how wonderful his old life was—but *it was wonderful.* When we went somewhere, it impacted. At first, he wanted the world. But I guess somewhere along the way he decided he just wanted to be average.

"I trusted him so completely that, even now, four years later, it's very hard for me to put trust into another human being. I've learned to live alone and I've learned to value my privacy, but it would not be my life of choice. I enjoy sharing too much. I want to give to someone. I want to. But I just have to be so sure that if, indeed, I should ever marry again that it's very lasting and very special. I don't want to grow old alone, but it's going to take me a while to get my emotions healed to the point that I can really put total faith into someone again."

Far from being finished, she was just warming up. She had lost none of the energy that made Joe Browning exhausted every time he thought about her, lost none of her charm, and none of her quick-fire temper that had driven so much anger into Jay's soul.

"How can he live with himself?" she demanded to know. "Or with anybody else? If he had such a fear of disappointing me, then why did he do it this way?" She had asked that question many times before, and she was asking it still, knowing that she would probably never get an answer from him. "If he wanted to *punish* me so much, why did he ask Dom and Colonel Loeliger to take care of me 'for a while'? And why does he continue punishing me now with this appeal? As I told you, I may have frightened him with all the optimistic talk about the summer, but he *never* let on that he was unhappy. If he made his decision because he couldn't face confrontation, then once he made it, it seems to me, he had to busy himself and fill his mind with justification for it. He had to take some little thing and make it into a major one.

"Rationalization, after all, is human behavior. But you can go overboard, the way a narcissist or someone like that would. And if you're going to do something like this and you know you're going to do it for a long, long time, and you know that it's going to tear up a lot of people, you've got to have more and more reasons why you've got to do this in order to keep living with yourself. I don't mean to dwell on the deceit, but it certainly is there. And I am truly sorry he wasn't human enough, man enough, to talk to me, to say 'Hey, Nance, let's talk about x or y or z or whatever.' . . .

"I mean, here I was, trying to nurture him through a difficult time, and he knew *exactly* what he was going to do. I tried to get him to get help for his drinking, but he just shut me out, and then he turns around and testifies that he was drowning in booze, that he thought he would die if he didn't leave. He's *got* to think that. He's *got* to rationalize that behavior."

SHE WENT INTO the kitchen to pour herself a drink. The phone rang and she said she looked forward to lunch on Wednesday in Baltimore, and would it be okay if she stayed the night? It rang again and yes, a dinner party two weeks from tonight would be fine. And as soon as she hung up, it rang once more.

But even though she was, as always, in demand, Nancy was finally thinking of selling Green's Inheritance. She was still proud of it (in fact, she would soon be getting it ready for a spring tour of historic houses), but she had been wondering if it really made sense for her, a single, childless woman, to go on living in an area so oriented to families, and in a house she could not really afford, even if the court's decision was upheld. Since she and Jay had been synonymous with Southern Maryland for so long, maybe it was time for her, too, to move on, to forge a new life somewhere else. Though she would never admit it, there was really nothing left for her to prove. With everyone's help and support, she had survived, as everyone told her she would.

And survival was what she wanted to talk about when she came back into the den, cigarette in one hand, drink in the other.

"I DON'T THINK that Jay will ever, ever know the grief that he put me through," she said, tears welling up. "I don't think he has any idea. It's been very hard to be the left person and deal with total rejection and not understand and try to pick up the pieces and start again.

"I can't tell you how tired I got of everybody telling me I was a survivor, when they had no idea of how many nights I would just put on the answering machine and hole up here, unable to face people, wondering if I could go on, wondering if I even wanted to go on. After all, nobody wants to be around a sad sack. Everybody sees me, I think, as this lively, vivacious redhead going here, there, and everywhere, but always I knew he was back there, in the wings, supporting me. *Nobody* could possibly know how much I loved and depended on that man, and how terribly hurt I was. Even though I was always out front, I don't think anyone knew how much I was Jay's foil—I'm not even sure that I did—how much he controlled me, not the other way around. I thought it was he and I against the world. When did that change?

"You ask what I feel I might have contributed to his leaving and I tell you that I have done an awful lot of self-examination. I got very down on myself, thinking *how* could I have made things better, *what* I might have done, but I really don't think there are any answers. If it was the whole thing about the child, I still say, How can you push too hard for something you really want and believe in and is sort of a woman's . . . I mean, *I wanted to have a child.* Jay and I are both strong-willed people, and as I've said, I could never get him to talk about it, other than his saying he didn't want a twenty-year commitment. So when I'd heard that he said he wouldn't have left if there had been a child, that really hurt. . . .

"Everybody thinks I forced him to do things for me, but he *wanted* to do them. I could have driven to Baltimore or Annapolis or Delaware, but he always said he'd take me. He was so good at playing a role, maybe that's how he lived his marriage with me—being what he *thought* a husband should be. I don't know, but I certainly fell for it, hook, line, and sinker. I gave up a lot of my personal drive and career to be supportive of him and he really pulled my strings."

MAYBE IT WAS the somewhat skeptical expression on her visitor's face, a look that said, *Come on, Nancy, level with me, there must be more to it than that,* or maybe it had nothing to do with that at all. Maybe it was just one of those moments when one's guard slips—slips enough that one's own thick layer of rationalization, one's own version of "truth," peels away and exposes a new layer, a layer of brutal honesty often too upsetting to confront. After all, nobody likes to admit culpability, least of all someone as proud as Nancy.

"Maybe we took each other for granted," she admitted, leaning her head back for a second and closing her eyes. "If so, that will never happen to me again. Jay and I spent so much time pleasing those around us, I do think that introspection probably got lost in the shuffle, and that, too, will never happen to me again. I know this sounds trite, but I do realize now that relationships, no matter how good, have to be worked at, and maybe Jay and I had forgotten that.

"When I care for someone again, I have to be able to let them know that, and I must be able to do little things to constantly, you know, reinforce that. And if you try to take advantage of somebody, you lose them. I see that now. But, of course, this goes back to the whole communication thing, and I certainly know now how important that is, and how it is also not good to totally surrender yourself to another person.

"In that sense, I guess, there have been some positive things that have come out of Jay's leaving. It's made me stronger, for one. For the first time in my life I have been truly on my own, not under the protectorate of a man. But the total aloneness scares the hell out of me. No children, no brothers, no sisters, no parents, really [her mother was on a life-support system], and no husband—all gone.

"With the men I've been with, when things get close or intimate I withdraw, because I'm afraid. But I eventually want to give to someone. When I drove back from seeing my mother in Indiana last autumn, it really hit me when I stopped along the way to see the trees. And even though I always worried that Jay could never appreciate things like that to the degree that I could—at least he could never express it—he was always with me."

ONE MONTH LATER, who should turn up at Green's Inheritance but Gordon Brumfield. It had been years since he and Nancy had seen each other, but he would get news of her through his parents, who stayed friendly with Nancy's mother. As for the news of Jay's disappearance, he hadn't heard about it until a year after the fact (like Homer and Bea, Nancy's mother had, for the longest while, kept it from her friends). Having gotten married and divorced a second time, he had two sons and was living near Baltimore, working as a building contractor.

He hadn't called Nancy when he learned what happened because he felt that if she needed his help she would let him know. Having recently found out where he was living, she had phoned and said how nice it would be to see him again. He said that he was living with someone and would want to discuss it with her first. She was somewhat insecure, he said, and he wanted to explain it in the right way.

"Why, Gordon," she laughed, "somehow I don't see you with an insecure woman."

"Why not?" he said. "That's the only kind I've ever gone with."

Two days after their conversation, on the kind of fine spring morning Jay had left on, Gordon came up the long, wooded driveway. He had once gotten a Christmas card with a sketch of the house on it, but he was not prepared—not at first, anyway—for its size and surrounding land. And yet once he was inside and sat with Nancy, saw her in her element, he knew, of course, that this was precisely the kind of grand place he should have expected to find her in. And even though he came right out and told her, having nothing to lose, that he could never be comfortable living in a museum, he also found himself, as so many have, falling under her spell yet again.

"You know what amazed me?" he said later. "When I was there she said something about putting the house on the market, and I almost offered my help. Can you imagine? After all these years? I sure as hell could never have explained that to Emily.

"Anyway, I still feel a great deal of tenderness for Nancy, and guess I still love her, with qualifications. She's a very easy woman to spoil and do things for. But whatever Nancy might have contributed to his decision—I'm sure she ran the debt up way too high—I still don't think it was right for Jay to do what he did. It just doesn't square with the person I knew."

SIXTY-SEVEN

THE REASON IT MADE Evelyn Hungerford so sad when she talked about Nancy's long, frantic search was because she, and Nancy's other friends, felt that Nancy was running away from life, that she wasn't really looking for anything beyond the fleeting, superficial pleasure of being entertained and made a fuss over, day after day, night after night.

To hear Karen Sprague tell it, it was all very simple: Jay changed and Nancy didn't. It didn't mean that people felt any less bad about what had happened to Nancy—or any less upset at the way Jay had deserted them. It just meant that the way Nancy appeared to deal with the men who were now in her life served as further proof to her friends (one of whom, Jane Zantzinger, had tried to turn to Nancy after her husband left her for another woman) of how Jay must have felt: that he had given far, far more than he had ever received.

If Evelyn Hungerford was right, though, could the same thing be said, in a somewhat different way, about Jay? That by taking a job that would keep him constantly on the move, happily living out of a suitcase as John Sine said, he, too, was running from life?

Or could the opposite be said? That his taking the Troy job was perfectly in keeping with his image of himself as a rainmaker, and with his underlying fear of getting backed into the sort of well-paid administrative position that would not only squeeze the life out of him—*process and procedure, year after year*—but one in which the vicious cycle would invariably begin again, the treadmill of more and more achievement meaning more and more responsibility, greater and greater expectations and, inevitably, the disappointment to others that would come when their hero occasionally failed and showed himself to be human after all. The very disappointment that had, in part, made Jay flee in the first place and could send him on his way again.

AS FAR AS people like Joe Browning were concerned, Jay's decision to go gallivanting around Europe was temporary. He was simply on a sabbatical, Joe felt; sooner or later he would be thirsting to get on the ladder and "back into the fight" again.

To Dom Monetta, the Jay Carsey who had "brought me into this world," as Dom so often said, was a different person now, someone who would require relearning. And even though they would correspond from time to time (and almost got together in Spain for Thanksgiving in 1985), Dom's feeling of sadness and abandonment was unchanged from the moment he got back from New Mexico and read Jay's first note, the note, Dom now grudgingly conceded, that signified the end of their day-to-day friendship. It wasn't that Dom didn't feel good about having been a loyal friend, first helping Nancy out, then Jay. And it wasn't that he didn't feel pleased that Jay appeared to be so happy with Dawn. It was just that Dom had needs, too, and when Jay left on May 19, a large part of Dom's life went with him.

As time went on, John Sine's anger—and understanding—grew. Quite apart from his feelings about Jay's pursuit of the estate, he felt that Jay's leaving the college in the way he did was a form of "human and moral bankruptcy." On the other hand, he had been the president of the college long enough to see, as Bob Shepack and Jay did, how such jobs can come to seem lonely and undoable, that no matter what decision you make, someone is going to vilify you for it. But since John's need of other people's approval is practically nonexistent compared to Jay's—and since, like Shepack, he has a strong family life to turn to—he goes on.

John wasn't in town on the occasions Jay came back to Charles County to contest the estate, but wouldn't have gone to the courthouse even if he had been. That was a private matter, John felt, and besides, he and Jay were corresponding with each other. But in all their letters, there was one thing that John had never said to Jay, the one thing that represents his hope for Jay in the future.

"You know," John said one day in his office, gazing out the same window he had stood by the day he received Jay's postcard, "Jay is kind of like any hero—unless you recognize what it is you suffered through, and unless *he* recognizes what it is he did. Simply the experience of it is meaningless. Willy Loman is not a tragic figure. He's empathetic. He never does understand what he's going through. My hope for Jay Carsey is for him to understand what he's gone through. That's all."

Not quite. Just as Jay had had a p.s. for John on the postcard, John had one for him.

"It's funny," he said, "but just the other day I was thinking that if Jay ever did decide to come back here, it sure would be fun to do the play again."

SIXTY-EIGHT

From across the ocean, thousands of miles from the college he had built and the county where, despite all his efforts, he was still missed, Jay laughed hard when he heard that. Why, just the other day *he* had been thinking that it might be fun to take Dawn to Charles County sometime and show her around. Since he didn't have many go-back dreams anymore, or so he said, it was hard for him to know if the play he had dreamed about that time, the one that had to be canceled because of all the varmints that had infested the moundlike stage it was to be performed on, was *The Rainmaker* or not. But since John had mentioned it, it started Jay, ever the schemer, wondering if the best time to put on the play wouldn't be in the year 2008 (marking the fiftieth anniversary of the college), when they could be assured of a great turnout.

And since John had mentioned it, it had started Jay's visitor wondering—wondering how fitting it would be for Jay to finally perform the role in art that he had played for so long in life.

In the end, so much had contributed to the shaping of Julian Nance Carsey—genuineness and fraudulence; charm and deception; emotional superficiality and depth; stubborn conviction and guilt; expectation and disillusionment; strength and vulnerability; blind, hardscrabble ambition and introspection—into who he appeared to be, needed to be, and thought he should be, and into who he was (and is): victim and victimizer, hero and coward, dutiful son, brother, husband, and mischievous little boy, bent on adventure.

John Sine was right. If Jay didn't understand all that he had gone through, the experience of it would, on some level, be meaningless. Just as he was stubbornly attempting to triumph over his alcoholism himself (despite Joe Browning's plea that he go into AA, he was, with Dawn's help, partly succeeding, having given up hard liquor), he was searching for answers in books as opposed to therapy.

"Anomie," he announced one day, in response to a question about what *he* thought might lie at the heart of what he had done. "Total rootlessness—that's what you're dealing with as much as anything. As I've said before, I have no sense of links. It's funny, but I used to be slightly suspicious when I would look at someone's résumé and see fourteen jobs in fourteen years in fourteen different places. Now I understand. There's a good chance, for instance, I may go the rest of my life without seeing people from Southern Maryland again. If Buddy Sprague were to show up on my doorstep, it would be great to see Slick. But I *won't* seek him out. If he were to die, I might send flowers to the funeral, but I won't *go* to the funeral."

But when he was told that anomie meant more than just rootlessness, he seemed somewhat taken aback. If he had simply consulted the dictionary (or even absorbed more fully what he had read in *Contemporary Social Problems*) he would have realized that in addition to "rootlessness," anomie also meant "lack of purpose, identity, or ethical values in a person or in a society."

Fine, Jay said, not the least bit defensive, that fit too, and it wasn't long before he had found a passage in Walter Lippmann's *A Preface to Morals* that he thought expressed things better than he could:

At the heart of [modern man's discontent] there are likely to be moments of blank misgiving in which he finds that the civilization of which he is a part leaves a dusty taste in his mouth. He may be very busy with many things, but he discovers one day that he is no longer sure they are worth doing. He has been much preoccupied; but he is no longer sure he knows why. He has become involved in an elaborate routine of pleasures; and they do not seem to amuse him very much. He finds it hard to believe that doing any one thing is better than doing any other thing, or, in fact, that it is better than doing nothing at all.

It occurs to him that it is a great deal of trouble to live, and that even in the best of lives the thrills are few and far between. He begins more or less consciously to seek satisfactions, because he is no longer satisfied, and all the while he realizes that the pursuit of happiness was always a most unhappy quest.

Lippmann wrote that in 1929, six years before Jay was born, but it seemed only right that it would last, at least long enough for Jay to get around to reading it.

DAWN HAD BEEN listening intently to the conversation Jay was having, and she had something to say—especially when the devil's advocate suggested to Jay that, beyond all the sociology and newly discovered passages, by doing what he was doing, what he himself called "this ten-week gypsy process of dismembering one habitat to go to another," he was doing nothing more than running from life. He had left Maryland without any sense of what he was moving toward, only running from, but once he found, in Dawn, what he claimed to be looking for, why was he still on the run?

"He's not running *from* life," Dawn said defensively, her eyes wide, "he's running *toward* it. Is 'life,' whether it's in Maryland or El Paso, sitting there and watching everybody start planning their retirement fifteen years ahead of time, or sinking into alcohol? That's not living. Is that what he's running away from—that kind of living?

"And that's how I felt, too. I could have become a fat, frumpy housewife by now with four kids if I wanted to get into life—being responsible in capital letters—and then become PTA Mother of the Year, or something like that. That's not life. That's some weird definition of it. You're smart enough to know that."

BUT SHE WAS not without complaints about the man she had first glimpsed across the pool table at the Back Door one hot Texas night and who had now become her husband.

"Jay's hardest lesson, I think, continues to be his difficulty in accepting the financial limitations of his new life. Instead of telling Dom the real reason we couldn't meet him and his fiancée in Spain for Thanksgiving—we couldn't afford it—he wrote and told him we would just be getting to Greece, and that the base might require us to be there. It puts me in the position of nag, having to always say, 'We're too poor, we can't do that.' How do you think I feel?" Then, turning to Jay, who was staring down at the floor, she said, "Goddamnit, Jay, you abandoned it. Why can't you face up to it? Why can't you remind people of that?"

Getting no response, she went on.

"It makes me feel like the 'poor person connection,' the one who caters to you when the high-flying wife won't because she's doing the important things, like buying a service of china and stuff like that. Makes me feel like I'm really settling for the bottom of the barrel when this guy is really still living at the top of the line in his mind."

Fearing disapproval and confrontation, as always, Jay got up from his chair and, without a word, went over to the corner of the room and put a tape on.

"He forgets how desperate things were in the fall of '82. For the longest time he didn't bring a cent into the support system and he assumed it was going to be all right. He has this absolute belief in his charmed life. I could have pushed him to get something else, but it wasn't a good time to push him, and I knew that. But even though he makes money now, I still take the responsibility for the level at which we live. He put it on Nancy—*You tell me how much we need to make and I'll make it.* With us, he doesn't know the cost of things, how much it takes to live at a certain level. He depends on me for that. If you let him on his own, he'd be a goddamn Bowery bum because he couldn't cope with the reality of coming to grips with what he did."

The thought that life could be better
is woven indelibly into our hearts and our brains.

Whether it was hearing Paul Simon in the background, or seeing Jay, beatific smile on his face, mouth the words to the song, or whether it was simply a desire on her part, as it had been on Homer's, to set the record straight, something kept spurring Dawn on.

While she still felt it was very brave of Jay "to go looking for something better," she worried that he had stopped too soon, that he had found something comfortable and decided just to rest for a while. "What really gets me," she said, "is how he can sit there pontificating about the life he left, but can't expend the same kind of effort about learning his new one. That annoys the fuck out of me. Makes me wonder if he's just nesting without being honest enough to say 'I've got to finish things.'"

Did that mean she was fearful that he might pick up and disappear again? Or did it mean that—despite her worry, despite his fleeing from El Paso that Friday in November of 1982, and despite all the jokes Connie and Phyllis had made about not letting him go to the dentist alone or not trusting him if he said he would be home for lunch—she continued to feel sure that she was an exception, that what had happened to Nancy wouldn't happen to her?

"Well, obviously, I've thought about all that, and people like Wendy Bruck have reminded me that if he did it once, he could do it again. I'd be a *fool* not to think about all that, especially when he talks about the guillotine and everything. But I've got to tell you, I've got faith he won't. I do believe that he knows and feels secure that I love him for who he is, not for what he can provide. Our lack of money now bothers him a hell of a lot more than it troubles me. When we found out that the appeal was turned down, he went on a tear emotionally, got drunk, and had three or four very bad days. But what bothered him, I think, was less the fact he wanted some of that than his feeling he had really failed me somehow, and failed his father—failed the people who had some faith or trust in him, or dependence on him."

Like a schoolboy whose teacher had singled him out for misbehaving, Jay got up at that point and stood against the wall. It was now dark outside. He had said nothing since Dawn had begun to talk, and he continued to say nothing when it was suggested, to both of them, that perhaps he was still the same person, that no matter where he went, no matter what he did, he would carry the burden of other people's expectations—and the fear of not meeting them—with him always.

"I've said it before," Dawn said, "and I'll say it again. Jay is the most perfect other-directed person I've ever seen." As long as they both recognized that, she said, they would be all right. "Our covenant, as I call it, is that I understand how cold-blooded he can be and I can recognize when he's being flip, or reaching his limit with something, or when I am. But when he is being serious or when he's feeling emotion or when he's trying to cover up emotion I can tell how he feels about me then. I have to try to make myself not become something he likes less. And I work hard at trying to make him not let himself become something that I like less."

"You said before," she was reminded, "that you didn't feel that Jay could ever really be yours until he had some communication with Nancy. Do you still feel that?"

"I still feel he's very cruel, because it's such a complete and thorough rejection. My first sense was, Well, she must have really hurt him badly, really stabbed him someplace critical. He takes a lot of pride in the fact that he hasn't ever said anything to her, and I guess I continue to feel that that duel cannot be finished—that he won't really be mine until he stops being hers—until he is willing to talk to her one on one. That scar must still be very deep."

APPARENTLY, THIS WAS the moment he was waiting for. He put down the beer he was drinking and moved forward from the wall. At first, he talked about a "failing of the human spirit" that prevented him from contacting Nancy now. But then he talked about guilt and stubbornness, admitting that once he made a decision, "even if I'm wrong, I'm going to continue along with it."

Like going back for the estate?

"I'll admit that was a mistake. It was something I did very purposely, but I probably shouldn't have gone through with all that —it was a total waste of energy, money, and time."

And what about his whole theory of the guillotine, wasn't that just shot through with contradiction?

"In a lot of ways, I guess, nobody's past is totally closed out. We can only pretend that it is—or elements of it, anyway. But as far as I'm concerned, and I can't stress this strongly enough, Southern Maryland is shut down for me. I might tell anecdotes and I might see John Sine again, but that life is gone. The *only* reason the door got opened again is that I had to get back to my real name, with references and all that. But for Joe Browning to say that I'm on a sabbatical, that I'm going to come back to the bureaucratic world of making one hundred twenty, one hundred fifty thousand dollars a year, the answer is no. I've got *no* regrets. If I were in an alfresco jail in Juárez, I might say I'm in a terrible position and wish I hadn't done it. But the results are so satisfying to me—I've got a marriage and a job I enjoy—that the method worked. And I don't care whether you interpret this as selfishness or callousness or shame or however you want, but I am *never* going to have any contact with Nancy for the rest—"

"So when you're tired of me," Dawn broke in, "you mean you're just going to leave. You're not going to say to me it's over."

"It's not the same thing," he said.

"Well, why isn't it? Why isn't it the same thing?"

Visibly agitated, Jay began pacing back and forth, frustrated and silent. The only light in the room now was provided by the moon, and the only sound came from Paul Simon, eerily reminding the three people who were there that *Everybody loves the sound of a train in the distance, everybody thinks it's true*. And even though the message held a particular truth for Jay, he didn't allow it now to speak for him, as he had allowed his letters, his tape, and the *New Yorker* cartoon to speak for him when he walked away from Maryland. No, this time, he reached down and found a way to speak for himself.

He stopped pacing and went over to where Dawn was sitting. He took her hand, and then, looking straight at her, answered her question.

"Because you're completely different from any other woman I've ever met. If it ever came to that point—and I hope it doesn't—I think we'd have a long discussion about it."

EPILOGUE

Dom Monetta returned to the Naval Ordnance Station in the fall of 1986 to become technical director, and Nancy threw a big party for him.

Joe Browning, who paid for that party, continues to live in Miami, and continues to hope that, some day, Jay will contact Nancy.

Susie Duncan, Jay's sister, finally saw her brother at their mother's funeral in 1984, but has not seen him since.

Homer Carsey, now ninety-four, still lives in Bryan, Texas, and is as fiercely independent as ever.

In the end, Nancy did put Green's Inheritance on the market, but as of February 1989 no one had come forward to meet the price she asked. Meanwhile, she found a part-time job raising money for the handicapped, and continues to travel at the speed of light.

As for Jay—after three years in Europe, years in which he and Dawn moved from Air Force base to Air Force base, living in Greece (twice), England (three times), Turkey (three times), the Azores (twice), Holland, and West Germany, years in which they visited many other places in between—he came back to the United States in the summer of 1988. The main reason, he said, was that he didn't want to become an expatriate for the rest of his life—a life of modest means that he wouldn't exchange, he continued to claim, for any other.

AFTERWORD

"Dr. Livingstone, I presume?"

One week before Thanksgiving of 1985, I stood outside the entrance to an apartment building in the Greek seaside town of Voula, just outside Athens, and this was the first question Jay Carsey asked me, the legendary question that I should have been asking him, even though I hadn't "discovered" him—at least not in the way that the American journalist H. M. Stanley had found the British explorer David Livingstone in a remote African village in the nineteenth century.

But I had the thrill of discovery nonetheless. Since I had lived with the story in my mind long after I had reported it for CBS News, it was an odd feeling to come face to face with the person who was its subject. Somehow, I think I always knew that I would write about Jay Carsey—provided he ever turned up *and* was willing to talk with me. As in my first book, *At Mother's Request*, I was obsessed with human behavior, with why people do what they do, with the various elements that bring them to such a point that they act in a certain way, a way that, in larger and lesser degrees, has an impact on others.

Jay seemed to me an Everyman, someone, Dom Monetta said long before I ever met Jay, "just like you and me." If he had been a celebrity, I would have had little interest in writing about him. Besides, if a celebrity had done this, the story would have been exhaustively covered long before anyone sat down to write a book about it.

Jay was reluctant when I first broached the idea with him, but said he had seen the piece I had done and felt it was fair and responsible. I explained that I had no idea how the book would eventually turn out, but that I could promise him I would follow the story wherever it took me, and that I would write it with the care it deserved. I made that same promise to Nancy and everyone else I spoke with, and made it clear that that was all I could promise. I knew—and they knew—that it probably would never align with the way they saw it. That rarely happens—unless the story has been subject to certain guidelines of approval.

It will always be somewhat of a mystery why one person agrees to let another probe his or her background, actions, and motives. But in Jay's case, I came to the conclusion that he was allowing me into his two different lives for, more or less, the same reason Nancy did: he wanted to explain himself (and, perhaps, as one person said, "have you do his work for him"). Then, again, maybe the real reason is among those things he is determined to take to the grave with him.

In the preface to his book *Among the Missing*, a comprehensive look at some of the most famous and not-so-famous disappearances of our time, Jay Robert Nash wrote that "there is in most of us a wide-eyed fascination with the baffling world of the vanished . . . and for those whose lives are touched and changed by the disappearance, there are undying memories and unrelenting apprehension."

Nash was right. Of all the people I spoke with who were not connected to Jay Carsey in any way, I didn't find one whose expression didn't change, whose mask didn't slip for a moment, when I casually mentioned what I was working on, or who didn't know of a friend who had a friend or relative who had done something similar.

Fear and fantasy, it seems, make interesting bedfellows.

J.C.
February 8, 1989

· SOURCES

Since this is a work of nonfiction, it couldn't have been written without a certain amount of reporting. From the time I first began this story for CBS News until its completion as a book, I interviewed nearly 150 people, many of whom graciously allowed me to intrude upon their lives numerous times. With few exceptions, everyone spoke on the record. None asked that their name be changed, but I decided to protect the privacy of two people—"Jessica Ross" and "Lois Sorenson"—by giving them pseudonyms.

In addition to the interviews I conducted, nearly all of which were tape-recorded, and my own observation, I drew on a vast array of other primary and secondary sources: letters; books; newspaper and magazine articles; photographs; police reports; appointment calendars; telephone logs; depositions, court transcripts, and exhibits; school yearbooks; and other memoranda and documents.

Since this book is not intended to be a scholarly work, I did not feel that a page-by-page notes section (or index) would either serve a useful purpose or be appropriate to the story I have tried to tell. As often as possible, I identified my sources within the text itself; for the instances where I felt to do so would interrupt the flow of the narrative, I list those additional sources of information here:

Burt Adams; Jynx Adams; Sally Barley; Pat Billeter; LeAnne Bongiorno; Margaret Braun; David Brown; Ed Digges; James Edwards; David Fogle; Ed Foster; Chris Fraga; Rava Gigere; Jenny Giron; Aida Guzman; Ceil Haislip; Hilda Herbert; Pamela Hungerford; Vince Hungerford; Belva Jensen; Clark Kerr; John Kopp; Betty Gayle Laughlin; Carol LeFleur; Susan Light; Ed Loeliger; James Manuso; George Morales; Joe Mullen; John Thomas Parran;

Charles Roberts; Elaine Ryan; Bob Schaumburg; John Schaumburg; Jim Scott; Carmen Sloat; Earl Sloat; Leila Smith; Enrique Solis; Ellie Straus; Jerry Stroud; Jay Thornburg; Diane Troyer; Sean Wallace; Bill Williams; Charles Wise; Billy Zantzinger; Jane Zantzinger.

The background reading I did proved so interesting and helpful that I want to cite the following books and articles especially:

Barbara Ehrenreich's *The Hearts of Men: American Dreams and the Flight from Commitment* (Anchor Press, 1983); Gloria Emerson's *Some American Men* (Simon and Schuster, 1985); Daniel Goleman's "The Strange Agony of Success" (*The New York Times*, August 24, 1986); Daniel J. Levinson et al.'s *The Seasons of a Man's Life* (Ballantine, 1979); David Riesman's *The Lonely Crowd* (Yale University Press, 1950); Maggie Scarf's *Intimate Partners: Patterns in Love and Marriage* (Random House, 1987); John Updike's *Rabbit Run* (Fawcett Crest, 1962); Geoffrey Wolff's *The Duke of Deception: Memories of My Father* (Penguin, 1986).

ACKNOWLEDGMENTS

As much as a writer might like to think that he alone has written a book, it is simply not the case. Sometimes it is a small gesture (the use of a phone or an office), or a casual comment, or a long conversation devoted to something blissfully removed from the subject in question, or something that the "collaborator" is entirely unaware of: whatever it is, without it, the author's job would be infinitely more difficult.

Many, many people who figure in this story gave of their time and hospitality, and nearly all of their names appear in the pages of this book. To them—and to those whose don't—I offer my thanks. I shall remember that John Sine made me feel as if I were a colleague, that Joe Browning made me aware that the financial markets take a great deal of learning, and that Homer Carsey not only enabled me to relive an era with him, but that I'd still be in his living room listening to him hold forth if I hadn't found a graceful way to exit. I shall remember the passion of Susie Duncan's convictions, the unguarded way that Bob Shepack spoke of his job, and the way that Buddy Sprague shook his head when he said that Jay would always be willing to listen to your problems but you could *never* get anything out of him. And most of all, I shall remember how they, and everyone else, cared enough to help me immeasurably in my effort to understand this story. They will not, of course, agree with everything they read here, and I take full responsibility for that.

When I first went to Maryland in 1982 to do this story for CBS, my colleague Jody Perkins came with me, shared my curiosity, and continues to root for me from a tiny place in Texas called Sealy.

When I told Tom Stewart at Atheneum that I wanted to do a book on this story, he was enthusiastic and supportive. And even though he was no longer there when the manuscript was delivered, I feel confident that this was the book he wanted. And when it was delivered, Robert Stewart (no relation), Lee Goerner, Barry Lippman, Bonnie Ammer, Susan Richman, Sharon Dynak, Harry McCullough, Lee Wiggins, Polly Goode, and Cathy Fox read it and responded with the sort of enthusiasm that authors long to have.

As for many of the people who provided the various things I spoke of in the first paragraph, they are Ann Beattie, Joan Bingham, Sydney Blair, Liv Blumer, Angus and Sheila Cameron, Mike Carter, Michael Coleman, Kathryn Court, Ruth Estep, Joni Evans, John and Mina Ferguson, Michael and Elaine George, Ashbel Green, Ian Hamilton, Don Hirsch, Louise Kaplan, Robert Kellogg, Andrew Lack, Sandy Lindsey, Jerome and Anne McGann, Victoria Munroe, Sheila Parker, Paul and Mary Rooney, Eric Saltzman, Dawn Seesler, Elisabeth Seldes, Al and Rosa Silverman, Frances Sternhagen, Elizabeth Swados, Nan Talese, Bettina Volz, Leslie Walker, Howard Weinberg.

The Virginia Center for the Creative Arts provided a haven and Carol Marcum's excellent food for two months in the summer of 1987.

Erika St. Dennis made endless phone calls and trips to the library, and never, not once, lost the sunny disposition that makes her special.

No stranger to anxiety, Bob Lindsey was, as always, urging me on.

I don't see Irene Webb, my "second agent" and friend of fourteen years, as much as I would like, but she is always there.

In my first book I wrote that Owen Laster, my agent, is "one of the most decent and professional people I have ever known." In the four years since that book was published, he has somehow managed to soar even higher in my estimation.

It is hard to adequately describe the many contributions that

Amy Lemley has made to this book. But it should be said that without her fine mind, her probing questions, her sharp pencil, and her indispensable good cheer, I would still be struggling to finish this. It's not always joyous living with a writer, especially this one, but she rose to the occasion.

JONATHAN COLEMAN was born in 1951 in Allentown, Pennsylvania. A graduate of the University of Virginia, he is a former senior editor in book publishing. From 1981 to 1983 he worked for CBS News, where he first began investigating this story. His first book, *At Mother's Request*, was published to critical acclaim in 1985, became a bestseller, and was nominated for an Edgar Allan Poe Award. In 1987 he made a cameo appearance in a miniseries based on that book.

Mr. Coleman lives in New York City and in Charlottesville, where he teaches writing at the University of Virginia.